I0887129

SUPERSPY

SUPERSPY

Hans Tofte, Intelligence Officer for SOE, OSS, and CIA

DAVID A. FOY

CASEMATE

Pennsylvania & Yorkshire

Published in the United States of America and Great Britain in 2025 by
CASEMATE PUBLISHERS
1950 Lawrence Road, Havertown, PA 19083
and
47 Church Street, Barnsley, S70 2AS, UK

Hardback Edition: ISBN 978-1-63624-576-8
Digital Edition: ISBN 978-1-63624-577-5

A CIP record for this book is available from the British Library

Printed and bound in the United Kingdom by CPI Group (UK) Ltd, Croydon, CR0 4YY

Typeset in India by Lapiz Digital Services, Chennai.

For a complete list of Casemate titles, please contact:

CASEMATE PUBLISHERS (US)
Telephone (610) 853-9131
Fax (610) 853-9146
Email: casemate@casematepublishers.com
www.casematepublishers.com

CASEMATE PUBLISHERS (UK)
Telephone (0)1226 734350
Email: casemate@casemateuk.com
www.casemateuk.com

Front cover image: Hans Vilhelm Tofte. (US Army)

The Publisher's authorised representative in the EU for product safety is Authorised Rep Compliance Ltd., Ground Floor, 71 Lower Baggot Street, Dublin D02 P593, Ireland.
http://www.arccompliance.com

Contents

Introduction		vii
1	A Danish Boy	1
2	The "Dynamic Dane" in World War II	5
3	Yugoslavia and Operation *Audrey*	27
4	Man of Action: Austria, Scandinavia, Mason City	51
5	The Korean War	73
6	The "Dynamic Dane" and Regime Change	107
7	Mason City Interlude	131
8	Apartment to Let	143
9	Life After Langley	159
10	Looking Through a Glass, Darkly…	167
Epilogue		171
Endnotes		179
Bibliography		201
Index		209

Introduction

It all began so innocuously—a man simply wanted to rent out the basement apartment in his home in the most fashionable quadrant of the nation's capital in 1966. However, by its denouement, a prominent figure's accomplished career in the intelligence community would be at an abrupt end, a national agency already facing harsh scrutiny would be embroiled in controversy, and America would be reading all about it as the case progressed through the judicial system.

***

Much of the relatively little we know about Danish-American intelligence officer Hans V. Tofte comes from the research and pen of Danish author Henrik Kruger who, in 2005, published *Den danske krigshelt, der kom til tops i CIA* (*The Danish War Hero Who Rose to the Top of the CIA*), a misleading title. While it could be argued that at times Tofte glimpsed the mountaintop, he never reached it. It is also worth noting that the bulk of the extant information about Tofte focuses on his OSS activities and, to a lesser extent, his CIA career, though his obvious talents contributed to success in other areas in life as well. The earliest records of his OSS activity and achievements were not declassified until the 1980s, and those of his CIA activity did not begin to see the light of day until 2003.

Kruger had the opportunity to interview Tofte while the former worked as a journalist for the Danish newspaper *Politiken* in Washington, DC, in 1970—Tofte had been willing to freely discuss his World War II activities, but the only part of his CIA career he would discuss was his first two years in Korea. Kruger had first envisioned writing a biography of Tofte in the 1980s, but Tofte died before Kruger could recontact him. However, he did manage to interview several key family members and also received a serendipitous gift—thanks to an unnamed National Archives and Records Administration (NARA) employee in College Park, Maryland, who had known Tofte, Kruger was able to bring home approximately 300 documents discussing Tofte's activities.[1] The final wrinkle in knowing what there is to know about Tofte is that Kruger's volume is in Danish and has never been translated into English, though such is now possible due to modern technology. In addition to Kruger, this author is especially indebted to fellow Army Counterintelligence veteran and writer Joseph C. Goulden, and personnel at several archival facilities: to Gry Scavenius Bertelsen, the curator of the National Museum of Denmark, in Copenhagen; and to Todd Crumley and Alexis Hill, Still Pictures Branch; Sara Graff and Matthew Novick, Cartographic Branch; and Paul Brown and Suzanne Zoumbaris, Textual Records Branch, all at National Archives and Records Administration (NARA) II, College Park, Maryland.

Here then is the first English-language biography of a little-known but significant figure in the history of 20th-century military and civilian intelligence, a foreign-born patriot who came to the assistance of several other nations in a time of need and did his best to help them. Tofte was an imperfect but accomplished role model, whose factual and nuanced story should be told and appreciated.

CHAPTER I

A Danish Boy

Hans Vilhelm Tofte was born on April 4, 1911, in Copenhagen, Denmark. His father, Hans Henrik Ludvig Tofte, a ship captain for the East Asiatic Company (EAC), was 32 years old when baby Hans was born, his mother Ulla Vilhelmine Agnes Christensen only 22. Hans was soon joined by a younger brother, Per Ludvig Thorkild Tofte, born in 1914.[1]

Tofte's father, known to everyone as "Ludvig," was frequently gone while Hans and Per were growing up, which meant that they essentially were raised by Ulla, a firm but loving woman who never came to grips with her husband's infidelity, which was encouraged by his ability to spend time with female passengers on one of the EAC's few passenger ships. Not surprisingly, both boys were very close to their mother. Ludvig spent the years 1918 and 1919 sailing between the East and West Coasts of the United States, with the Tofte family settling in San Mateo, California, near the elder Tofte's homeport of San Francisco. However, their pleasant existence was shattered in 1921, when Ulla died. Hans was so devastated by the sudden loss of his beloved mother that he barely spoke for a year. To help in the healing process, Ludvig brought a Danish-speaking German professor to live with them, though Ludvig soon became bored with being a landlubber, becoming increasingly restless and irritable. So, he farmed Hans and Per off to the grandparents in Denmark and returned to sea, an example of the headstrong behavior that would arise periodically in the life of his eldest son.[2]

Once Hans decided to speak again, he returned to school in Frederiksberg and became an avid Scout, a member of the 2nd Vesterbro Troop. Hans spent the rest of his formative years at the Stenhus *Kostskole* (boarding school) in Holbaek, Denmark, receiving both his primary and secondary education there. Hans proved to be more academically minded than his younger brother and was one of eleven students entrusted with living in a self-governing unit, left unsupervised when it came to completing homework, going to bed at curfew, and abiding by the ban on smoking, though he noted that "self-discipline was a matter of honor." As Kruger noted, "Hans did not let anything get him down, and after he had shaken off his mother's death, he was well on his way to developing into an adventurer, a man of the world in his guise." Hans wanted to be a sea captain like his father and applied to EAC while still in the 3rd grade at Stenhus, when he was likely eight or nine years old, despite recalling "when you went overseas for the company, you did so with the understanding you would be there twenty-five years or so, with marriage not permitted for the first ten years." His headmaster penned this recommendation:

> Hans has very good abilities, which he uses sensibly, is clear and quick in this thinking, and his memory is also good. His circle of interests is quite a bit larger than is usual at high school and he uses a part of his free time to get a sensible understanding of the problems that have caught his interest by reading and talking. He is in every respect an appealing and reliable student who interacts with both his peers and teachers in an open, trusting and personal way, and there has never been any recourse on his part to…petty misconduct. I therefore think that his development is in a good direction, and since he is also practical and quick for practical employment, I believe that he has all the conditions to fulfill himself wherever he may find his employment when the schooling is finished. We all like him very much and I recommend him highly.[3]

Besides the idea of plying the seven seas, there were at least two other noteworthy interests that fascinated Hans during his teens. One such interest was sport, most notably boxing, which provided him with enhanced physical strength and speed, two characteristics that would serve him well later. Another—somewhat predictably—was girls. As Kruger put it, "Hans loved girls, and when he found one, he turned the charm on full blast and it almost always worked." In 1929, Hans graduated from Stenhus, leaving him with the question of how to proceed with his life. As time passed, however, and the thought of entering a profession which compelled him to leave his homeland and his romantic interests became less attractive, Hans temporarily put away his dreams of becoming a sea captain like his father and instead enrolled at the University of Copenhagen, with an interest in philology. However, he voluntarily left his studies in 1930 in order to fulfill his military service obligation in the navy, and it was while in uniform that he met the first girl to seriously turn his head—Iris Elizabeth Rand, known as "Musse." But the lure of the sea proved strong and he left Musse behind, reluctantly, once he was invited to EAC for a free education. At the time, the promise of a fulfilling career seemed to compensate for the enforced 10-year marriage ban.[4]

In the spring of 1931, the 20-year-old Tofte was working for the EAC, not only his father's employer, but also the largest business in Copenhagen. The EAC dispatched the young Tofte to Peking to learn Mandarin at the North China Union Language School, the initial step in a planned overseas career. However, Hans chafed under the discipline enforced at the school and when the counselor of the Danish Legation in Peking, Henrik Kauffman, offered Tofte a room in his house instead, Tofte gratefully accepted the offer, and the two men became lifelong friends.

Tofte spent the next two years learning Chinese before relocating to Kirin and later Harbin, Manchuria (modern Jilin, PRC)—in northeast China—for the next six years, watching over EAC interests in the region. During this time, Tofte travelled throughout that part of Manchuria and in northern Korea for his employer, acquiring knowledge and experiences that would pay dividends later in life. He not only developed strong ties with a community of anti-communist White Russians living in the area, but also became intimately familiar with the local road and rail network, which again would aid his later espionage efforts. He also became fluent in Japanese and Russian, as well as improving his Chinese and learning some Korean as well. Tofte also went on big game hunts and became a skilled rider and marksman, at home in the wild regions of Manchuria, Siberia, Mongolia, and northern Korea, gaining knowledge that would prove more valuable than he could ever realize at the time. He also had Danish friends in Manchuria, most notably the Director of the Danish Asiatic Company (not the EAC) Thor Ibsen and his wife Sonja—their relationship became so close that Tofte referred to them as "uncle Thor and aunt Sonja."[5]

The year 1931 also proved to be a prophetic one for Hans, for reasons not at all obvious at the time. In December, during his tenure as an ice-skating waiter at the prestigious Peking Club, Hans met "a very beautiful and feted young American woman" named Marlys Leister Calcina. She had married a young US Marine Corps captain named Julian Brown, who had been posted to China in 1929, along with Marlys. But their marriage lasted only until 1930, when she divorced him, and stayed in Shanghai, only to soon marry again, this time to "an immensely rich Italian financier and industrialist," Piero Calcina. Marlys soon settled comfortably into Shanghai's elite, becoming friends with the Danish director, Lieutenant Colonel Erik Nyholm, and his wife Betty. It was at their invitation that Marlys found herself at the Peking Club for lunch that day. Upon sighting Marlys, Tofte was so taken with her that he smoothly vaulted over their table and the sideboard, while on skates, to stand immediately in front of her, positively smitten. Though five years older than the impetuous young Dane, Marlys was equally struck in a meeting that would prove fateful, though not for some time.[6]

In 1938, Hans returned home to Denmark on leave and recontacted Musse. The pair wanted to marry, but her father was opposed, inspiring Tofte to commit an act of "voluntary romantic kidnapping." Hans stole his father's car and took a willing Musse to Egypt, where they spent several months living together, an act tantamount to a life of crime in that day and age, but not inconsistent with Hans's true nature. When the young lovers announced they were returning home, their families demanded that they wed immediately, which they did, in Berlin on the return trip. By the following year, 1939, Musse was pregnant with their son Finn. Tofte should have headed to Malaysia in 1938 for the EAC, but Musse's father insisted that Hans stay home and got him a job as a secretary at the Copenhagen Fruit Auctions. As one observer noted, this job was "something of a letdown after being his own boss in Manchuria for so many years."[7]

CHAPTER 2

The "Dynamic Dane" in World War II

"In a global and totalitarian war, intelligence must be global and totalitarian."
—Colonel William J. Donovan (Office of Strategic Services, National Park Service)

As the Nazi juggernaut spread throughout much of Europe, beginning in the fall of 1939, Denmark declared its neutrality in 1940 and cut the size of its army in half, hoping to avoid the fate of other European nations. German forces invaded anyway and demanded submission from the Danes; King Christian acquiesced, but did not surrender, meaning that technically Denmark was still a sovereign state. As an indication of what was to come, on July 4, 1940, 1,500 Danish citizens gathered to sing patriotic songs, to remember the 1864 war with Germany, and to recall the bravery of Danish soldiers during that conflict.[1] Such displays of patriotism were enough to bolster national pride and identity but not enough to prompt German reprisals. By 1941, a Danish underground element was operational and an embryonic anti-German press effort was growing.[2]

A restless Tofte channeled his energies into fighting against the German occupiers from 1940–41 as an active member of the Danish underground, though he realized that the Nazis could never be defeated from within an occupied country. So, at Easter 1941, he bid Musse and young Finn farewell and headed for Berlin, intent upon transiting to a location where he could join some sort of resistance group. Once in Berlin, he had to report to the Gestapo office on Alexanderplatz to get a stamp on his passport. When the wait proved to be long and the simple process proved tedious, Tofte affected the demeanor of a boorish Nazi and loudly demanded his stamp immediately. Surprisingly, he not only got his passport stamped at once, but he also got a Gestapo man to carry his luggage to a waiting car. When the Gestapo man asked Tofte's destination—apparently more out of helpfulness than interrogation—Tofte thought quickly and realized he could not say he was going to the American Embassy, though that was indeed his intent. So, he instead said he was going to the Eden Hotel, at the time one of the finest hotels in Berlin. Once he arrived, he took his bags, marched boldly through the lobby, and out the back door—right into the American Embassy.[3]

With the aid of the Americans, which—according to a 1977 resume compiled by Tofte—included "the Grosvenor family of the National Geographic Society in Washington, D.C.," Tofte exited Germany, using forged papers, flew to Lisbon, Portugal—a neutral country—and then on to New York City. Here he sought out the Scottish-Canadian William Stephenson, the head of the British Security Coordination Office (BSCO) and later Special Operations Executive (SOE), the United Kingdom's intelligence element in America. Since the United States was an intelligence infant in the early days of the war, it had to rely on its more experienced cousins across the pond for assistance—like Stephenson, a wealthy and influential Canadian industrialist, who worked from a non-descript suite of offices in New York's Rockefeller Center, labeled "British Security Coordination." (Stephenson, who had a larger-than-life existence, was a millionaire, a former champion boxer, and a fighter pilot and double ace during World War I before becoming a POW and then escaping. A close friend of Prime Minister Winston Churchill, he became increasingly concerned with the rise of Nazi Germany. Seeing the need to bolster the US-UK "special relationship," Prime Minister Churchill had sent Stephenson to New York City in 1940 to run the BSCO.)

Wartime portrait of Sir William Stephenson, head of British Security Coordination Office (BSCO) in New York, 1940. (Alchetron, the Free Social Encyclopedia)

Tofte, who first arrived in the United States in June 1941, found a kindred spirit in Stephenson, who seemed equally impressed with him: the latter said, "The young Dane's radiance and eagerness to get into battle made a strong impression on the spy chief." Indeed, Tofte's linguistic skills and his extensive experience in the Far East made him invaluable for British intelligence, which was actively "recruiting personnel for hazardous missions." As Tofte soon learned, SOE had already recruited another Dane—his Peking acquaintance, Lt. Col. Nyholm, who would become a good friend to Tofte in the near future. Before Tofte and Lt. Col. Nyholm left San Francisco—Lt.

Col. Nyholm to China, Tofte to Singapore—Betty Nyholm threw a small party and invited her friend, Marlys Leister Calcina. Marlys had fled China in the wake of the Japanese assault and was now in Reno, Nevada, to divorce her husband, with whom she had had a daughter, Teresa. This was not the last time that Tofte and Marlys would bump into one another.[4]

Stephenson encouraged Tofte to enlist in the British Army and then promptly dispatched him via Australia to Singapore. In a moment of likely unintentional levity, the British gave Lt. Col. Nyholm the code name "0700" and Tofte "0701," which to future generations looked suspiciously like "007." Upon his arrival in Singapore, Tofte's first job was to recruit a group of young Danish EAC personnel, who would join him in training at Special Training School (STS) 101 at Tanjung Balai, on the Johore Straits outside Singapore. The school was in a large, Art Deco-style bungalow, the former estate of an Armenian millionaire, secluded, inaccessible, in short, perfect. Here, the Danes learned how to use explosives, shoot, and kill with their bare hands from instructors who had learned such techniques from their acknowledged master, Lt. Col. William Ewart Fairbairn, a man whom Tofte would get to know much better shortly.

Known as "Dangerous Dan," Lt. Col. Fairbairn had certainly come by the nickname honestly—the former assistant commissioner of police in Shanghai, China, he had reportedly learned 50 ways to defeat an enemy in hand-to-hand combat. The STS 101 recruits, who all received the rank of lieutenant in the British Army, learned that the favorite targets when engaging the enemy were the eyes and testicles, allowing you to then "quickly and efficiently" kill the enemy with the soon-to-be-famous Sykes-Fairbairn fighting knife. The training Tofte received prepared him to oversee the transport by indigenous people of supplies over the Burma Road to Chinese forces fighting Japanese troops in the interior. The intention behind the school was also to train stay-behind teams that would be dispersed throughout Southeast Asia to not only conduct sabotage operations, but also to start relaying intelligence information to British forces and to recruit indigenous people to fight the Japanese.[5]

Many years later, when in his late 60s, Tofte looked back and summarized in written form the situation in the Far East at the time. In 1978, he recorded his recollections:

> In the summer of 1941, well before "Pearl Harbor," it was imperative in the interest of the British Empire in the Far East that Generalissimo Chiang Kai-Shek and his Chinese government-in-exile be given all possible military help to fight and tie down large Japanese occupation forces in the interior of China…There was no relief in sight unless the Chinese, somehow, could be activated against the Japanese by sheer weight of numbers. There was only one answer: massive guerrilla warfare.

> The interior of China was crawling with guerrillas, hundreds of thousands of them, all the way to Peking. But there was no leadership, no organization and no coordinated effort against the Japanese enemy mainly due to lack of equipment and military supplies. The Japanese invaders were too well entrenched. Only very hard-hitting guerrilla forces would be able to throw the occupying enemy off balance and keep him busy with self-defense to the point where he would be unable to go any place or do anything.[6]

But Japanese war plans and their execution in early December 1941 forced the British and their allies, which would soon include the United States, to shift from supporting Chinese guerrillas to fighting for their lives. Fellow Dane Lt. Col. Nyholm, who would soon play a major role both in the war in China and in the life of Tofte, described this dramatic period in his diary. On December 8, 1941, Lt. Col. Nyholm was in Singapore and recorded his experiences:

> At 4:15 a.m. Japanese aircraft came over and bombed Singapore...Dodged second bombing attack at entrance to airfield, taking shelter in ditch, and scooted out of Singapore in Sunderland flying boat low above the water with R.A.F. fighters, Jap planes and plenty of ack-ack [antiaircraft gun fire] still in the air. Landed at Penang 8:00 a.m. but were sent off immediately to avoid expected Japanese attack. Flew far out to sea, every-body on lookout for enemy aircraft. Landed at Mergui in lower Burma at 2:00 p.m. on last drop of fuel... Southbound flying boat from Rangoon already there...Our two Sunderlands zoomed out of Mergui Hell for leather and wing tips in the water! Landed at Rangoon on the Irrawaddy River at 5:00 p.m...listened to news over the radio: The Japanese are attacking all over the East from Hawaii to Singapore, Pearl Harbor [Honolulu] heavily bombed and U.S. Pacific fleet badly battered, Hongkong bombed, Manila Bombed [*sic*], Singapore bombed, and Japanese invasion of Thailand is in progress meeting little or no resistance. Wake, Guam and Midway islands in the Pacific are also being attacked...Japanese troops have landed in Malaya just outside the border. Complete blackout in Rangoon tonight; Japanese air raid expected, however, there are no air raid shelters available.[7]

From August 1941–May/June 1942, Tofte, sporting the rank of a British/Indian Army major,[8] was in Australia, China, and Malaya on "Official Business for the British Government, Special Branch." But by early 1942, the war was moving quickly—the Japanese occupied the entire northern half of China and the entire coast up to Hong Kong, took Singapore in February 1942 (meaning the abandonment of STS 101), and Chiang Kai-Shek's Nationalist government had fled to Chongqing (Chungking).

Although there was no British diplomatic presence in China at this early date, SOE was represented by Sir John Keswick, KCMG, an SOE veteran and influential businessman in China and Hong Kong then serving as the first secretary at the British Embassy in Chongqing. In Lt. Col. Nyholm's diary entry for December 12, 1942, he described Keswick as "a young Shanghailander, one of the three brothers who own Jardine Mathes & Co. of Shanghai. He seems very pleasant and told of his interesting flight out via Gibraltar, Malta[,] Cairo and India. He had just been to Singapore…absolutely all of our military equipment had been bombed to Hell in Rangoon, also he had spent New Years eve with the boys in Lashio and found, that George Soderbom had lost control there and morale was low." However, dissatisfaction with Keswick and his attitudes and actions set in not long after this initial positive impression. On January 5, 1942, Lt. Col. Nyholm and a colleague had

> serious talks in the afternoon: we feel that John Keswick is taking [a] funny attitude and that he has made various mistakes in Lashio adding to the confusion by introducing himself as "the new boss"! I will have to go to Lashio very soon to straighten out matters—we feel that the British have let us down very badly with their inefficiency and lack of cooperation. John seems to think he is coming to take over the whole show, and "save what can be saved." He even suggests that our outfit might be called "Keswick's Brigade"! Furthermore we are to blossom out as a purely British unit and are to be reinforced with a lot of the officers from Singapore. Told Erik [another Erik—NFI] exactly how I feel about this and how all the boys will feel about it as well—someone will have to tell John a few things one of these days.[9]

Despite the growing animosity between Tofte and Lt. Col. Nyholm on the one hand and Keswick on the other, even after Keswick went on to his next assignment—at the British Embassy, Washington, DC—he was still empowered to answer any further questions about Tofte's British military service in the Far East.[10]

***

The British were well aware that there were some 300,000 Chinese eager to fight the Japanese—the rub was in how best to utilize them in the war effort. SOE suggested using a group of Danes with close ties to China to use them to full advantage. Chiang Kai-Shek accepted the SOE proposal, laying the groundwork for a secret organization known as the China Commando Group (CCG). The CCG was a joint SOE and Chinese intelligence and special operations project stood up in the summer of 1941, intended to benefit both the United Kingdom and China in thwarting the Japanese. The mission of the CCG was to activate sizable guerrilla forces against Japanese occupation armies in the Chinese interior by supplying them with modern military equipment suitable for underground resistance on a large-scale nationwide. Unit personnel would also co-locate with guerrilla leaders, to help plan and execute operations and exercise overall supervision of anti-Japanese resistance. The CCG teams were expected to remain with the guerrillas for at least a year, relying for support on a CCG forward headquarters at Kweiyang. In a later recollection, Tofte described the significance of supplying Chinese guerrillas to thwart the Japanese advance:

> That was the job, top priority and with all possible speed on [an] emergency basis. I was selected for it at New York City, recruited for it by "A Man Called Intrepid" as soon as I landed in America as a war refugee from Europe, and sent straight to Singapore by air across the Pacific to report to the chief of the British Secret Service in the Far East. Because delivering war supplies...to China had to be a secret, undercover operation that no Englishman could handle [*sic*]. It had to be done by neutral people with what is professionally known as natural cover. I was neutral as a Danish citizen. And by happenstance I had a bona fide status as representative of American Madsen Corporation, Inc., a subsidiary of the internationally known Danish Rifle Syndicate.

Thirty-eight-year-old Lt. Col. Nyholm was appointed the CCG head and given the rank of lieutenant colonel in the British/Indian Army, maintaining the thinly veiled subterfuge. Tofte was to be his second, the field commander of the mission and a major in His Majesty's Indian Army, once he had led the first transports of British weapons and explosives through Burma to China. Tofte developed the overall plan of getting aid to the Chinese guerrillas with the assistance of the colorful figure chosen as the chief of all transportation and the top caravan leader, K. G. Soderbom, a Swede from Mongolia experienced in exploration in Central Asia. Weighing in at more than 350 pounds, he was ironically known as "Baby."[11]

The plan was to deliver eight convoys of arms and explosives to the CCG, along the critical, but dangerous, Burma Road. One of these explosives was the brand-new P808, or Nobel 808, since it was produced by Nobel Chemicals Ltd. Easier to handle than TNT or dynamite and more powerful than anything they had used up to that time, it looked like green Play-Doh and smelled faintly of almonds. P808 proved especially effective for anti-personnel operations, sabotage of communications, disruption of rail traffic, and use against all kinds of installations. As one contemporary document put it, "It provided tremendous striking power for small units of well-trained men." These arms and explosives arrived by ship in Rangoon, were then transported by rail to Lashio, near the Chinese frontier and the entrance to the Burma Road, and from there the Danes would transport the cargoes by truck to Kweiyang, south of Chungking, location of CCG headquarters.[12]

The group left the training camp in early December, but Tofte was to stay in Singapore for a few days before flying out. However, the war did not wait for him and the Japanese bombed Singapore while he was staying at the Strand Hotel. When Tofte finally got out and flew to Rangoon, he and Hugh Williamson learned that the Japanese had attacked Pearl Harbor, Hawaii;

Hong Kong; Manila, in the Philippine Islands; the Pacific Islands of Wake, Guam, Midway; and Thailand. Tofte was now certain that the United States would enter the war and, as always, he wanted in on the action. Fortunately, in an instance of clairvoyance, before he left the United States, he had struck a bargain that if that nation declared war, he could switch to US military service. The problem was that his Danish colleagues were still waiting for him at Lashio, compelling him to delay his transition to US service. Furthermore, he learned that while some of the intended supplies for the CCG had reached Lashio intact, some had been lost, and so Tofte and his men spent three weeks scouring Rangoon for loose weapons, trucks, and whatever else they could find to support the Chinese guerrilla movement. Just after New Years, 1942, Lt. Col. Nyholm and Keswick also fled to Rangoon, where the former told Tofte that morale was very low, that Soderbom had lost control, and that Tofte needed to return, which he did, taking a convoy along the Burma Road to Kweiyang. Tofte described the harrowing trip as follows:

> The Burma Road was a disgustingly narrow, stony and in some places muddy road with steep rock walls or deep ravines on the sides, with hairpin bends and violent temperature swings. In the morning we could drive in snow and fog at an altitude of over 3000 meters and in the evening in a warm and humid valley full of cursed mosquitoes. We lived on quinine pills in those days. Lively black market trading had caused the road to develop into something of a clone dyke with many outlandish vehicles and characters. There was no room for two trucks to pass each other, so I had given orders to my people not to hold anyone back. Oncoming traffic had to give way, and if they refused, we threatened simply by running them over the [edge]. In that case, they would not be the first. A place on the road was called "The Rolling Thirties," because deep down in the abyss lay 25–30 wrecks of trucks that had slid [off]. It was an inaccessible place, so the remains of the drivers were still safely in the wreckage.[13]

But Tofte's return proved no panacea for the ongoing supply problems—or for the deteriorating relations with the British. Despite the Japanese bombing of Rangoon, which had sunk two ships carrying arms and supplies for the CCG, and the fact that supplies at Lashio were way down, the British continued to reassure all concerned that additional supplies were on the way. However, delays and foot-dragging exacerbated the problems, as did the growing conflict between Tofte and Lt. Col. Nyholm on the one hand and Keswick on the other. Such sustained conflict brought some of Tofte's lesser qualities to the forefront—as one observer noted, Tofte proved "impatient, impetuous, self-willed, [a man who] had very little faith in authority and had no sense of financial costs, qualities that would later lead him to both success and failure."[14]

Back at Lashio by January 14, 1942, Tofte often had reason to go through Kunming on his various travels, where he formed a friendship with US General

Claire Lee Chennault, leader of the famed "Flying Tigers," and his Chinese wife, "the beautiful but powerful and feared Anna Chan Chennault, nicknamed 'The Dragon Lady.'" By early February, Tofte and his men were in Chungking to train Chinese guerrillas with the meager supplies they had. He also took the opportunity to set up three training camps and was personally responsible for establishing the camp in Chuchow (present-day Chao'an), in eastern Guangdong Province, northeast of Hong Kong. When Tofte complained to Gen. Chennault about British "inefficiency and broken promises," the latter suggested that the CCG ask the US government for arms. On February 20, 1942, Tofte wrote a memo about the current situation of the CCG which, after summarizing problems with "lack of gasoline," "lack of supplies," "lack of standing," "red tape London," and "lack of transport," closed with a "Conclusion" and a "Suggestion." The "Conclusion" paragraph began:

> Although hampered by allied war adversities we may still be able to carry [out] our great plan with regard to guerilla [*sic*] activities in China, if we are given adequate support and left to carry through our own plans in accordance with promises and charter given to us upon arrival at Singapore. This, however, necessitates a complete shake-up and reorganization in our supply base and rear Head Quarters…
>
> Every man in the China Commando Group (Danes) have [*sic*] voluntarily given up personal considerations, run risks not only with regard to their own personal safety, but also with regard to the safety of their families, possessions and connections in Denmark. Ever since they joined the British war effort in the far East they seem to have been frustrated and curtailed in their work. Fortunately they are still full of the right spirit.

In good staff officer fashion, Tofte supplemented his list of complaints with several suggestions:

> (A) That our leader, E. Nyholm, contemplates the possibility of obtaining American assistance under reference to the offer already to hand from Donovan at Washington. (His assistance also seems to have been extremely nonchalantly treated by the British).
>
> (B) That E. N. considers the possibility of a personal visit by himself to the U.S.A. in order to follow the matter up properly. The far East is really America's war theatre and it should be possible to interest American authorities in our show both with regard to funds and equipment.
>
> (C) Meanwhile I could hang on at Chungking as E. N.'s representative. Also we could send our expedition to Chekiang and use up our present stores during the coming 4 months—while E. N. works in the States.

What neither knew, however, was the intense opposition to the CCG and John Keswick by a group of Chinese generals and warlords.[15]

On March 19, 1942, the CCG chief, Lt. Col. Nyholm, wrote a detailed letter to Keswick, SOE's Oriental Mission representative, which laid out the situation as Lt. Col. Nyholm saw it at the time:

Dear John:
Considering the events of the last few days concerning gasoline and Kweiyang and especially the general attitude of our Chinese partners, I feel it is essential that clear lines on which the China Commando Group will have to work be established, as otherwise we are continuously running up blind alleys and controversies will occur with the Chinese.

...it seems as if [the Chinese] are not at all interested in obtaining results with regard to harassing the Japanese. Political intrigues behind the scenes seem to be their main occupation...So far everything we have asked them to do, or which they should have done, or promised to do for us, has not been executed...

...if we continue in the same uncertain manner as we are now doing,...I am afraid we will only continue to incur heavy expenses, but show no results of causing harm to the Japanese...

...unless we can obtain a suitable arrangement it will be better to disband gradually and give up the whole scheme. I for my part do not feel justified in continuing to take the responsibility of the China Command Group and wasting time unless satisfactory results can be obtained...

...I therefore recommend that it is time for the C.C.G. and the contemplated American help to be put directly under the supreme command of the United Nations War Council, under General Stillwell, and taken away from the sole command of General Chow.

An attachment to Lt. Col. Nyholm's letter provided a handy list of CCG foreign personnel by name, nationality, British rank, and duties. The listing indicates that there were 18 Danes who were members of SOE, 16 Brits, 10 Chinese, five Americans, one Belgian, one Frenchman, one Swede, and one Jewish refugee, a truly international undertaking.[16]

Keswick responded on April 15 with an overly warm letter, given the generally frosty relations with the British at times. He wrote:

Dear Erik:
Many thanks for your kind, wise and sympathetic letter. I too have a heavy heart at the misfortunes that have overtaken us, for which I must take all the responsibility.

First I must say that there is no blame attaching to us because circumstances were beyond our control. We have worked hard and no man could have tried more unstintingly than you have to make a success of the Commando Group...

...I have no doubt that one of these days the tide will turn and we shall be able to make some little progress in this land of frustration and complexity. I hope when that day comes we shall be together.

If time permits I hope to write to each member of your group to thank them personally, particularly our friend Hans [Tofte] for whom I have the highest regard, and it is one of my greatest regrets in this affair that I cannot continue to work hand in glove with him and you. I could not wish for happier companions or people who think and work more upon the same lines as I do.

This is a personal letter but I wish to take the opportunity of thanking you most sincerely, not only as a friend, but as a representative of the British Government, for all the hard work and unselfish effort you have put into our cause during the last 6 months, if any man could have made cooperation with the Chinese possible here it was yourself. It is a sad parting but

> I am sure that the same enthusiasm which has carried you along in China will bring you the success which you richly deserve in America. I know you will leave with the knowledge of my true friendship and esteem and you go with the full confidence of the British authorities.
>
> Yours ever,
> [signed] John Keswick[17]

In early 1942, General Joseph Warren "Vinegar Joe" Stillwell had been dispatched to serve as chief of staff to Chinese Nationalist leader Chiang Kai-Shek and he was no friend to intelligence services in general and especially not to Colonel William J. Donovan, the Coordinator of Information. He also had little patience for generals who colored outside the lines, which meant that relations with Gen. Chennault and the Flying Tigers deteriorated as well. His arrival proved to be a death knell for the CCG, as Chiang Kai-Shek ordered the CCG out of China a month later. Begun with such enthusiasm, the 8-month-duration CCG turned into a fiasco, thanks to policy failures in London, mutual suspicions between the British and the Nationalist Chinese, and the chasm between British colonial and Chinese nationalist mindsets. Thus, the Danes, including Tofte and Lt. Col. Nyholm, were compelled to leave China with a bad taste in their mouths—"they had voluntarily risked life and limb for a cause that was suffocated in intrigue." Just two days after the CCG left China, the American Special Operations Group was created, managed by Stillwell, a reluctant Col. Donovan, and Chinese General Tai Li (Dai Li), who became the head of the Sino-American Special Technical Cooperative Organization (SACO, pronounced "Socko"). A top-secret group of 2,500 US Navy personnel dedicated to helping their Chinese allies fight off the Japanese, they transmitted classified information to Allied planners on the disposition of Japanese troops, raided Japanese vessels on Chinese rivers, and, like the CCG, trained Chinese guerrillas in irregular warfare. The offbeat unit, more colorful than even OSS, was known for its "What the Hell?" banner and its pennant with three question marks, three asterisks, and three exclamation marks on a white background.

Nationalist Chinese leader Chiang Kai-Shek. (Library of Congress)

A resourceful group, SACO was led by US Naval Academy graduate Captain Milton "Mary" Miles, who had served in China in the 1920s and '30s, on patrol boats plying the

Yangtze River. A passionate supporter of China, Capt. Miles was plagued not only by persistent supply problems but also by the incessant bickering between the Army, Navy, and OSS. To aid in conducting their operations, Capt. Miles formed an unlikely alliance with Gen. Li, who was the leader of China's Military Bureau of Investigation Services and one of Chiang Kai-Shek's right-hand men. Once the COI became OSS and Col. Donovan gained sufficient power, he was able to install Keswick as the liaison officer to SOE at OSS headquarters, thereby poking Stillwell and Gen. Li in the eye. Meanwhile, Tofte and Lt. Col. Nyholm found themselves in India, where British Colonel Orde Charles Wingate was mobilizing a force, primarily composed of Burmese tribesmen, to fight the Japanese in Burma. Tofte assisted Col. Wingate in organizing this force, but otherwise washed his hands of the British, at least for the time being. Before heading to the United States to render his services, he ensured that his Danes could fight on under Col. Wingate. Thus reassured, Tofte benefitted from "friends among high-ranking military personnel" who made arrangements for Tofte to come to the United States by military plane via Egypt and the Gold Coast. As his personnel file noted, he had "worked under extremely dangerous conditions in effective operations against the enemy. He was among the last to escape from the Far East when the circumstances of war compelled such action."[18]

***

But fate was about to deal Tofte an unexpected hand—immediately following the Japanese bombing of Pearl Harbor, President Franklin D. Roosevelt had summoned Col. Donovan, then attending a baseball game, to the White House. At the time, Col. Donovan was serving as the nation's Coordinator of Information (COI), a grandiloquent title for a humble enterprise that had begun on July 11, 1941, with Col. Donovan and seven assistants sharing one telephone in the Office of the Budget. However, in just a few months' time, the COI had grown to several hundred employees. But the president now

Chinese Nationalist General Tai Li and Captain Milton Miles, USN, Chongqing, China, December 1942. (https://warfarehistorynetwork.com/article/bringing-the-war-to-the-japanese-in-china, accessed January 19, 2024)

informed Col. Donovan that the nation was standing up a force known as Office of Strategic Services (OSS) and that he had appointed Col. Donovan as its first director; OSS would include all of the COI, save the overt propaganda side, which became the Office of War Information (OWI). According to the official language of the day, the "Office of Strategic Services is an agency of the United States Joint Chiefs of Staff charged with collecting and analyzing strategic information and secret intelligence required for military operations, and planning and executing programs of physical sabotage and morale subversion against the enemy in support of military operations."[19] Subordinating OSS to the JCS might have seemed bizarre at the time, but the rationale was that such was necessary to better coordinate activities with the military.

Both Col. Donovan and OSS were larger-than-life, with the former described as a man "who could visualize an oak when he saw an acorn," arguably just the man for such a daunting mission. The OSS—which drew many of its recruits from America's social and intellectual elite—was commonly referred to as "Oh So Social" and was informally divided into scholars, collectively known as "Choirboys," and field agents, known as "Cowboys." Even the ranks of Hollywood gave up some of their own to serve in OSS, notably Quentin Roosevelt, Teddy's grandson and Col. Donovan's personal representative to Chinese Nationalist leader Chiang Kai-Shek, as well as Lieutenant John Hamilton, better known to moviegoers as actor Sterling Hayden, who would help supply Yugoslav guerrillas during the war. In the minds of many, however, the heart of OSS consisted of two distinct divisions—Secret Intelligence (SI) and Special Operations (SO)—the former focused on foreign intelligence and modeled on Britain's MI6, while the latter conducted sabotage and espionage operations and was modeled on His Majesty's Special Operations Executive (SOE).[20]

OSS member and future DCI William J. Casey once spoke at length as to the nature of OSS and also Major General Donovan's wisdom in learning from the British how to establish and operate a professional and capable intelligence service. In his December 5, 1974, remarks upon receipt of the William J. Donovan Award at the OSS Veterans' Dinner, Casey observed:

> What was the OSS and what was it all about? It was probably the most diverse aggregation ever assembled of scholars, scientists, bankers and foreign correspondents, tycoons, psychologists and football stars, circus managers and circus freaks, safe-crackers, lock pickers and pickpockets—some of them in this room tonight. You name them, Donovan collected them. What did he do with them? Well, he unleashed them—and [they] delivered magnificently.
>
> Now, General Donovan unleashed this talent in a very intelligent and perceptive way. He knew he had a bunch of rank amateurs going into a very professional game. He knew the British had run an intelligence service for five centuries and had been working for three

> years to carry out Winston Churchill's dramatic order "to set Europe ablaze." So, Donovan either set up joint operations with the British...or he set up parallel but closely related organizations and arranged for an appropriate degree of British tutelage...Donovan grasped the value of the clandestine side of war as no other American of his time. But, its potential was realized not by his OSS but by the combined effort of British and American clandestine services...OSS, coming into the European war three years late, would not have been able to do very much at all if the British had not taken us in as junior partners and so generously taught us all they knew.[21]

Donovan statue at CIA headquarters. (CIA)

While the decision to stand up OSS brought numerous actions in its wake, one of the most pressing was the need to identify and procure secure, secluded, forested training areas close to Washington, DC, where live-fire exercises could be conducted in a safe environment away from prying eyes; if potential properties already belonged to the federal government, so much the better. Two distinct areas seemed ideal—the 15,000-acre Chopawamsic Recreation Demonstration Area (RDA), now Prince William Forest Park, in northern Virginia, and the 10,000-acre Catoctin Mountain Park in western Maryland. Both were not only Federal properties but already had a number of structures on-site, thanks to the efforts of the Civilian Conservation Corps (CCC) and the Works Progress Administration (WPA) during the Depression. Major General Donovan promptly directed the War Department to secure leases for both properties. The latter property would become Area B for basic special operations training, including Special Operations (SO), Secret Intelligence (SI), and Operational Groups (OG); Area C was the training area within the Chopawamsic RDA for the Communications branch, though it was actually administered by the Special Operations element; and Area F, the former site of the financially strapped Congressional Country Club in Bethesda, Maryland, would—along with other facilities—train the OG soldiers in sabotage techniques.[22]

As a Special Operations brochure put it, "Special Operations Branch plans and carries out operations of physical sabotage, its primary objective being the destruction of enemy personnel, materiel and installations by subversive attack. Resistance groups are organized, supplied and equipped with the weapons and special implements they require. Resistance groups are instructed in modern forms of sabotage and provided with special devices for all forms of subversive assault."[23] In encyclopedic terms, the mission of the Operational Groups was "to organize, train, and equip local resistance organizations, and to conduct 'hit and run' missions against enemy-controlled roads, railways, and strong points, or to prevent their destruction by retreating enemy forces." Unlike their Special Operations brethren, members of the OGs always operated in uniform; trained in infantry tactics, parachuting, guerrilla warfare techniques, and the use of foreign weapons; and had organic medical assets. On paper, most Operational Groups had four officers and some thirty enlisted members, though in reality most OGs were half that size. During World War II, they operated in Burma, China, France, Greece, Italy, Norway, and Yugoslavia.[24]

Tofte and Lt. Col. Nyholm returned to the United States at the end of summer 1942, and Tofte moved into Lt. Col. Nyholm's apartment at 4 E. 74th Street, Manhattan. Both sought to continue their war against the Nazis as OSS officers, preferably together, and preferably in Sweden. But repeated queries to OSS brought no response—not only was OSS leery of taking recruits off the streets, even experienced ones, but Tofte and Lt. Col. Nyholm's old nemesis John Keswick was still in Washington, DC, as the OSS liaison to SOE and as unfavorably disposed towards the pair as ever. However, other British citizens were more supportive—on August 25, 1942, Sir George Moss wrote a complimentary note summarizing Tofte's aid in the Far East. As Moss wrote:

> Hans Vilhelm Tofte was employed by His Majesty's Government from August 15th, 1941 to June 1st, 1942, on special war work of a confidential nature in China and the Far East [emphasis in original here and where it appears in other quoted matter].
>
> While in China Hans Vilhelm Tofte acted as major in the British Army and displayed loyalty and considerable resource, ability and qualities of character in carrying out the duties entrusted him.
>
> In recognition of his services I have very great pleasure in making this statement and in wishing him the success he deserves in any new undertaking.

Not until November 20, 1942, did Tofte and Lt. Col. Nyholm finally receive an audience with OSS Colonel Ellery C. Huntington, Jr., which went well. An illustrious figure in his own right, Col. Huntington was a World War I veteran who had played football against future general and president Dwight Eisenhower as a star quarterback at Colgate University and knew the future president personally. He had earned an LL.D. degree at Harvard and was a highly respected New York attorney who specialized in corporate law. Well-traveled, he spoke French, Italian, Spanish, and some German. The pair clearly impressed Col. Huntington, as other interviews followed over the next two weeks, but both were still foreigners and SOE wanted no Danes in Sweden, since the British service viewed Scandinavia as an exclusive area for British operations.

One thing that did become abundantly clear in the course of this process was that OSS was more interested in Tofte than they were in Lt. Col. Nyholm—while the latter, whom they described as "a coordinator behind a desk," had been tilting at windmills with the British, Tofte had been training Chinese guerrillas in combat, experience that OSS sorely needed. Initially there were thoughts of sending Tofte back to Denmark as an operative, but OSS finally decided that he was of even greater value as a trainer. A late December 1942 memo explained that "Tofte was one of the Danes of the China Commando Group…there is no ill feeling against any of these Danes, in spite of the failure of the plan…<u>Tofte would probably make a good instructor in one of our schools here, especially in demolition work, as he seems to have been very well trained in this, and had, I believe, some practical experience in the field</u> [emphasis in original]."

On New Year's Eve, 1943, Tofte was informed that he could not go directly into OSS as an officer. But he definitely wanted to fight, and as an American, so he opted for the only course of action that seemed open to him, namely, enlisting as a private in the US Army. His formal enlistment date in the US Army was February 11, 1943, in New York City—he was living at 923 Fifth Avenue at the time—and the future seemed set for the bearer of military serial number 32801604. In a letter Tofte wrote to a Mr. Howland, he explained, "I shall consequently join the American army, obtain my citizenship after ninety days of basic training and then endeavor to have myself placed in a position where I feel I can be most useful." Tofte referred to the "citizenship after 90 days" process as "a procedure which is now very common."[25]

Not surprisingly, he was soon ordered to report as a recruit to an infantry base in Virginia, likely Camp Patrick Henry, which opened in late 1942. A week after reporting, he was promoted to sergeant and tasked with training his fellow recruits. During one such training session, he was observed by none other than "Dangerous Dan" Fairbairn, who had already heard of Tofte and his exploits in Burma and China and concluded that he had a real affinity for close-quarters combat. Impressed by what he witnessed, Fairbairn went directly to Col. Donovan and requested that Tofte be assigned as his assistant; on February 18, 1943, Tofte was told that he would be transferred to OSS as an instructor and assistant to Fairbairn.[26]

Arguably one of the most illustrious trainers at the various OSS facilities, Fairbairn relied on a 12-inch-long, 7-ounce, double-edged "OSS dagger" in training recruits, which he dispensed to them with the serious admonition, "Keep it sharp, it may save your life." The so-called "Fairbairn System" involved slashing motions which targeted an enemy's jugular arteries, abdomen, heart, and either below the shoulder blade or above the wrist. As one trainee noted, "It wasn't pretty, but it was effective." Tofte felt qualified to serve as Fairbairn's assistant, given his early youth in the Far East, where he had fended off Manchurian bandits and Chinese outlaws by employing the lethal self-defense measures he had learned from Fairbairn in Shanghai. Tofte's plum assignment likely was due to his unique background—and perhaps also to the fact that the two "Bills" (Stephenson and Col. Donovan) were close friends. Tofte served as a trainer in guerrilla warfare at the OSS facility at the failing Congressional Country Club in Bethesda, Maryland, just outside Washington, DC, formally known as Area F. In his tenure as a trainer there, he instructed such noteworthy Jedburgh candidates as future Director of Central Intelligence (DCI) William Casey and future father of the US Army Special Forces Aaron Bank. It was also in this training environment that he first met two future illustrious colleagues and friends, Tracey Barnes and Desmond Fitzgerald.[27]

The training focus at Area F was clearly on silent killing and sabotage. Appropriately, trainees arrived at the secret camp blindfolded. "Agents were to stand with their backs to the target, and on command, within three seconds, they were to turn around and hit two targets moving in opposite directions. Fairbairn was the master of the art of killing, but he was well into his years," which meant that much of the actual training was conducted by Tofte rather than Fairbairn, who was 58 years old in 1943. The "Dynamic Dane" trained not only OSS personnel, but also FBI agents and US Marine Corps non-commissioned officers (NCO). As Tofte recalled, "I drew up a training program which should make each agent a perfect fighting machine. He had to be able to not only attack and defend himself in every imaginable way, he had to be able to operate behind enemy lines, inflict maximum damage, and avoid capture. If he was caught, he should be able to break free and make it back to his own lines." Within six months, Tofte was recognized as the world's second-best silent killer after "Dangerous Dan," who had to frequently remind Tofte, "Now,

Lieutenant Colonel William Fairbairn, British Royal Marine at Camp X, Canada. (Camp X)

remember, it's only training." The two grew close in that environment, as indicated by a postwar letter Fairbairn wrote:

> My dear Hans:
> Before severing my connections with the Office of Strategic Services and returning to England, I want to thank you for your wonderful assistance during the training of the Italian Operational Group at Area "F" in 1943. Although I held the post of Chief Instructor, it was you as my assistant who really built up the Training Staff to such a height of perfection that they were, very rightly so, soon the "The Talk of the Town." I have since met many of the students on their return to the States and you will be pleased to know that they openly state that many of them are alive today, owing to the type of training they received…Your Training Schedule was later copied and sent as a specimen to all Training Areas in the O.S.S. This I maintain is the highest praise that could be given to anyone, and I am personally very pleased to have been associated with you…In saying goodbye and the best of luck always, I have only one wish—That is, in the near future we shall have an opportunity to work together again.[28]

While Fairbairn was impressed, the harsh methods Tofte employed at Area F also made enemies, notably a prospective officer, Major Robert Koch, whom Tofte assessed as "completely impossible" during training and whom he described in a report as "completely unsuitable" for Special Operations. But Maj. Koch had powerful friends, who not only ensured that he saw Tofte's report but also that he ultimately was sent to Italy as a Special Operations officer and major. He would remain a thorn in Tofte's side for some time to come.[29]

When he wasn't training SO recruits, Tofte spent time with his friend Kauffmann in Washington, DC. He was once invited to a small, private party at Kauffmann's house but was strictly ordered never to divulge who he saw there—the "mystery man" proved to be his recently escaped countryman and world-renowned physicist Dr. Niels Bohr, who had won the Nobel Prize in Physics in 1922 and was part of the British mission to Los Alamos, where he paid periodic visits to Dr. Robert Oppenheimer, in charge of the atomic bomb development project at Los Alamos. Tofte also spent as much time as possible with Marlys, but she was in New York, so their time together was limited. They both wanted to marry, but an employee of Kauffmann's convinced Tofte that they should wait until his divorce from "Musse" was finalized, though he was increasingly convinced that Marlys was the woman for him.[30]

Meanwhile, he was waiting, most impatiently, to make a more direct contribution to the United States' eventual victory in the war, making a pest of himself cajoling Col. Donovan to deploy him as an OSS officer. He didn't need to convince OSS of his value and potential for greater contributions—as an entry in his personnel file notes, "Because of his military proficiency and his wide knowledge of guerrilla warfare, OSS recommended to the War

Department that his talents and ability could be more fully utilized as a commissioned officer." Furthermore, several friends either volunteered or were asked to provide written appeals to get Tofte the direct commission they thought he so richly deserved. On February 22, 1943, both State Department officer Cabot Coville and Colonel William Mayer sent letters to the Officer Procurement Division of the War Department testifying to his suitability for such. Coville wrote:

> I wish to record with you my full endorsement of his [Tofte's] qualifications and my recommendation that the application be approved. I have closely and personally known the applicant since 1932 and am thoroughly acquainted with his extraordinary capacity for leadership…In the accomplishment of the assignments which have been given to him he had shown tact, rare leadership, and competence. His gift with people is equalled by few…I take pleasure in unqualifiedly recommending Hans Tofte for the responsibilities both of American citizenship and of service as an officer of the United States Army.

Colonel Mayer's letter did not address Tofte's bid to become an American citizen, but was equally laudatory in terms of his capabilities as a US Army officer. Colonel Mayer penned these words:

> I hereby unreservedly recommend Mr. Hans V. Tofte for commission in the United States Army. I have personally known Mr. Tofte for over two years, and he has been known to friends of mine for over ten years. I saw him on duty as an officer of a British-Danish commando unit in Burma and in China. He has high qualities of leadership, and the necessary professional attainments and high moral character required of an officer in our army. I should be very happy to have him serve as an officer under my command.[31]

Dated the same day as the letters of Colville and Col. Mayer was one from Lieutenant Colonel J. M. McHugh, USMC. Lieutenant Colonel McHugh, an "old China hand," had graduated from the US Naval Academy in 1922 and went to China the following year to study the country and the language. He wrote a textbook on China and a Chinese-English dictionary, both of which were used by the British and American embassies and the military in China until the Japanese took Shanghai in 1937. He spent some 20 years in China, serving as an intelligence officer for the 4th Marines and the US Asiatic Fleet, as well as the Naval Attaché for Air and a special representative of US Navy Secretary Frank Knox to Chiang Kai-Shek, who was a close friend. In his recommendation for Tofte to the Personnel Procurement Division of the War Department, Lt. Col. McHugh wrote:

> 1. I certify that I have known Hans Wilhelm Tofte, Danish citizen, since 1933 when he was employed by the East Asiatic Company in Manchuria. Mr. Tofte returned to Denmark in 1937. He again came under my observation in November, 1940, when he returned to China as a member of a secret British Mission. In my capacity at that time as Naval

> Attache and Naval Attache for Air to the American Embassy, China, I was intimately acquainted with the nature of his mission and had occasion to observe him closely. He had just graduated from a course in "Commando Warfare" in Singapore and was holding the position of second in command as a Major (temporary), British Army, of a group of alien volunteers, chiefly of Danish nationality, under the auspices of the British Army with a view to supplying the guerrilla forces in China with modern military equipment and active military assistance against the Japanese.
>
> 2. I know Mr. Tofte to be a man of the highest integrity and to possess great force of character and executive ability. He has a pleasing personality and high qualities of leadership. He speaks the following languages:
> Danish (fluent), English (fluent), German (fluent),
> Chinese (fair), Russian (fair), Japanese (slight).
> 3. I consider Mr. Tofte to be especially well qualified for special work either in Europe or the Far East.[32]

On May 11, 1943, a memo from Lieutenant Colonel Kenneth H. Baker, OSS Schools and Training Branch, stated, "Pursuant to the request of the Board of Officers, this is to certify that Sergeant Hans Tofte is to be commissioned and assigned immediately to foreign service. There are operations both in SO and ON, for which his qualifications make him eligible. Both these branches have asked for his assignment upon completion of his commission." But while Tofte's receipt of a direct commission worked its way through the system, the Army was astute enough to realize that it could make better use of their foreign-born NCO in the meantime. On May 18, 1943, Major Philip G. Lovell wrote to Brig. Gen. Donovan concerning OSS training at Area F and recommended "the transfer of Sgt. Hans Tofte from Schools and Training Branch to OSS Operational Groups, having him put in charge of building and supervising the various training courses." Major Lovell specifically wanted Tofte left at Area F to instruct 101st Cavalry NCOs in "fieldcraft, close combat, physical training, [and] small arms." Several weeks later, Tofte received a likely surprising letter from a Captain Werner Michael Iversen, chief representative of the "Free Danes" in London, the collective term for all able-bodied Danish citizens living outside Nazi-occupied Denmark, who were encouraged to join especially the American or British armies. Several thousand Danes who fought on the Allied side during the war were later decorated with the Danish Medal of Freedom, and Tofte would be among them. As Iversen's letter explained:

> The British authorities have informed me in details of the splendid work you did as a fighting Dane in the Far East 1941–42 in your, as I understood, recognized capacity as an officer in the British Service.
>
> …It is with a feeling of pride we Free Danes in London hear that a countryman, whenever he can, is willing to stake his own life to help achieve victory for the cause of freedom.

> Although not in personal touch with us your record of service has been followed with great interest and by the instigation of the British Authorities I have been very glad to inscribe your name on the Free Danish Role [*sic*] with honorable mention…
>
> Yours sincerely,
>
> sgd, Captain W. Michael Iversen

Whatever else could be said about Tofte's wartime service, it seemed especially appreciated by his freedom-loving countrymen.[33]

Whether he was convinced or worn down, Brig. Gen. Donovan eventually relented—on June 14, 1943, Tofte received an Honorable Discharge as a sergeant in OSS, the very same day on which he received a temporary appointment as a captain; as the document read, "By the direction of the President you are temporarily appointed and commissioned in the Army of the United States, effective this date, in the grade and section shown in the address above." The commission would remain in effect for the duration of the war and for six months thereafter, unless terminated earlier. Enclosed was an "oath of office" form which he was to "execute and return promptly to the agency from which it was received by you. The execution and return of the required oath of office constitute an acceptance of your appointment. No other evidence of acceptance is required." Interestingly, the appointment letter also included a medical item that otherwise could have been problematic—"Waiver is granted for removal of semilunar cartilage, left knee, on physical examination report dated April 27, 1943, made at General Dispensary, U.S. Army, Washington, D.C." It must have come as a relief to Tofte that neither his over-exuberant Cossack dancing nor a bona fide wartime injury to the same body part would derail his goal of becoming an OSS officer.[34]

In June 1943, a memo from Maj. Lovell to Col. Huntington read, "We have asked for the transfer to Operational Groups of Captain Hans Tofte, and if we do not have him as a permanent instructor we will be severely handicapped because he is the main man in our instructor staff…My suggestion is to make Captain Hans Tofte Chief Instructor after Major Fairbairn has completed the two weeks above mentioned." This back-handed compliment was supplemented by another memo to Col. Huntington just three days later, in which Lt. Col. Baker of the OSS Schools and Training Branch wrote, "He [Tofte] is extremely anxious for an assignment which will give him opportunity for action of a more direct sort than that which he gets as an instructor, and we have no desire to hang on to him if and when such an assignment should become available." Later that month, another memo from Maj. Lovell to Col. Huntington said "I am please [*sic*] to report that Hans has been commissioned a Captain and I think we are very fortunate to have such a man on our training staff. Unfortunately, due to an old knee injury Hans has been commissioned for limited service, but I am hoping that I can get this waived." To expedite matters, that same month Tofte volunteered for "an exceptionally difficult and dangerous mission," the purpose of which was the destruction of the Italian oil industry in Albania. He was placed in command of the unit and left for the Middle East on August 25, 1943, but the mission was cancelled after Italy surrendered on September 8, 1943, and joined the Allies.[35]

While Brig. Gen. Donovan sought to expedite his US citizenship, Tofte was released from duty with OSS in Washington and instead "assigned to station outside continental limits of US," which proved to be Cairo, Egypt, initially. On July 19, 1943, he was notified that he had been selected for OSS operations in Italy, once he had taken a course in intelligence work. But before he could head to the Middle East, there were a few other details to attend to—first, he had to lead 20 Norwegian officers and 96 privates at Camp Hale, Colorado, through a training program, as they and a small group of US officers were to constitute a special operations unit in Norway, the Norwegian-American 99th Infantry Battalion (Separate).

The 99th, which had a complement of 1,001 men at full strength, was an elite unit, limited to Norwegians and Americans with direct Norwegian descent; members were expected to have a working knowledge of Norwegian and preferably already know how to ski, since Camp Hale was at an elevation of 9,200 feet. The Norwegians were at Camp Hale to learn the finer points of ski training alongside the US Army's 10th Mountain Division and, while they were there, OSS had asked for volunteers from the 99th, ultimately selecting 12 officers and 80 enlisted for the Norwegian Special Operations Group (NORSOG). Second, and more importantly, he wanted to marry Marlys before he deployed, a pleasant task he took care of on July 24, 1943, the same day he received written verification of his US citizenship. His letters to her had "tenderized her," and he was convinced she was the woman for him. Then he was off to Cairo.[36]

CHAPTER 3

Yugoslavia and Operation *Audrey*

In July 1943, the Allies launched Operation *Husky*, an amphibious landing on the island of Sicily, the beginning of a long and bloody advance up the heel of Italy's boot. Donovan, who had been promoted to brigadier general in March, was convinced that maintaining control of Yugoslavia was key to the European war. German forces had invaded Yugoslavia in spring 1941, but a robust, albeit badly divided, resistance movement had sprung up quickly, centered in the sparsely populated mountains of the country. The goals of OSS operations in Yugoslavia fell into several different categories—first, to assist resistance members in sabotaging German rail lines carrying supplies back to the *Vaterland*; second, to tie down tens of thousands of German troops that otherwise would be on the front lines threatening Allied forces; third, to rescue the downed American aviators, primarily from the 15th Air Force's B-24 bomber fleet and its assigned fighter escorts, from bombing missions originating in Italy and bound for the critical oil fields of Ploesti, Romania; and fourth, to possibly deceive Hitler into thinking that the long-anticipated Allied assault on Hitler's "Fortress Europe" might come in the Balkans rather than Normandy. To this point in the war, Yugoslavia had been considered part of the British wartime orbit and SOE had the responsibility of supplying the Yugoslav partisans by air; however, this method proved slow and ineffective, and the supplies were often intercepted by the Germans or their Croatian allies, the Ustashi.[1]

Although most Yugoslavs were united in their hatred of, and determination to fight, Hitler, that was often the extent of cooperation with their countrymen. The German occupation of the country basically divided the population between the communists of Josip Broz, a Croatian better known as Tito, whose partisans held sway over the mountains and forests of northern Bosnia, and the royalist Chetniks of General Draza Mihailovic, a Serb, whose forces operated from a base in the wooded mountains of southern Montenegro. By fall 1943, Allied forces had invaded Italy and Tito's forces had gained control of the Dalmatian coast and several offshore islands. Allied leaders realized it was in their best interest to assist the Yugoslav partisans by delivering supplies to them to support the fight against the Nazis; the ideological rub was that some were communist-leaning, like Tito and his followers, while others were the monarchist guerrillas of Gen. Mihailovich, an issue that would become a sizable thorn in the sides of British and American leaders alike.[2]

But Brig. Gen. Donovan, not known for his patience, had already secretly sent in two OSS officers to assess the situation in Yugoslavia first-hand—baseball star Morris "Moe" Berg and Major Linn Farrish—both of whom concluded that the Allies should back Tito. Significantly, Prime Minister Winston Churchill argued the same and convinced President Roosevelt to forbid OSS from supporting Gen. Mihailovich. On July 26, 1942, Brig. Gen. Donovan traveled to London to meet the SOE chief—General Colin Gubbins—and the two spy chieftains agreed that Yugoslavia would remain in the British command sphere, but that OSS could have agents in-country and support resistance movements. The following month, Brig. Gen. Donovan decided to openly send OSS personnel into Yugoslavia, preferring to rely on information collected by his own intelligence personnel rather than those of the British.

In the third week of August, two OSS officers were airdropped into Yugoslavia—appropriately enough, one into each of the two warring factions' camps. Thus, US Army Captain Melvin O. "Benny" Benson landed in Tito's headquarters, while US Marine Corps Captain Walter R. Mansfield came down in Gen. Mihailovich's camp. Captain Mansfield was a Boston native, a Harvard graduate, and a former member of Brig. Gen. Donovan's New York City law firm, who had joined OSS as a civilian but who was also a USMC Reserve officer; he had learned demolitions and guerrilla warfare techniques at OSS Special Operations training facilities in Maryland, Virginia, and in the United Kingdom. He landed with 15 canisters of supplies, including small arms, radios, and 3 tons of ammunition. He was later joined by Lieutenant Colonel Albert B. Seitz and Captain George Musulin, the latter an American of Serbian ancestry. All three OSS officers were very impressed by the Chetniks.[3]

Captain Benson became an equally dedicated supporter of Tito, and was joined by Lieutenant Colonel Richard "Bob" Weil, who despite his tender age of 27 was the former president of Bamberger's department store, a division of the renowned R. H. Macy & Company. In November 1943, they were joined by the "Alum" team of OSS personnel, headed by Lieutenant George

Wuchinich, a second-generation American from Pittsburgh, whose parents were Orthodox Serbs from Serbia. The "Alum" team jumped into partisan-held territory near Ljubljana in Slovenia, the first OSS team to land in northern Yugoslavia. Lieutenant Wuchinich was accompanied by a Greek-American radio operator, Sergeant Sfikes, and four other enlisted men. Lieutenant Wuchinich and his men were not initially trusted by the partisans but joint combat actions removed any doubts on both sides and Lt. Wuchinich compared the partisans to Continental soldiers fighting in the American Revolution.[4]

As the Allies moved from Sicily across the Straits of Messina, Tofte and his colleagues sat in their hotel in Cairo, thoroughly bored, waiting eagerly for missions in southern Europe and the Balkans. It was while cooling his heels in the hotel that he met another OSS officer who would become a colleague and friend, 1st Lieutenant Robert E. S. Thompson, described as "a glorious fellow with a terrible tongue. He could curse continuously for five minutes without repeating himself." Ironically, the Jerusalem-born son of a missionary couple, 1st Lt. Thompson had been a reporter for *The Philadelphia Inquirer* prior to the war. As Tofte recalled, "He had a fantastic flair for obtaining things, often by sheer trickery, an ability that was to prove very valuable." It was also during this interlude that Tofte first met another OSS officer who would even more powerfully affect his future, Lieutenant Commander Frank Wisner—as Tofte's first biographer put it, "Tofte and Wisner's friendship came to link their destinies for many years to come." Despite the fact that Tofte was not an American and didn't have the same academic background as the University of Virginia-educated lawyer Wisner, the two were nevertheless brothers-in-spirit.[5]

Key to enabling the Yugoslav partisans to resist the Germans was their ability to be consistently and ably resupplied by the Allies. It occurred to several observers that the Allies could deliver an increased volume of supplies more rapidly by sea than by air, the current method practiced by the British; as Tofte characterized it, the British operation was "too slow and too limited in nature." Also, a number of Yugoslav ships and crews had been interned on Italy's east coast and as these were liberated in the Allied advance, the ships could be used to transport ammunition, weapons, supplies, and freed Yugoslav partisan POWs; from eastern Italy, the distance to Yugoslavia was only 150 nautical miles. But OSS realized that haste was necessary, before the Yugoslav ships and personnel, now freed, escaped their grasp.[6]

This was the basic plan that the 33-year-old Captain Tofte and 32-year-old 1st Lt. Thompson submitted to their Cairo-based immediate superior, Major Louis Huot, on September 12, 1943. Major Huot liked the plan and approved it within six days. On September 16, Brig. Gen. Donovan dispatched the following generic note:

> TO WHOM IT MAY CONCERN:
>
> On or about 16 September, 1943, the following named officers are proceeding on a secret mission of great importance to SICILY and the ITALIAN MAINLAND on behalf of my command, the OFFICE OF STRATEGIC SERVICES, United States Joint Chiefs of Staff:
>
> H.V. TOFTE, Capt., AUS, O-525313
>
> R.E.S. THOMPSON, 1st. Lt., AUS, O-923962
>
> Your assistance in expediting their mission and their return to this Headquarters will be in the interest of the prosecution of the war and will be deeply appreciated by me.
>
> WILLIAM J. DONOVAN
> Brig. Gen., Inf.
> Director of Strategic Services.

The final approval was that of British Army General Henry Maitland Wilson, the commander in chief, Middle East, since February 1943. This labyrinthine chain of approvals was necessitated by the fact that Yugoslavia lay within the geographic jurisdiction of Wilson, while Italy was within the control of Gen. Eisenhower as Allied commander in chief of the North African Theater of Operations, areas of control neatly bifurcated by the Adriatic Sea. In strategic terms, "The plan was roughly to establish an advanced OSS base on the Adriatic coast of Italy by having officers of SO, M E [Special Operations, Middle East] follow the British Eighth Army, then fighting its way up the 'Heel' of Italy, and select a suitable site from which contact could be made with [Tito's] Army in Dalmatia with a view to organizing a supply line across the Adriatic." Thus began Operation *Audrey*, the shipborne resupply of Yugoslav partisans, whose operations, if successful, could potentially tie down a substantial portion of German and Italian manpower and supplies.[7]

On October 5, 1943, Maj. Huot and 1st Lt. Thompson were dispatched from Cairo to Algiers, to meet Tofte, expected shortly, and to establish a new OSS headquarters at Bari, Italy, commanded by Lieutenant Commander Turner McBaine. According to a report written by the chief of the Yugoslav desk at Bari at the time, "These three officers [Tofte, Thompson, and Huot] were in charge of shipping supplies to the Partisan Yugoslavs. They were busy day and night, and without adequate help they were doing an excellent job." As Maj. Huot and 1st Lt. Thompson were staying busy hurriedly collecting Yugoslav ships—just ahead of Tito attempting to do the same—Brig. Gen. Donovan ensured that a portion of Bari harbor was reserved for Operation *Audrey*, and that would become the storage location for supplies bound for the Yugoslav guerrillas.

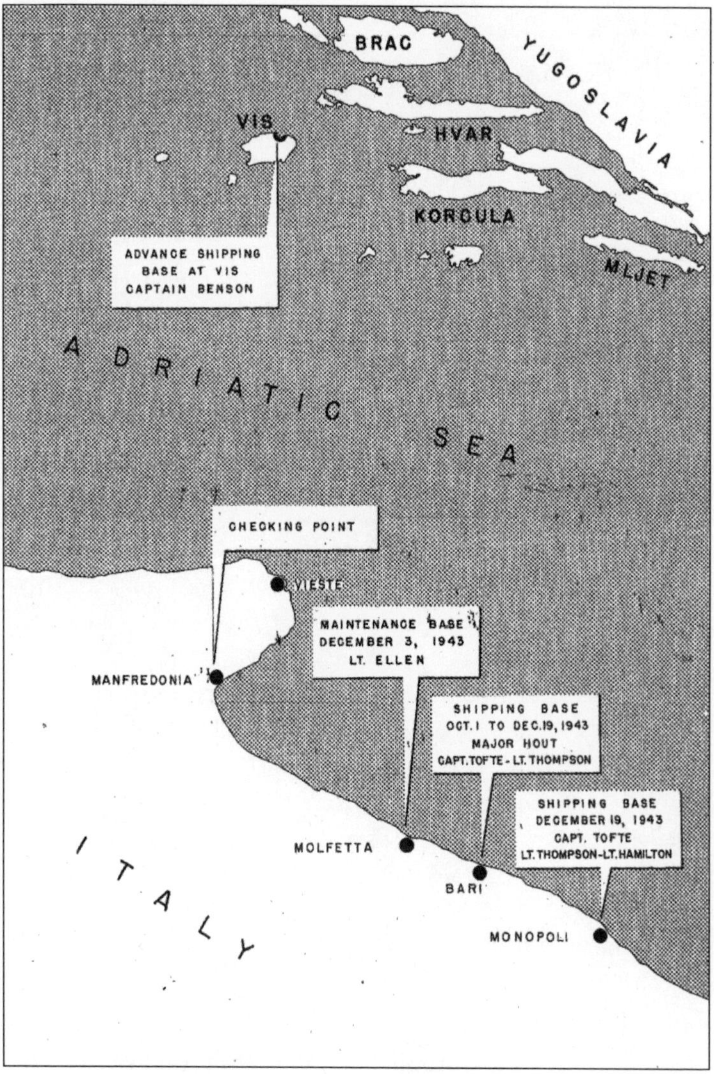

New OSS bases in Italy, 1943. (NARA)

To effectively supply Tito's partisans, Tofte needed to be able to parachute in, a realization which soon resulted in his being sent to a crash course at the Royal Air Force Parachute School in Ramat David, Palestine. As Colonel J. E. Toulmin, director, OSS-Middle East, noted in an October 18, 1943, report submitted to Brig. Gen. Donovan, "Capt. Hans Tofte returned from Ramat David, having successfully completed the British parachute course there,

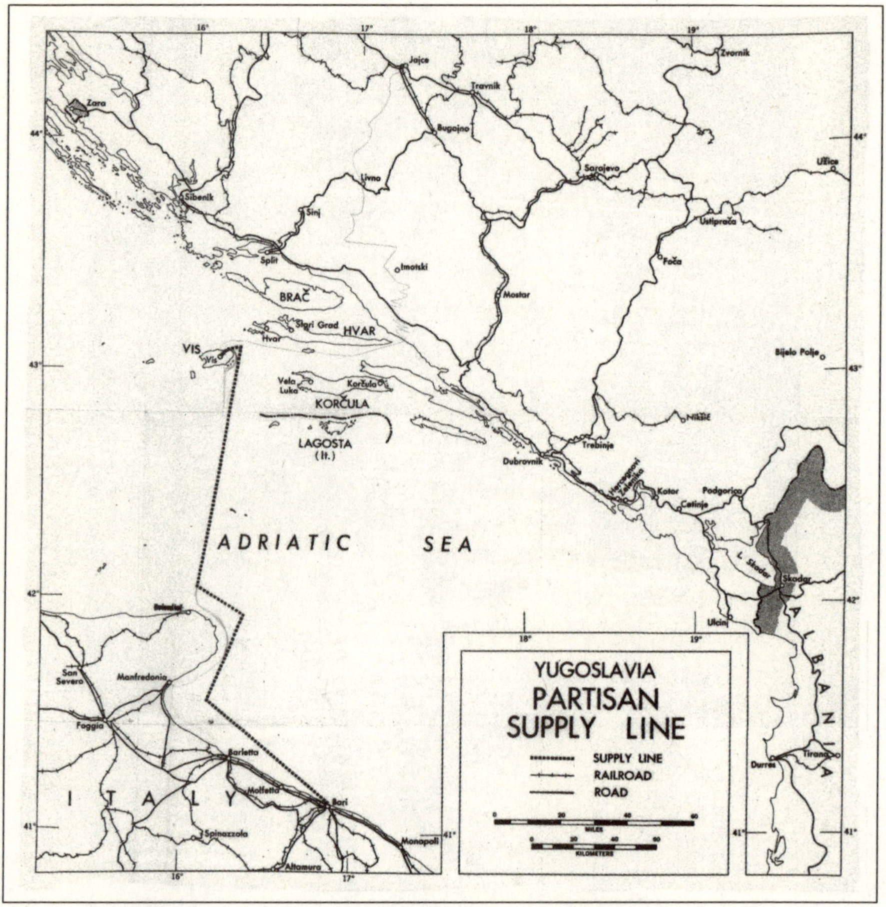

Map of partisan supply lines, 1944. (NARA)

and will be infiltrated into Occupied Territory from the Advance Base at an early date. He left Algiers with Major Carleton Coon, accompanied also by Mr. Larry Post who will be his interpreter in the field." A week prior, Maj. Huot and 1st Lt. Thompson had sailed to the Yugoslav island of Vis, then to Podgora, where they met with Tito's right-hand man, Colonel Pavle Ilic, commander of the 8th Partisan Corps. The three agreed on how the resupply operation should be conducted and where supplies should be off-loaded to be most effective.

Major Huot described Tito as "a force to reckon with, a leader men would follow through the very gates of hell." Sharing the opinion of Tofte and others,

Col. Ilic described the British efforts to-date, under the command of the officer in charge of the British mission, Brigadier Fitzroy MacLean, a member of the landed Scottish gentry and a swashbuckling veteran of Britain's Special Air Service (SAS) in North Africa, as "something close to a disaster"; for his part, Tito regarded British officers as "a bunch of fools who thought more of their own convenience than of doing anything in the common struggle." In sharp contrast, Capt. Benson had won Tito's trust, and the latter was eager for the Americans to take over the delivery mission. Pavle then invited Maj. Huot to accompany him to Tito's headquarters at Jajce, high in the mountains, a seemingly innocuous but ultimately fateful invitation.[8]

With regard to the often-touchy relations with the British, Tofte noted, "Details with regard to Anglo-American cooperation were to be worked out at Cairo upon the return of a British survey party, which was to follow the OSS officers to Italy during the first half of October." Tofte was soon brought in to handle mountain transport logistics, but wound up taking over the OSS Bari Mission and its shipping operation when Maj. Huot was relieved of his duties effective November 7. As Tofte's personnel file notes, "because of his extensive civilian experience in shipping, he was placed in command of all OSS shipping operations" in the immediate area. Major Huot's unauthorized visit to Tito's headquarters had complicated the delicate dance between the United States and Great Britain in dealing with the Yugoslav guerrillas. Brigadier MacLean lodged a formal protest with OSS headquarters, resulting in Maj. Huot's sacking.

Initially sent home to the United States, Maj. Huot was later fired from OSS "on the grounds that he was too self-willed and impossible to manage." The downside, however, was that "the Americans came to realize that Tofte was at least as difficult as Huot, but at the same time he was more efficient, enterprising, and cunning, so he was difficult to get rid of." The new second-in-command in Bari proved to be Tofte's training nemesis, Maj. Koch who, while a Signal Corps member and not a member of SI, was "very diplomatic in dealings with the people," according to the chief of the Yugoslav desk in Bari at the time. This talent did not sway Tofte's opinion of him, especially after he tried desperately to get rid of him, to no avail. Tofte and 1st Lt. Thompson were both saddened by their friend's sudden departure, but Tofte asked a favor—would Maj. Huot check on Marlys when he returned to the States? He agreed, exceeding his mission to such an extent that Marlys had difficulty getting him to leave, even after three weeks.[9]

Operation *Audrey* enabled Tofte to use his maritime background to great advantage, to set up a shipboard supply system across the Adriatic Sea, between Bari and the island of Vis, off the Yugoslav coast, in waters deemed too dangerous for the Royal Navy. But the Yugoslav "fleet" he inherited consisted largely of "battered, leaking fishing schooners," which had to be made seaworthy, carefully loaded, and camouflaged before they could be of service. Tofte managed to accomplish all this with no naval personnel to assist him; since he had only one junior US Army officer to help, who was often patrolling the coast, Tofte was also responsible for the housing and feeding of 600 partisans serving as stevedores; the procurement of equipment and supplies for the base; and the coordination of shipping activities with US, British, and Yugoslav authorities. But by October 1943, Tofte's makeshift fleet consisted of some 44 low-profile vessels, which made nightly supply runs, weather permitting, from Bari to Vis, usually heading north along the Italian coast for a bit before heading straight to Vis; each such run delivered a higher tonnage of supplies than the British were airdropping monthly.

Most of the partisan ships were of the schooner variety, with a capacity of 50 to 100 metric tons each. Any ships of the OSS-Partisan fleet too large to conceal among the various islands were used to ship supplies from Bari to Sicily. Since the *Kriegsmarine* (German Navy) still had a presence in the Adriatic, Tofte's convoys had to sneak through the blockade under cover of night with their cargoes of small arms, mortars, machineguns, rifles, ammunition, and medicine. Tito gladly accepted such supplies, which enabled his partisans to tie down thousands of German troops. To protect the vessels of Operation *Audrey*, the Royal Navy provided four motor torpedo boats (MTBs) and gunboat 361; any ships over 50 tons were routinely accompanied by an MTB. When either Tofte or 1st Lt. Thompson personally went to Vis on one of these missions, they routinely stayed aboard an MTB.

Although the Germans frequently flew reconnaissance missions over the islands of Vis and Hvar to spot guerrilla resupply operations, the number of small coves in the area ensured that the Germans seldom saw anything. The one rub with having the MTBs along for protection was that they were unable to carry sufficient amounts of fuel to enable them to both do escort duty and attack German vessels. Tofte was "largely instrumental" in setting up and maintaining naval bases in the Dalmatian Islands, to house the MTBs to patrol the clandestine supply line to Yugoslavia, thereby minimizing partisan losses. He also suggested that his convoys deliver fuel, so that warehouses could be built on Vis and Hvar to refuel the MTBs, which ultimately delivered over 150,000 gallons of 100 octane gasoline to the Dalmatian Islands bases. He further suggested that each MTB should take one of his experienced Yugoslav captains aboard as a pilot through the treacherous waters around the islands, a suggestion the British adopted. In the next two weeks, the MTBs sank the German cruiser *Dalmatia* (actually the SMS *Niobe*, a late 19th-century German Imperial Navy vessel that had changed hands several times over the years), three German gunboats, and three armed freighters.[10]

In mid-November 1943, Brigadier General Fitzroy McLean, commanding officer, Allied Military Mission to Partisan Forces, summed up the partisan situation and significance in a report. He noted that the partisans had a force of some 26 divisions (220,000 troops), an efficient system of political administration and, perhaps most significantly, the "wholehearted support of the civil population." He also remarked on the "immense enthusiasm of all concerned for the new Yugoslavia, which they are building and to their unshakable confidence in the future." But from the Allied perspective, it was another characteristic that was most significant—providing the requisite supplies to maintain the fight. As Brig. Gen. McLean emphasized, "The need for the rapid organization and despatch [*sic*] of supplies by the Allies cannot be emphasized enough. In particular the dispatch of supplies by sea is of the greatest urgency."[11]

In mid-November 1943, Capt. Benson messaged Tofte that Tito had requested to meet the head of Operation *Audrey* at the latter's headquarters in Jajce, high in the mountains. A few days later, Tofte sailed one of his "partisan navy" ships to Vis, from which he was transported to Makarska, about 5 miles north of Podgora, along the Adriatic coastline. Since Capt. Benson was already in Jajce, Tofte had to rely on a young, green partisan to drive him there, along the "Burma Road," Tofte's nickname for the main supply route from the coast. They left Makarska at midnight and the inexperienced driver turned the wrong way and they wound up in Mostar, which was full of Germans. They drove past three inebriated German officers, who stared at them before they had the presence of mind to pull out their Lugers and begin shooting. In the resulting firefight, Tofte shot two of them before the driver turned around and got them out of town.

A few hours later, Tofte was standing in front of Tito, who was holding an Al Capone-era tommy gun, and Tofte took an immediate liking to the partisan chieftain. Captain Benson had provided Tito with the tommy gun, which he let go of only when sleeping; his other favorite possession was a German shepherd, ironically, named "Tiger," who was always at his side. Tofte learned that there were some British officers at Tito's headquarters, but they were not well-regarded and generally kept to themselves—one of these was Prime Minister Churchill's son Randolph. At Tito's urging to find him a job, Tofte set him to providing daily weather reports from the mountains behind Split.[12]

In November 1943, the Germans made an attempt to destroy Tofte's successful shipping operation to the Yugoslav partisans. In preparation for such an attack, he personally reconnoitered the Yugoslav coast from Split to Dubrovnik, and assessed that an immediate shipment of 500 tons of food, clothing, arms, and ammunition would be needed to stave off the anticipated enemy strike. The only available ship that could carry such a load was the SS *Galeb*, whose top speed was only 3.5 knots, about 4 miles per hour, making it essentially a sitting duck. A Royal Navy armed motor launch escorted the *Galeb*—which Tofte decided he personally would take across the Adriatic to Yugoslavia; as he put it, in a classic example of understatement, "The trip was a hazardous one, fraught with many vicissitudes." Despite storms—the heaviest gale in the Adriatic in 10 years—and air attacks, the *Galeb* delivered her cargo of arms on November 26, "plus miles of barbed wire and thousands of land mines." When the two buffeted ships were spotted by German aircraft, RAF fighters came to their rescue off the Yugoslav coast. As a result, every possible landing beach on Vis Island was heavily fortified. An entry in Tofte's personnel file noted that "later interrogation of enemy prisoners established the fact that Vis was to have been the focal point of the enemy attack. Had it not been heavily fortified, the Allies would have lost their one foothold on the Balkan coast, a foothold which was later built into a strong air and naval base and was the only avenue for supplying the Partisan forces."[13]

Tofte also received a note of appreciation from Lieutenant Commander Morgan Giles, Royal Navy, for his assistance after two British warships—the destroyer HMS *Quail* and the minesweeper HMS *Hebe*—struck mines in mid- and late November. Though the two ships ultimately sank, Tofte and his partisans were able to save most of the crewmen—witnesses reported seeing Tofte in the bow of one of the ships, personally directing the rescue. The grumpy British were suddenly all smiles, referring to Tofte as a "good old chap." For his efforts, Tofte received a written thank-you note and a certificate of honor from the British High Command. "The Naval Officer in Charge, Bari," the note began, "has made a signal expressing his gratitude for the prompt and efficient work carried out by small craft when *H.M.S. Hebe* was sunk. Please convey this message to Partizan [*sic*] ships who were concerned upon this occasion and also when *H.M.S. Quail* was mined."

The British minesweeper HMS *Hebe* hit a mine and sunk on November 22, 1943, with a loss of 37 sailors. The ill-fated HMS *Quail*, a Royal Navy destroyer whose active career lasted less than a year, was based at Bari, to support military operations and escort convoys. It struck a mine—part of a barrage laid by German submarine *U-453* on October 25—on November

15 while on patrol in the Adriatic, killing one sailor. Beached the next day, it was towed to Bari for temporary repairs, then first to Taranto and then to Malta for permanent repairs, but sank in the Gulf of Taranto on June 18, 1944. While the details of Tofte's exact contributions are undisclosed, they were clearly significant enough to merit a commendation from his British allies; furthermore, jumping into the fray was characteristic of Tofte's nature.[14]

Not long after, Tofte had another opportunity for heroic action when the Germans unleashed a disastrous and unexpected bombing attack on the port of Bari on the night of December 2, 1943. The attack was launched by 105 Ju-88 bombers and caught the city of 200,000 fully illuminated so that stevedores could unload supplies for the ongoing offensive to take Monte Cassino. Bari was under British control because it served as the major port for the Eighth Army but had recently become the new headquarters for the US Fifteenth Air Force, deployed to take pressure off the Eighth Army. The attack surprised British authorities, who believed the Luftwaffe was stretched too thin for such an ambitious offensive; nevertheless, the attack was "officially described as the most terrible and successful German bombing raid carried out at a low level during the War" and as the "second Pearl Harbor," with heavy damage to the docks and the port, including 17 Liberty ships and tankers set on fire among the 30 Allied ships in the harbor, anchored so close together that they almost touched.

Making the situation even more dangerous was the fact that the ships were loaded with 100 octane gasoline, bombs, ammunition, and—in an event that would prompt a secret, high-level, international investigation—one US Liberty ship carried 100 mustard gas bombs in its hold, potential Allied retaliation should German forces resort to chemical weapons use in Italy. According to eyewitnesses, the resulting conflagration "burned fiercely for several days"; the initial death toll was at least 1,000 Allied military and merchant marine personnel, as well as 1,000 or more Italian civilians. In official language, Tofte "distinguished himself outstandingly by courageous conduct while directing and participating in voluntary rescue work in the port of Bari throughout the night." More specifically, Tofte "mobilized a fleet of trucks and ambulances manned by his Partisans and, with complete disregard for his own safety, led them directly into the blazing inferno of burning and exploding ships. Working side by side with his men, he directed the evacuation of scores of wounded; assisted in hauling the dead and wounded out of the water, and had improvised first aid stations set up on the docks."

One of the Liberty ships carrying chemical weapons had sunk in the harbor, spreading mustard gas over a large portion of the water's surface—the deadly mix of mustard gas with fuel oil and gasoline resulted in severe and often fatal burns, both immediately and in the days to come. "Disregarding the danger of contamination which caused several hundred casualties during the night," according to the account in Tofte's personnel file, "Major TOFTE continued his rescue work...It is submitted that for this portion of his work alone, Major Tofte is deserving of the highest recognition."[15]

By the end of December 1943, the OSS Mission in Bari, led by Capt. Tofte and 1st Lt. Thompson, consisted of eight US officers and four enlisted personnel. The junior officer of the team was the emotional, "tall and handsome" 28-year-old Lt. Hamilton, better known as actor Sterling Hayden, who would come to play a major role in the resupply operation. As an established actor, Hamilton/Hayden had left the US Marine Corps Reserve to join OSS anonymously via a friendship with William Donovan's son, thrusting the former merchant seaman and overnight movie star into intelligence operations. It was his expertise as a mariner and sailor that made him attractive to OSS and he would conduct what records described as "a series of harrowing missions" in Greece, Italy, and Yugoslavia. He also penned a lengthy narrative asserting that "infighting between British and American officers was undermining the mission." But, despite winning several medals, Hamilton/Hayden was generally able to maintain his anonymity throughout the war. Lieutenant Hamilton was described as "a man to Tofte's and Robert Thompson's liking, and the three became close friends and almost inseparable." For his efforts, Lt. Hamilton was awarded the Silver Star.[16]

Lieutenant Hamilton left a rich narrative written in November 1944—approximately a year after the events—explaining the day-to-day activities of the partisan resupply operation originally based at Bari. He attributed much of what happened—good or bad—to the personalities involved. He wrote, "After an unsatisfactory meeting with Major Koch and Major Weil, I met Captain Hans Tofte and through him I was assigned to the Shipping Section at SBS [Special Boat Service]. Three hours after arrival at Bari I was working on the docks with Captain Tofte and Lieutenant Thompson on the Partisan shipping line. This was the first time since joining OSS I was associated with men who were really doing a job." Eager to do his part for the war, Lt. Hamilton had his opportunity, noting that Tofte, 1st Lt. Thompson, and Lieutenant (JG) Ward E. Ellen—all of whom had arrived in Bari from Oran—were working an average of 16 hours a day, 7 days a week. But when not working, Tofte and 1st Lt. Thompson sought to enjoy themselves—they lived on a wrecked steamship in port, the *Ljubljana*, which they dubbed "Hotel Ljubljana," where they drew up plans and met with the captains of their fleet, usually accompanied by a few bottles of *rakija*, Yugoslav grape brandy.[17]

Tofte had taken over shipping operations from the recently relieved Maj. Huot and had established, in Lt. Hamilton's words, "A magnificent liaison with the Yugoslav Partisans. They had implicit faith in his judgment and the whole operation was exemplary in every respect." Captain Benson certainly agreed with that assessment—in his report entitled "Liaison with Tito and Operations in Yugoslavia," he commented, "Americans, generally speaking, are thought of as their friends whose actions speak louder than words. They do not think of us as having any intentions other than a desire to be friends. Our British allies do not enjoy the same confidence accorded the Americans." Clearly, Tofte and his staff had more than simply a working relationship with the partisans, who were amused that he referred to the main supply route as his previous one in China—the Burma Road. Tofte also won the loyalty and respect of the partisans by fighting to give them free rein in town, rather than being sequestered to the base, but, as a result, was responsible for their conduct. He also argued that they should be able to fly whatever flag they chose on their vessels, regardless of their individual political leanings or the ultimate disposition of Yugoslavia post war—not surprisingly, they chose Tito's star-spangled flag.[18]

In addition to the straight shipping operation, Capt. Tofte was fighting an uphill battle with the Royal Navy and with various British officers in Bari who were jealous of the American position at that time. He was greatly handicapped in having absolutely no support from his organization, SBS; and, in fact, Maj. Koch, Lt. Cmdr. McBaine, and Lt. Col. Weil "did everything in their power to hinder the operation." A communications snafu threatened to add fuel to the fire—at one point, OSS headquarters in Bari had tried to contact Tofte for four days. He showed up on day five, explaining that the ship he was traveling on had been attacked and he had to hide out in a cove. Their prompt return to Bari was impeded by the lingering presence of German patrol ships in the area. Although one of the Yugoslav captains supported Tofte's explanation, both Lt. Cmdr. McBaine and SOE were convinced he was lying but were unable to prove it.[19]

The day after his return to Bari, Tofte again sailed to Vis, on *MTB 297*, and met the partisan chief of staff, Colonel Srecko Manola. Based on information he gleaned from Col. Manola and Tito, Tofte drafted an intelligence report that assessed that during the coming winter, the partisans would concentrate on interrupting land-based supplies headed for German divisions deployed in Dalmatia. The partisans assumed that the German objective was to control the entire coast, which made holding on to the islands of Vis, Hvar, Brac, and Korcula especially critical. Expecting a very cold winter in the mountains, the partisans were in dire need of warm boots and uniforms. Tofte not only got busy with satisfying that request, resulting in increased sailings to Vis, but also proposed equipping some 2,000 liberated Yugoslav POWs with weapons and uniforms and sailing them to Vis and Hvar so that they could help defend the islands. Despite some objections from both British and American officers, the proposal was ultimately adopted.[20]

Prior to the beginning of this major German offensive, civilian refugees from the Yugoslav mainland began flooding the offshore islands, hoping to stay ahead of the combat. This predictable response further strained already tight resources and by mid-December, the situation was critical, with Capt. Benson relaying an urgent plea from partisan leaders for food. Tofte presented this request to senior OSS and SOE figures at a meeting, but no one seemed disposed to act immediately, with some expressing uncertainty that they should even be assisting civilians. Tofte was enraged by such an attitude, prompting him and 1st Lt. Thompson to secretly persuade one of the few capable British officers there to release 500 tons of food from a reserve stock to feed the starving partisans. On December 15, the Yugoslav ships *Hrvat Danica* and *Jastreb* set sail with the emergency supplies.[21]

The Germans had assigned the 7th SS Volunteer Mountain Division Prinz Eugen to gain control of the Dalmatian coast, but Tito's partisans had brought the division's advance to a halt by blowing up bridges and rail lines. Elsewhere across Yugoslavia, seven other German divisions were delayed by partisan victories made possible by the supplies provided by Operation *Audrey*.[22] As the offensive ground on, the number of badly wounded partisans rose sharply, with the British claiming they had no hospital space for them. So Tofte and his colleagues again stepped into the breach, scrounging medical supplies and abandoned properties to use as hospitals. They told Tito they needed 20 Yugoslav doctors and 60 nurses—they had them within a week. Tofte also thoughtfully provided oranges and cigarettes as Christmas gifts for the wounded and then had a creative idea—after acquiring a box of postcards with President Roosevelt's image on them, he then printed on each one, "Thank you for your heroic efforts during the war." As he noted at the time, "It was pure fakery, but I didn't care, and I figured the president would too. In any case, the wounded were happy with their gift and their card."[23]

But due to the damage at Bari, Tofte was ordered to move all his ships and the entirety of Operation *Audrey* to the port of Monopoli, a port 35 miles to the south—a move which Tofte anticipated, which was why he had already reconnoitered the site. Monopoli would become the new OSS shipping operations base, and Lt. Hamilton was tasked with establishing the new facility. On December 18, Lt. Hamilton was joined by 1st Lt. Thompson and two enlisted members while Tofte remained in Bari to "fight the Royal Navy and to try to reduce the damage being done to the Partisan cause by Major Koch, Lieutenant Commander McBa[i]ne, and Major Weil."[24] As Tofte reported to OSS headquarters, by late December 1943, there were four partisan bases in full operation—at Bari, Monopoli, Molfetta, and Manfredonia, all under the command of OSS officers, augmented by a staff of 600 partisans.

He also noted that OSS officers had collected valuable intelligence on partisan and enemy locations in Yugoslavia; as a result, the towns of Moster and Metkovic were bombed by Allied aircraft, enemy columns on coastal roads had been strafed, and one large German supply steamer sunk. He was doubtless glad to report that no OSS personnel had been lost in operations, and partisan losses had been light—two partisan ships lost, several vessels strafed, but less than 25 partisans killed in enemy encounters.

The same report cheerfully added, "Close liaison and cooperation with British 'Special Force 133,' the Royal Navy, and other authorities were maintained throughout the operation"—it is difficult to ascertain if Tofte actually believed this or was merely giving headquarters the information he knew they wanted. In light of future events, it is ironic that Tofte would have such a rosy view of relations with the British ally. An assessment Tofte included later in this same report may more accurately portray the true situation: "The British tried," wrote Tofte, "in many subtle ways to gain control over the sailings and thus over the Partizan fleet and the delivery of supplies to Yugoslavia. It is at least of academic interest to note that if these attempts had not been diplomatically and persistently realized, the American side of the OSS-SOE partnership would have rapidly decreased in importance. Also, the speed of the operation would beyond any doubt have decreased considerably."[25]

For Christmas 1943, it appeared that the stockings by the fireplace were filled—with personnel reassignments. Just before Christmas, Lt. Cmdr. McBaine was recalled to Cairo and transferred to another command. Unfortunately for Tofte, Maj. Koch was appointed to replace him, with Lt. Col. Weil as his second. Tofte felt confident he could handle Maj. Koch, but there were more changes in the offing. On December 26, Capt. Benson was removed from Vis, ordered back to Cairo, and reassigned, leaving no US personnel operating along the Yugoslav coast. The sudden reassignment of Capt. Benson irritated both Tofte and the partisans—Capt. Benson was "capable, efficient, and restrained," and they needed more like him. Without checking with Maj. Koch, Tofte then dispatched Lt. Hamilton to the island of Hvar, northeast of Vis, from which he then moved south to the Italian-occupied island of Korcula to help fend off a major attack by German and Ustashi forces, who fought to keep control of the Adriatic coast and protect their southern flank from Allied attack following the Italian capitulation. The German offensive proved successful, however, and Korcula had to be evacuated on December 29. Three days later, Cairo dispatched Major Linn Farish to Tito's headquarters for a few months, to make "a political assessment of the situation."[26]

On January 2, 1944, Tofte sent a report to the director of Strategic Services which summarized the accomplishments of the OSS Shipping Operations section from October 1943 to January 1944. In the report, Tofte noted that the

> principal function has been the procuring, loading, dispatching, and distribution of military supplies. Shipping Operations has also conducted nine reconnaissance voyages to Yugoslavia. Among these were the first landing by Allied officers on the Dalmatian Islands, the first landing by Allied officers on the Yugoslav mainland, and the conducting of the Royal Navy to the Dalmatian coast on their first operation. Shipping Operations also initiated the mobilization of a regiment of Yugoslav troops from Italian Prisoner of War camps. These troops are now aiding in the defense of our supply base at Vis Island.
>
> Hans V. Tofte, Capt., AUS
> Chief, Shipping Operations
>
> Robert E. S. Thompson, 1st Lt., AUS
> Executive Officer

The report continued with details of the liberated Yugoslav troops and statistics which more categorically described the accomplishments of Shipping Operations during the period. Tofte explained that 2,086 partisan troops had been recruited from internment camps in southern Italy, had been equipped at Bari, and then shipped from Bari to the Dalmatian Islands, actions accomplished during the period from November 25–December 31, 1943. These partisan troops had been fully outfitted with British-issue equipment, with each soldier receiving two blankets, an Italian rifle, 150 rounds of ammunition, and five grenades.

Lieutenant Steven T. Jacobs, an OSS officer, was responsible for "organizing and dispatching said troops for camp." Shipping Operations was also responsible for transporting 2,479 refugees from Dalmatia to Bari during the week of December 25–31, 1943, and for the transportation of 800 wounded partisan troops from Dalmatia to Bari between October 1–December 31, 1943. Tofte concluded the report by listing all of the US personnel involved in shipping operations as of January 1, 1944, to ensure that all received the credit due them for their efforts—besides Tofte himself, that included Capt. Benson, 1st Lt. Thompson, USMC Lt. Hamilton, and USN Lt. Ellen.[27]

When Hamilton/Hayden returned to Bari, he found Captain Tofte and 1st Lt. Thompson in an open clash with SBS officers, who were deciding who the officer-in-charge (OIC) would be in Bari. The personnel wrangling reached a crescendo on January 4, 1944, when Lt. Hamilton, Tofte, 1st Lt. Thompson, and Lt. Ellen decided the present situation was intolerable and told Maj. Koch that unless they were granted the freedom to operate and to depend on requisite support from SBS, they collectively would have nothing to do with assisting the partisans. Although Tofte, the ranking officer, presented the group's argument in what Lt. Hamilton referred to as "a very cool and quiet and absolutely straight-forward manner," Maj. Koch responded as if he were dealing with a mutiny. He pushed to have the troublesome Tofte removed, not only from Operation *Audrey* but also from Special Operations as a whole, and to deny him any further promotions.

Lieutenant Hamilton and Lt. Ellen were ordered to OSS headquarters in Bari and told to have nothing more to do with the situation; Maj. Koch told Lt. Hamilton that Tofte had misled him and to have nothing to do with Tofte or 1st Lt. Thompson, both of whom were relieved of their duties, replaced by Lt. Jacobs who, Lt. Hamilton asserted, neither knew nor cared anything about the situation. Major Koch further ordered Tofte and 1st Lt. Thompson to abruptly leave the partisans without telling them, which they did; 1st Lt. Thompson became the new finance officer at Bari, while Tofte was put on the shelf for the time being—not only awaiting reassignment but also recuperating.

In early January 1944, when Tofte was on his way home from Bari, where he had appeared as a witness at a judicial inquiry, his driver had swerved into a ditch. The car had overturned, and Tofte was slightly injured, wrenching the knee that he had earlier injured in Cossack dancing. But there was no time to be lounging around in the hospital—the personnel brouhaha had become so serious that the "big guns" of Col. Toulmin and Lieutenant Colonel West were called in from Cairo to deal with what became known as the "Tofte-Thompson-Hamilton situation." The two senior officers decided that 1st Lt. Thompson and Lt. Hamilton would remain in Bari, while Tofte would return to Cairo for reassignment.[28]

Despite its ignominious end, surviving documentation suggests that Tofte's resupply operation worked well. Although estimates vary, Tofte reported that the total amount of supplies sent to the Yugoslav partisans between

October 15–December 31, 1943, was 6,500 tons. To put it another way, in less than 3.5 months, OSS had provided more supplies than SOE had provided to all the resistance forces in Yugoslavia since late 1941. In a June 1944 memo, Capt. Benson, liaison officer at Vis and Hvar, Yugoslavia, discussed his work with Tofte, formally identified as OSS chief of shipping operations, and 1st Lt. Thompson, noting that they "handled things on the Bari end," a reference to the OSS/SOE operation there. Captain Benson added that Tofte's routine reports "adequately covered…the extent, nature, and effectiveness of these 'Shipping Operations'" and that Tofte and 1st Lt. Thompson made "frequent" trips to the two Yugoslav islands, which afforded an opportunity for "direct discussion of all problems." He noted further that since British radio communications were "not very satisfactory," the frequent trips by Yugoslav boats or British MTBs to and from Bari made the necessary exchange of notes between Capt. Benson and Tofte "very expedient."

While Capt. Benson, on Vis, used a radio contact from Hvar to Bari operated by SOE Cairo (Force 133), signals from Tofte were received at Hvar and passed to Capt. Benson via telephone after decoding. The information passed typically included ship arrival times, type of cargo aboard, course, and related data. Both Tofte and Capt. Benson were vexed by such a situation, prompting frequent complaints from the latter, who commented that it seemed the British were deliberately trying to sabotage Operation *Audrey* because they were jealous of American success. As an experienced intelligence officer, Tofte realized that neither his communications nor his operations were unknown to the enemy. He noted that war correspondents regularly visited the base and that in early November 1943 alone, more than 30 enemy agents with wireless sets were arrested in Bari. In a summary report, Tofte noted that "military security at Bari was non-existent for a considerable period of time after the establishment of the Partizan Shipping Base. The base was conspicuous, to say the least, and the OSS officers in charge of operations were known by name everywhere in Bari and beyond. The lack of security was not only deplorable but dangerous."[29]

Tofte's own personnel file also contains praise for his command of the shipping operations in support of the partisans. As an entry notes, "His [Tofte's] sound judgment, imagination, and foresight in the planning stages of the operation were responsible for the successful supply of thousands of Partisan forces thus enabling them to divert strong German divisions from the Western front [*sic*] thereby facilitating the rapid advance of the Allied Armies. The entire service of Major Tofte to the Government of the United States has been honorable."[30]

And the partisans themselves were grateful for the efforts of Tofte and his men in their fight. On January 1, 1944, the chief of the Delegation of the National Liberation Army, Sergei Makiedo, sent Tofte New Year's greetings from Bari, along with these words:

> Dear Capt. Tofte:
> At the occasion of the New Year kindly accept personally from myself as also from all our fellows connected with the Partisan work in Italy most cordial felicitations.
>
> I take this opportunity to thank you for your devoted work in the matter of sending help to our National Liberation Army during the last year. Your exceptional devotness [*sic*] with which you stood by to the work is best proving that you have thoroughly understood the importance of our work and the greatness of our National Liberation struggle. During the past three months of 1943 not sparing any fatigue or time you have connected yourself with our common work and have given all that you could in front of the innumerable difficulties to make all possible that our work might be carried on to its best results.
>
> Your work is deserving any praise and I feel obliged as representative of the Supreme Staff of the National Liberation Army and Partisan Groups of Yugoslavia to express to you our full appreciation with the hope that you will in the coming year continue your work and attain still greater successes enabling in that way our Liberation Army to increase its share for the final victory and the destruction of Hitler's herds.
>
> With the fellowly [*sic*] greeting:
>
> DEATH TO FASCISM—LIBERTY TO THE PEOPLE!
> The Chief of the Delegation
> /s/ Makiedo[31]

The same day, Tofte also received a thank-you letter from Dr. Josip Smodlaka, the Commissar of Foreign Affairs, Committee of National Liberation of Yugoslavia. Smodlaka wrote:

> Dear Captain,
> Upon your arrival in Italy I feel very glad to be able to thank you personally for your kindness towards my family when it arrived at Monopoli, and I ask you to be good enough to pass on my thanks to Lieutenants Thompson and Hamilton.
>
> At the same time I am pleased to let you know about my absolute satisfaction with the organization of the Yugoslav base at Monopoli, which I inspected in my capacity of Commissar of Foreign Affairs of Yugoslavia.
>
> I have ascertained that this base has been able—thanks to you and your colleagues of the United States Army—to continue with complete success the dispatch of War materials and food to Yugoslavia, a task started under the alert direction of Major Huot.
>
> ...I express the hope that you and your valiant assistants, Capt. Benson and Lieutenants Thompson, Hamilton, Geer & Ellen will continue and be able to bring to a fine conclusion your efforts towards the final victory of the United States over our common enemy.
>
> I ask you, dear Captain, to accept the expression of profound gratitude, which I address to you in the name of the Government of Yugoslavia, and at the same time the assurance of my high esteem.
>
> /s/
> DR. JOSIP SMODLAKA[32]

Similarly, on February 15, 1944, 1st Lt. Thompson sent a letter to Lieutenant S. G. Percy Wood, chief operations officer, Cairo, which further sang Tofte's praise. "All of the Partizans," wrote 1st Lt. Thompson, "have asked me to tell him [Tofte] of their unswerving belief in him and thanks to him. He is something of a national Hero among them, you know. Their moving tributes to him are almost beyond description."[33]

Nor were the plaudits limited to the Yugoslav partisans alone—in a letter from early November 1943, when many of Tofte's greatest achievements still lay ahead, Major John E. Burke, Essex Regiment, British Army, wrote Tofte, "Herewith my most sincere thanks for the material assistance you provided at such short notice to assist the Yugoslav Partizans in their splendid fight against our common enemy. I hope it may be possible for us to work together again in the way that we have done, the true definition, if I may say so, of Anglo-American cooperation."[34] Similar in sentiment was an after-the-fact letter from a Royal Navy officer, Lt Cmdr. Giles, who in January 1944, wrote:

> Dear Hans,
>
> ...Things have grown enormously, as you know. But I must say that they have never gone more smoothly than when we were working together at the beginning of the thing. It was always a pleasure to be able to pick up the receiver and speak to you or to Bob [Thompson], and straighten out the latest snag which had cropped up!!...I know that a great deal of the credit...is due to yourself, and once again I thank you for the very pleasant atmosphere in which all of our work together took place. All the best.[35]

But not everyone was so enamored of working with US personnel. One such critic was SOE operative Lieutenant Colonel Bickham Aldred Cowan Sweet-Escott, a former SIS member who joined SOE in 1940 and who served as the regional director for the Balkans and the Middle East in 1941. As he viewed intelligence operations in Yugoslavia between 1942 and 1944, he described them in these words: "Liaison with the Americans [is] like having an affair with an elephant: it is extremely difficult, you are apt to get badly trampled on, and you get no results for eight years."[36] His countrymen were also critical of Tofte for his "American" way of doing things and referred to him as a "cowboy" in derision. Thus, while some British memories of OSS's accomplishments in Yugoslavia were hazy or critical in retrospect, Maj. Huot, Tofte, 1st Lt. Thompson, and Capt.

Lieutenant Colonel Bickham Sweet-Escott, British Army. (Special Forces Club)

Benson were well-remembered in Yugoslavia and all were decorated shortly after the end of the war.[37]

Periodically throughout the war—and to some extent throughout his life—Tofte's stubbornness and willingness to "color outside the lines" brought problems, as had happened in late December 1943. On December 22, Lt. Cdr. McBaine, the head of the Special Intelligence (SI) section of OSS in Yugoslavia, assembled a five-man rescue team, including Tofte, to enter Yugoslavia and help extract a group of 25 American nurses, whose plane had been attacked by German fighters and forced to make an emergency landing on the border between Albania and Yugoslavia. Both Lt. Cmdr. McBaine and Maj. Koch suggested sending a plane in to rescue them, but Tofte was strongly opposed, pointing out that the area was rife with German antiaircraft guns. The plane was dispatched anyway, but was badly damaged, managing to drop supplies but barely making it back.

Tofte also had proposed to Lt. Cmdr. McBaine that Hamilton/Hayden replace one of the other officers. Since Lt. Cmdr. McBaine was scheduled to leave Bari in a few days, he suggested that Tofte broach the subject with Lt. Col. Weil, the mission commander, who refused Tofte's request. Tofte then went outside OSS channels to talk personally with the commanding officer of the nurses' unit. When Lt. Col. Weil became aware of this development, and remembering the similar tactic of Maj. Huot, he recommended that Tofte be recalled from Bari and given another assignment, that letters of censure be delivered to the officers concerned, and that any pending promotions be cancelled. There are no extant records to suggest that Lt. Col. Weil's suggestions were ever adopted.[38]

Predictably, a flurry of meetings and paperwork ensued to try to resolve what became known as "the Bari incident"—the conflict between Tofte and colleagues on one hand and Maj. Koch and his highly placed contacts on the other that had so negatively impacted the Allied war effort in Yugoslavia. As part of that process, the deputy director of SSO, J. M. Scribner, spent time with Maj. Huot and Major Carleton Coon, and less time with Capt. Tofte. But when Scribner again interviewed Maj. Huot and Tofte, he was concerned that the pair was "somewhat under a cloud concerning the situation which caused their return from Cairo." Although no charges had been placed against either man, Scribner was under the impression that the relevant OSS files "contain considerable comments of a derogatory nature," which in turn suggested that the "possibility of these individuals being accepted for a delicate or favorable assignment becomes remote and the opportunity they may have to perform, if they are successful in securing an assignment, starts off below par."

Instead of a court-martial, Scribner suggested that a hearing be conducted, once Col. Toulmin, chief of mission, OSS-ME, arrived. Scribner thought the hearing should be attended by Gen. Donovan; Col. G. Edward Buxton, Gen. Donovan's hand-picked assistant director of OSS; Col. Toulmin; and the two men, either individually or collectively. If the two—Tofte and Maj. Huot—were deemed culpable, Scribner suggested that they be given the opportunity to transfer out of the unit. However, should their innocence be established, "Appropriate steps should be taken to stop the circulation of rumors and comments," which Scribner believed might consist of something as elementary as a statement by Gen. Donovan at a staff meeting. He added that Gen. Donovan had already interviewed Maj. Huot and recommended him for several positions, "Tantamount to a clearance by General Donovan with respect to Major Huot's conduct."[39]

In mid-January 1944, Tofte was called to Cairo, where Col. Toulmin informed him that he had been fired in disgrace, both from Operation *Audrey* and Special Operations, and that he was being sent home to await further disposition. First Lieutenant Thompson and Lt. Hamilton had also been pulled from Operation *Audrey*, and Captain Steven T. Jacobs had been appointed as Tofte's replacement. This purging of personnel amounted to an unofficial end to Operation *Audrey*, although the resupply continued at a slower pace for another three months. While the stated reason for Tofte's removal was disobedience and lack of respect, others suspected a political maneuver. The declaration of a provisional government by Tito in early December and the approach of Soviet forces from the east had given the British—and especially the Americans—something to think about.

While most supported Tito's fight against the Nazis, fewer supported his civil war with the Chetniks, and fewer still the prospect of a postwar communist government in Yugoslavia. Tofte had often noted that while Tito was definitely a communist, he was one of the best people he had ever met and a born leader. Although some believed he and his men had gotten far too close to the communists, several OSS officers at HQ, Bari, strongly opposed the firings of Tofte and his colleagues. The head of the Yugoslav branch at headquarters, Major Francis Arnoldy, praised Tofte, 1st Lt. Thompson, and Lt. Hamilton for their labors and opined that their work was sabotaged by "group B men," who were "primarily interested in their own positions, their promotions, their ranks, comfort, safety, fame, and then in their work." This, in contrast to the "A" group, which consisted of "sincere workers and producers…who in the past showed complete disregard toward ranks, high salaries, advantageous positions, and above all, disregard of danger." Major Arnoldy believed that

"A" group members, such as Tofte, were seldom recognized by OSS and were often "kicked out" of their positions, despite being "men who did the utmost possible to further the operations, to get results." It was telling that another officer, OSS analyst and future renowned Eastern European historian Wayne Vucinich, commented that the partisans trusted no OSS men, save "Tofte men."[40]

A few weeks after the actual demise of Operation *Audrey*, in April 1944, the Germans attempted one last major offensive in Yugoslavia—Operation *Rösselsprung* (*Knight's Move*), a combined airborne and ground assault by the XV Mountain Corps and Ustashi troops. But in September 1943, Tito had taken advantage of the Italian surrender and increased both the size of his territory and his partisan army, now 200,000 strong. In November, he held a national congress at Jajce, proclaimed himself marshal and prime minister, and set up his headquarters in Drvar, Bosnia, within the German puppet state of Croatia.

The German operation's ambitious goal was to either capture or kill Tito at his headquarters at Drvar and also destroy his headquarters and support facilities, as well as collocated Allied military missions. The operation was scheduled for May 25, in the mistaken belief that that date was Tito's birthday (his birth date was actually May 7) and the connected thought that his partisans would be too drunk celebrating to mount any real defense. His personal headquarters was in a cave about 1 kilometer north of Drvar city center; in nearby villages were the British and Soviet military missions and US military officers on various assignments.

Perhaps surprisingly, the partisans underestimated the danger posed by the sizable German and Ustashi force—Tito's chief of staff swore that a German attack was "impossible." But attack they did, although the assault ultimately failed, due to the strength of the partisan resistance, the failure of various German intelligence agencies to freely share information, and the lack of contingency planning by the German airborne commander. As a result, despite the partisans suffering some personnel losses and organizational disruptions, Tito and all Allied mission personnel escaped unscathed, and partisan operations were quickly restored. The German gamble had come at a high price—the 500th SS Parachute Battalion, the major unit involved, suffered 576 killed and 48 wounded, with only 200 soldiers fit for combat the next morning.[41]

CHAPTER 4

Man of Action: Austria, Scandinavia, Mason City

About the same time as the denouement of Operation *Audrey*, Tofte involuntarily returned to the United States, feeling like an outcast—as Kruger put it, "He was left in a vacuum where the real reason for his dismissal remained a big question mark." The one bright spot was his continuing affair of the heart with the unforgettable Marlys Leister Calcina—the two had dated while Tofte was working on gaining his US citizenship and while he was an OSS instructor at Area F. They married on April 4, 1944, in part because he "was reluctant to let the beautiful one wander alone in New York's social life while he was gone indefinitely."

According to the information on their wedding license, Tofte was 33 at the time (the license was dated on his 33rd birthday) and Marlys was 37. Tofte listed his address as 1200 Greenleaf Building, noted that he had been married and divorced (in Jacksonville, Florida) before, and his occupation was a US Army officer. Marlys gave her address as 1115 5th Avenue, New York City, noted that she'd also been married and divorced before, and listed no occupation. But great as it was for Marlys to have her newlywed husband at home, within the first week, his "anger, frustration, and confusion" began to emerge. Thinking of the unceremonious way he had been dismissed from Operation *Audrey* and SO, he began to wonder why, if his actions had been so flagrant, had there been no formal investigation? Then at least he could have defended himself. But no such opportunity emerged. By early May, Marlys was so fed up with Hans's bad mood that she went to see Gen. Donovan, personally and unannounced, to plead his case. After hearing all he cared to, Gen. Donovan told her, "Stop, it's already being sorted out."[1]

What the newlyweds had no way of knowing was that since March, OSS leadership had been flooded with letters from officers protesting Tofte's treatment, arguing that instead of being fired, he should have been festooned with medals—Maj. Coon categorically listed eight reasons why he should be so recognized and the head of SO's security department in Cairo, Joseph M. Scribner, had written a letter of support for Tofte and sent it to Gen. Donovan's second, Col. Edward Buxton. But of all such letters, the one that would prove to be most meaningful for Tofte's career would be that written by the recently departed chief of SI, Stephen Penrose, to his successor, Whitney Shephardson:

> Dear Whitney,
> I am writing this letter as an introduction to a man who will soon pay you a visit. I hope you will find an opportunity to put him in touch with someone who can and will make use of his very large ability. The man is Captain Hans Tofte, about whom you may have heard somewhat unfavorably. He has just been sent home by the SO, more or less out of favor because of what was reported as his insubordination in Bari, where he was in charge of the SO's ship transports to the partisans. At the risk of getting one over the neck, I recommend him to you because I believe he has received treatment that his behavior does not warrant at all. SO is unlikely to use him again and I would be grateful if you would consider transferring him to SI.

Penrose filled Shephardson in on Tofte's problematic friendship with Maj. Huot and the resulting suspicions of Lt. Cmdr. McBaine and his replacement by Maj. Koch, whose negative reports about Tofte had eventually led to the latter's removal. He then continued,

> I will not excuse the instances of insubordination reported by Koch, but when you consider the history behind their relationship and Tofte's working conditions, I am sure his wrongdoings were nowhere near as serious as reported. Tofte also clashed with Major Weil over a proposed airborne rescue operation for American nurses stranded in Albania. Tofte spoke very strongly against Weil's plan...Both Weil and Koch later had to admit that Tofte was right. Yet Koch had included it in his report as one of Tofte's black spots...By now, I know him pretty well, and have made an investigation of his operation, and I am convinced that he is a valuable man [whose] skills it would be a shame to let go to waste without further ado...He knows the Far East extremely well and could do well in the Burma area. He himself would prefer to go to Scandinavia.
>
> Sincerely,
> Stephen B. L. Penrose, Jr.[2]

On May 16, 1944, Shephardson contacted Major Carl O. Hoffmann, chief, SO, regarding a possible transfer for Tofte. Shephardson explained, "We have a mission of some importance in ETO for which he [Tofte] is particularly qualified. Will you consequently accept this as a request for your approval of a formal transfer of Captain Tofte from the SO Branch to the SI Branch."

Thus, the deal was struck, and two days later Tofte learned that after a short training course in encryption and other intelligence specialties, he would be heading to London, to become the acting head of SI's Scandinavian branch, which naturally included his native Denmark—the letters of support had convinced Shephardson that Tofte was worth both salvaging and securing. In an ironic piece of foreshadowing, the details of Tofte's posting to London were taken care of by Major Richard Helms, with whom Tofte would have much more contact in the future. Tofte arrived in London shortly after D-Day, "after serving with great distinction with OSS in the Mediterranean Theater," just in time to move into SI's new headquarters, located at 72 Grosvenor St., Mayfair. By this point in the war, OSS was growing rapidly in manpower and influence and becoming more involved in the various European resistance movements. Not long after his arrival, Tofte would meet with three resistance fighters at the Hotel Dorchester and establishing a collaboration, as he had done so many times before.[3]

On September 29, 1944, Tofte met Anthony van der Steenhoven, whom OSS in the Netherlands had recommended as an agent. The idea was to send "Mr. Anthony," as Tofte referred to him, to Stockholm, where he had numerous acquaintances, and then on to Berlin, where he had Swedish contacts. But "Mr. Anthony" made a bad initial impression on Tofte and when he asked Steenhoven who his Swedish contact in Berlin was, it proved to be Bengt Fredin, a known German agent. His mistress, world-renowned Chilean singer Rosita Serrano, was also a known Nazi spy. As if that were not enough, Fredin's best friend, Count Karl von Rosen, worked at the German Embassy in Stockholm and was related to Luftwaffe chief Hermann Goering.

Not surprisingly, Tofte and his second—Capt. Benson, his Operation *Audrey* colleague—recommended that Fredin be questioned and investigated more thoroughly. Extant records suggest Tofte's initial doubts were only strengthened in the future—a November 11, 1944, memo indicated that Steenhoven was coming to the United States to engage in a propaganda mission for the Dutch minister of Foreign Affairs. The presumption was that he had been briefed by both the minister and the queen, but OSS opinion of Steenhoven remained low—"Our opinion of Van Der Steenhoven is none too high. He's very conceited and probably [a] none too intelligent young man who fancies himself as a slick operator."[4]

Tofte's new geographic area of responsibility included his native Denmark, so it was inevitable that he would pursue intelligence operations there as soon as possible. Until the fall of 1944, there was a "gentleman's agreement" that OSS/SI in London would not send agents directly into Denmark; rather, such individuals would be sent only through Stockholm, in collaboration with SOE and the Danish military intelligence services, collectively known as "the Princes." But once that informal agreement ended, Tofte agreed with

OSS Officer Bill Carlson in Stockholm that an acquaintance of Tofte's in Copenhagen, Lieutenant Colonel Ragnvald "Alfred" Roscher Lund, could be used to secure hiding places for OSS operatives in Denmark.

Lieutenant Colonel Lund happened to be the director of the Elizabeth Arden cosmetics company in Denmark, and could use some of the company's attractive female employees to scout out appropriate hide sites. While he was dealing with Scandinavia, Tofte also pushed for OSS involvement in Norway, historically a British bastion when it came to intelligence operations. On his own initiative, he invited Foreign Minister Trygvie Lie, Army chief General W. Hansteen, intelligence chief Lt. Col. Lund, and his second, Major F. Nagell, to a sumptuous luncheon on August 30, where they discussed issues and the removal of obstacles that might impede operations.[5]

Extant records suggest that Tofte excelled in his duties as chief of the Scandinavian Division. A note in his personnel file gushed that he

> displayed a keen intelligence and complete understanding of Scandinavian affairs while mastering the details of the varied projects initiated prior to his arrival…The responsibilities which Major TOFTE accepted…were exceptionally great, and added to them was the problem that any OSS mission to Scandinavia would only be established after successful completion of most detailed and delicate negotiations with the corresponding British agencies, with SHAEF, and with the American and British Army authorities concerned with the ultimate occupation or control of liberated Norway and Denmark. For some time, Norway and Denmark had been considered zones for exclusively British operations and it was due primarily to Major TOFTE's exceptional tact and his skillful handling of the necessary negotiations that the original attitude of the British on this subject was altered and the OSS was assured their full support on its operations in this area.

This glowing assessment was supplemented by additional laurels for a recurring talent for Tofte—namely, his ability to work effectively with virtually anyone and to inspire them along the way. He was lauded for "building up a competent staff to assist him in the highly critical operations which were envisaged. He proved himself an extremely astute judge of personalities…He fully utilized his own thorough knowledge of the Scandinavian countries." Praised for "his vision, enthusiasm, and keen sense of timing," he "faced the difficulties involved in initiating operations in a new area and in the handling of what might have been an extremely delicate international situation, with an ingenuity, intellectual and technical technique, and attention to the smallest problem which inevitably made his efforts successful."[6]

But all this proved too tame for the action-oriented Tofte, who spent only four months in the position. In August 1944, Supreme Headquarters Allied Expeditionary Forces (SHAEF) concluded that Allied intelligence activities within Germany were inadequate—in response, SI drew up the "Faust Plan," which would infiltrate agents into Germany to establish networks to monitor and report on conditions, morale, and troop dispositions within the crumbling Third Reich. Accomplishing this would involve working closely with the most active and credible underground and resistance groups, most of which were German socialist and communist labor unions.

The agents to conduct these operations were recruited from the Labor Division of SI in London, headed by future Supreme Court Justice Arthur Goldberg and George Pratt. Given past problems working with the British, the OSS head in Europe, William Casey, decided in November 1944 to create a new entity, the Division of Intelligence Procurement (DIP), and to fold the Labor Division into it. The task of the DIP was "to carry out the mission of evolving the plans for and directing a large scale agent penetration of Germany," and Casey chose George Pratt as its head. Pratt had the distinction of landing the first—and so far, only—OSS agent in Germany, Josef "Jupp" Kappius, on September 2, 1944, to organize sabotage against the military industry in the Ruhr, Germany's industrial heartland.

Pratt was acknowledged to be a "skilled leader and planner," but lacked operational experience. He "required the services of a highly capable deputy having both administrative and operational experience" and Tofte was selected due to his "extensive knowledge of conditions on the continent but also because of the rare executive ability, initiative, and devotion that he had demonstrated in directing the operations of the Scandinavian Section." Tofte was promoted to major and his friend Capt. Benson took his former post in the Scandinavian section. Pratt, described as a "quiet tolerant man with a good dose of humor," was warned of Tofte's inconformity and lack of respect for authority, but thought he could work with him.

Tofte insisted on having his old Yugoslavian colleague 1st Lt. Thompson on the team, as well as his new friend, Lieutenant Mike Burke. First Lieutenant Thompson actually had been transferred to First Army, whose commander was not fond of OSS people, but Tofte got him anyway. Tofte proved adept at DIP operations and managed to grow the division from an initial 4 personnel to 125. He was praised for his "skillful negotiation, persistence, tact, and qualities of personality and character" in working with the challenging British, resulting in what a superior described as "unusually fine cooperation and understanding between the two services."[7]

In October 1944, Tofte was presented with an intriguing piece of information, one that—if true—had the potential to delay if not preclude the by-then-inevitable Allied victory. On September 19, 1944, aircraft of Britain's Coastal Command flew a photo-reconnaissance mission over a port in southern Norway and photographed what appeared to be a U-boat modified with "special features," including a narrowing of the deck forward and "rails" on the deck running from the port side of the conning tower forward to the narrow neck of the deck. Another observer noted that the "rails" terminated "at a flat, rectangular surface," apparently modified to launch V-1 rockets. On October 26, SIS relayed a wireless message to the OSS Scandinavian Section that provided details on 15 new German U-boats "of a special construction," driven only by electricity, with a speed of 15 knots submerged and 23 knots on the surface. These new U-boats would be ready for operational use in the immediate future and reportedly were based in southern Norway, probably in Bergen.

The explosive part of the reporting was the claim that some of these boats were expected to leave shortly for New York Harbor—to launch V-1 flying bombs against New York City, for propaganda purposes. The following day, another telegram from the same source provided additional details—each U-boat was capable of launching six V-1 rockets. The telegram added the sobering message, "the greatest weight is attached to this statement as this source hitherto is absolutely sure." As Tofte explained the shadowy source, due to a "special arrangement with SIS," the Scandinavian section of SI at OSS had been receiving, for some time, "certain intelligence originating from a Danish military organization in Stockholm" that worked under the SOE auspices. The information the source provided was usually rated as "B" or better (with "A" being confirmed as true)—i.e., it was believed to be reliable, though admittedly the source's information on Danish matters was generally more trustworthy than on other Scandinavian topics.[8]

On October 27, Tofte discussed this matter with a Major Winklehorn, who had received identical information from the same source and who thought it significant enough to cable Washington. In the cable, SI indicated that a Danish source had reported on the 15 new U-boats with the same details as were privy to Tofte; the difference was that Maj. Winklehorn's information suggested that only *one* of the U-boats was headed to New York Harbor for the propaganda mission. A short time later, SI received a letter dated October 30, from Department 2 of the Norwegian High Command, providing identical information. The chief of Norwegian Secret Intelligence added a note which indicated that "the new submarine mentioned had been reported on previously." When Tofte personally checked with the chief, the latter confirmed that the information was from Danish Intelligence.

On November 3, Major General Clayton L. Bissell, assigned to the Office of the Assistant Chief of Staff for Intelligence on the War Department General Staff, cabled the Stockholm military attaché: "Have been advised through OSS that Tykander their representative in Stockholm has received reliable information that German U-boats are equipped with bomb launching platforms. Investigate and keep us fully informed." On November 1, Gen. Eisenhower sent a cable to the adjutant general, War Department (AGWAR), with the postscript "Following passed for what it is worth—'Special Force report quoting Danish source states U-boat will be leaving European waters shortly to launch V-1s against NEW YORK.'" On November 7, SI received a triple-priority telegram from Maj. Gen. Bissell, who "was greatly concerned" and asking for further information from the source; that same day, Stockholm cabled Washington, confirming that the source was Danish Intelligence. That same day, Gen. Eisenhower contacted SFHQ in London: "War Department G-2 have requested further evidence and any other confirmation of Special Forces' report of 30 October quoting Danish source who stated U-boat would be leaving European waters shortly to launch V-1s against NEW YORK. Most grateful your assistance including *re* evaluation source and report if possible."[9]

On November 8, Washington sent a priority telegram to Stockholm, asking for further information about the source and additional details about the U-boat's departure for New York. That same day, a note from OSS SO commented that identical information had been received by an SOE SO source in Sweden. Also on the 8th, the Americans and the British issued a press release of official War Department and Navy Department reporting on the possibility of flying bomb attacks on New York, a follow-up to information delivered in an address by President Roosevelt on November 6. On November 9, following a conference with a Mr. Gold, SI Reports Division, SI sent a cable to Washington indicating that SIS had transmitted the news about the U-boats to the British Admiralty with a rating of "B." Four days later, Gen. Eisenhower again cabled AGWAR, "Special Forces Headquarters reports same source reported 7 November that he believed 4 U-boats were to be used in operation against NEW YORK operating from BERGEN but course and rate unknown. Special Forces Headquarters grades source as (usually reliable) but comments that no other confirmation to possibility of such action received from BERGEN or elsewhere."[10]

And what did Tofte, the experienced, professional intelligence officer, make of all this flurry of seemingly circular reporting? He concluded, "The consensus of opinion would seem to be that the information concerning the new German U-boats should be correct. The possibility of an attack against New York…

would be quite possible from a purely technical point of view and should, therefore, not be overlooked by the proper Army and Navy authorities." A memo that he received from Maj. Winklehorn noted that on December 11, 1944, SI had sent a radio message to the chief of Danish Intelligence asking if there were any new information concerning the U-boats and a potential threat to New York. On the 19th, Danish Intelligence confirmed that the information was from an "old and new good source" and that although no U-boats had been seen since in Danish waters, the plans were undoubtedly ready; as the Danish service put it, "Preparation and execution may possibly take some time, Germans in doubt about reaction of Americans." Tofte summed up the entire affair in a classic understatement, noting that the subject "seems to have aroused some interest in Washington."[11]

Indeed it did, not only due to the significance of the topic itself, but also due to its connection to a major espionage case during the war. On January 8, 1945, FBI Director J. Edgar Hoover shared with leading FDR aide Harry Hopkins relevant details of an interrogation of German agent William Curtis Colepaugh who, along with a colleague, was landed by U-boat off the coast of Frenchman's Bay, Maine, on the night of November 29, 1944. Colepaugh had traveled to Kristiansand, Norway, on *U-1230* as part of his transit to the United States, where the pair was supposed to engage in sabotage operations. Colepaugh told the G-men that members of the *U-1230* crew had indicated in conversation that they had observed in one of the submarine ports near Danzig members of other submarine crews practicing in groups "with equipment of a rocket or gun type on the deck and these crew members presumed this equipment would be used against the United States." Per Colepaugh, the crew members "were pretty definite about this stating that the submarine would proceed to within 100 or 200 miles of the United States and then fire these rockets." Colepaugh added, however, that the crew members had no knowledge of the actual use of the rockets and made their presumptions simply based on what they had observed.[12]

The following day, January 9, Admiral Jonas H. Ingram, the new commander in chief of the Atlantic Fleet, described as not only "possible but probable" a strategically futile attack on New York or Washington by robot bombs within 30 to 60 days. "And we know very definitely," Adm. Ingram added, "that there are three ways in which he might get robot bombs within range of either city. He might sneak a half dozen submarines off the coast. He might launch robots from the long-range planes we know he has. Or he might sneak a surface ship, disguised as a neutral, within range." This dynamic story proved to have such legs that it continued to be a pressing concern, even after VE Day. A *New*

York Times article of May 15, 1945, quoted a story from, of all sources, *Stars and Stripes*—the US Army's own newspaper—which claimed that during the November 1944 presidential election, a German submarine tried to V-bomb New York, "Presumably with a jet-propelled or rocket-propelled weapon," citing "sources considered reliable."

The *Stars and Stripes* story reported that the projectile was launched from the deck of a U-boat lying off the coast and that it either fell short or was knocked down by patrolling fighter planes. Operators at Mitchel Field near New York City claimed that the bomb had fallen into the water. The article also reminded readers of the joint Army-Navy statement on November 8, 1944, that just such a V-bomb attack on the United States was entirely possible. However, a US Navy representative said that the report of the submarine attack was without foundation and a spokesman for the New York Police Department's bomb squad said he had no knowledge of any attempted bombing of New York last November. "Undoubtedly, if a robot bomb had been launched at New York from a U-boat, as reported, and had neared its objective, we would have been informed," he confidently asserted.

Skeptical observers, confident in the reputation of *Stars and Stripes* and stressing the reliability of the newspaper's sources, were not reassured by the US Navy and NYPD denials—they asked such penetrating questions as, "If the incident actually occurred, can it be clarified if the weapon was a sub-launched V-1 cruise missile or something else? If the weapon fell into the sea, was it ever located? Was the warhead a conventional explosive, or a chemical, biological, or nuclear weapon? A V-1 strike on a U.S. city with only a conventional warhead would have done relatively little damage and would have no strategic military value."[13]

An end-of-sorts to the immediate concern came with the publication on January 10, 1946, of a scholarly paper on "German Developments in the Guided Missile Field." In discussing various aspects of the V-1 development program, the authors noted two non-traditional applications of the technology—"an attempt to launch the missile from a ramp on the deck of a submarine and a project for a piloted V-1." They noted that in the first case a ramp was actually constructed, intended for use against coastal US cities and targets, but never used. In the second case, several models were built but, as far as is known, were never used, the idea being that the pilot would fly the rocket close to the target, set the controls, and then bail out. As a nearly 5,000-page report makes clear, however, German progress in rocket and missile technology during the war was impressive and more extensive than believed; furthermore, tests specifically involving firing rockets from

U-boats had been underway since 1942, when wolfpacks still roamed the North Atlantic.[14]

***

Between October 1944–April 1945, Tofte was assigned to the Danish desk at OSS headquarters in London and was later commended by William Casey for contributing to filling the intelligence gap created by the rapid movement of US troops into Germany without the behind-the-lines intelligence that the French had so ably and profusely provided. Now-Major General Donovan, who received his second star in November 1944, stepped into the breach and pulled intelligence veterans from throughout Europe—including Tofte—to prepare a number of agents, primarily Belgians, Dutchmen, Frenchmen, and Poles, to go into Germany, masquerading as foreign workers while collecting and transmitting to the Allies critical intelligence information. As Casey noted, "These brave men went into Germany blind and it was remarkable that over 90% of them came out alive."[15]

As the DIP deputy, Tofte's initial job was to evaluate and train foreign agents, a challenging though not unfamiliar task. Captain Jan Lavergne, an OSS man in Holland, had sent Tofte two Dutchmen, Hoofdorp and Wicklius, both of whom were well-regarded members of the Dutch resistance. But Tofte assessed both as "spoiled prima donnas, who sabotaged the teaching at the agent school and damaged the morale of the other future agents." Tofte was irritated by the fact that they refused to try on the German clothes and uniforms recommended for the mission because they were "used"; as he put it, "Much indicated that they did not really want to be sent to Germany."

Tofte was very suspicious of the pair, especially after reading a report from Polish intelligence that the Germans had infiltrated Nazi sympathizers from the Netherlands into OSS London and, on December 24, when all the newly graduated agents were afforded access to operational materials, Tofte denied the two Dutchmen access. While there were no specific charges against the pair, one report described them as "unreliable, lying, secretive, arrogant, and unwilling to cooperate." As protection for OSS, the two were sent on a long, compulsory guarded holiday on an island in the Caribbean, where they could do little harm. Meanwhile, as the war wound down, DIP personnel were working nearly around the clock, sleeping on cots in the office in case deployed agents needed to make contact urgently.[16]

Tofte and 1st Lt. Thompson thought that the standard system of sending one aircraft to drop one agent was inefficient and could be improved upon, much as the shipborne supply of materiel to the Yugoslav guerrillas had done. So, they developed a "new and special technique" that consisted of dropping off agents in "bus flight" fashion—i.e., they would drop one agent and all necessary equipment at one location, then fly on to another location to drop another agent and load of equipment, and so on, all during one flight. As Colonel James Forgan, OSS chief of the European Theater of Operations, noted in his report, "Such an operation theretofore had been considered impractical and had never been attempted." Back at headquarters, agents dropped were marked by red pins on a map of Europe and seeing lots of red pins suddenly pop up on the map enraged the British, who were used to seeing individual pins added rather than groups of them. Also abandoned during the Tofte-Thompson "upgrade" were the aircraft themselves—the heavy, slow B-24 Liberator bombers that had been used up to that point were later (March 1945) dropped in favor of the A-20 Havoc medium bomber, the A-26 Invader light bomber, and the British Mosquito night fighter/bomber.[17]

On December 26, 1944, Tofte presented Casey with a report which outlined the future flights and agent drop-offs; each team of two or three individuals would have a code name for select identification. Per the report, five teams were to be inserted in January 1945 and nine in the first half of February, when lunar conditions were expected to be optimal. In reality, in the period ending January 7, 1945, Tofte dispatched eight agents to Munich, Kassel, Stuttgart and Karlsruhe, in Germany; and Wiener Neustadt, Austria; during the lunar period in February, 19 agents were actually deployed. Allied advances in the war also meant that the origins of the flights could be nearer to Germany—Namur, Belgium, became the point of origin for drops in northern Germany, and Dijon, France, for those in southern Germany.

At a critical stage in DIP operations, Tofte personally went to Dijon to establish an air base there to insert agents into Germany. "The efficiency and speed with which Major Tofte set up the new base and began operations was outstanding and the unit served as a model for other such bases," wrote Col. Forgan. But Tofte was glad to escape London and get back to the action, where he was always happiest. His headquarters was the stunning Chateau Brochon, in Gevrey-Chambertin, approximately 10 kilometers south of Dijon, home to some of the world's finest and most expensive red wines. The chateau belonged to a single, elderly nobleman who, when informed that his home had been appropriated by OSS, sourly remarked, "I've been possessed by many different ones, and one kind is as bad as the other." As a man of similar appetites, Tofte felt bad for his forced host and allowed the nobleman to move his most valuable items to a wing of the castle reserved for him. The only exception was the chateau's outstanding wine cellar—Tofte had a good appreciation for fine wine and argued that retention of the cellar was good for morale, not least his own.[18]

As the Allied advance pressed farther into Germany, there was increased pressure on Tofte and his network of agents for more and better information on the enemy. Soon, Tofte was dispatching four flights every night to insert agents. He was present for every takeoff, and spoke encouragingly and urgently to each agent—his final words to each of them were, "See you soon." But from mid-March on, the weather deteriorated and Tofte was reduced to sending out two-man teams, composed of an observer and a reporter who was expert in using the ingenious "Joan-Eleanor" system of communication. This revolutionary system, which had been introduced in the Netherlands and Germany in late 1944, involved the first-ever use of the Very High Frequency (VHF) band (200–300 megahertz [MHz])—since most radio traffic used a band of 100 MHz or less, using the VHF band instead made it more difficult for the enemy to monitor radio transmissions.

An agent on the ground would use a small, handheld radio ("Joan") to communicate with an airborne radio operator in a plane 6 miles aloft equipped with a transmitter/receiver ("Eleanor"). This new communications technique was a critical advantage for the Allies—voice communications replaced telegraphy, and use of the VHF band obviated the need for encryption and decryption. Thus, the "Joan-Eleanor" system was more timely and more secure—in the assessment of the joint chiefs of staff, the system was one of "the most successful intelligence gathering operations" of the war.[19]

On Monday, March 19, 1945, two teams were sent out on important missions in the Munich/Alpine Redoubt area in southern Germany and the Austrian Alps, where Allied leaders feared the Nazis might be waging a last bloody stand. These agents were to report on German troop movements and also on the *Werwolf* movement, a late war guerrilla movement composed primarily of Schutzstaffel (SS), Gestapo, and Sicherheitsdienst (SD) members, who tended to be the most fanatical elements within the Nazi construct.

According to some accounts, *Werwolf* members were ready "to strike down the isolated soldier in his jeep, the MP on patrol, the fool who goes a-courting after dark, the Yankee braggart who takes a back road." Hitler and some of his subordinates, notably Minister of Propaganda Josef Goebbels, had tapped into a long history of fascination with lupines in German mythology to create these forces, who represented "German strength and purity against interlopers"—such as the many Allied soldiers descending on Germany from east and west simultaneously. Although the Allies were truly concerned about this potential threat, that was all it proved to be—there were never many adherents, they had few weapons, no leadership or viable plan, and many of the acts attributed to them in the late war/postwar period had more logical explanations. As General George Patton put it, "This threat of werewolves and murder was bunk."[20]

One of the teams Tofte dispatched encountered several anti-Nazi German deserters, who were provided with supplies and weapons for the fight against their countrymen. Smet and Blonttrock's team sent 66 messages and became one of the most important agent teams, reporting on the disposition of German mountain troops; antiaircraft reinforcements south of Munich; oil and petroleum depots; a secret jet base; a large *Werwolf* group in Bluhnberg Castle led by Otto Raab; and the mobile headquarters of what appeared to be the entire *Werwolf* movement aboard a camouflaged train named *Krista*. The team known as PAINTER consisted of Emil van Dyck and Francois Flour, and was declared missing in action (MIA) after six weeks, but the pair had not been captured, shot, or turned. Rather, using false papers, the two had managed to get jobs in an SS mechanic's workshop in Munich. Predictably, the two acquired a great deal of valuable information but were unable to get it to London due to the proximity of Allied bombing, prompting them to turn their intelligence collection efforts to the postwar scene.[21]

The critical month of March 1945 was also the month in which the fired Maj. Huot's book, *Guns for Tito*, was set to be published (on March 15, to be specific). But several individuals were opposed to the publication of this volume, not entirely because they wanted to defend Tofte. For example, Conyers Read, of the OSS History Project, opposed it for reasons of security, distortion, inaccuracy, and its potentially negative effect on morale. Similarly, the editor (unnamed) in charge of a history of Yugoslav operations also protested the publication of Maj. Huot's manuscript, noting that he "magnifies his own credit and gives none to Thompson, Tofte, and Benson, who deserve more on actual performance than he." While the volume was published despite objections, it is noteworthy that a review of the finished book has no mention whatsoever of Tofte or 1st Lt. Thompson, and only a vague, indirect reference to Capt. Benson.[22]

Throughout these closing days of the war, Tofte was constantly traveling between London and Dijon, where his contributions were recognized, not least by Col. Forgan, who assessed, "The large volume of highly important strategic intelligence procured by these agents was the final proof of the success of Dijon operations, a success which was in large part due to the rare abilities, the consummate skill, and the untiring efforts of Major Hans V. Tofte." But by mid-April 1945 he was back at headquarters, preparing to dispatch three American "Jedburgh" teams—each consisting of a US officer, a radio operator, and a Danish guide to lead the team into northern Germany, via Denmark. But the end of the war brought a halt to such preparations, and on VE Day (May 8, 1945), Maj. Tofte, captains Thompson, Mike Burke, and Eddie Miller had "a party which none of them ever came to forget." The Norwegian manager at Claridge's Hotel, in London, provided lodging, while Miller managed to scrounge up 100 eggs, to make his colleagues their favorite drink—eggnog.

Tofte was still understandably hungover that night when he received a call from the Danish ambassador in London, Eduard Reventlow, who invited him to dinner with his old friend, Henrik Kauffmann. So Tofte dragged himself to dinner, only to hear that Kauffmann had been trying to fly to Copenhagen for some time—Tofte was planning to go the next day anyway and so invited his long-time friend to ride along with him in one of the Army Air Corps' C-47 Dakota cargo planes. Tofte had also loaded a jeep on the Dakota and was able to drive it into Copenhagen with an American flag laid across a cooler, with Kauffmann by his side and three sergeants in the back. As he recalled the scene, he said, "It was an absolutely incredible experience to come back to Denmark like that—even more wonderful than I had dreamed of. In the gutters on either side trudged the disheartened German soldiers, and [on] the pavement people stood in close ranks, waving and waving flags and shouting hurray. Some of them smiled, others cried, but they were equally happy."

Tofte also took advantage of the opportunity to visit his father, Ludvig, whom he hadn't seen in four years. Despite their differences over the years, Ludvig no doubt was grateful for the meeting with Hans, since he had been told three years prior that Hans had died during his transition from China to India; it had taken several months to dispel the bogus information. Although father and son had never been close, on this occasion they shared pleasant memories over a long lunch. Furthermore, Tofte took the time to meet with his ex-wife and their son Finn, now five, before he headed to the United States for a reunion with Marlys.[23]

In the immediate postwar period, Tofte, still an OSS officer, was able to reunite with his old Yugoslav colleague Capt. Benson, now also a major, a reunion spoiled by an unfortunate accident. The United States recognized the strategic role that Norway could play in the postwar game of chess with the Soviet Union and had dispatched Tofte on a secret mission there in summer

1945. Following the mission, Capt. Benson's driver, Henry Nordlie, was transporting Tofte to the airport, to fly back to the United States. Along the way Nordlie accidentally hit an elderly man who had stepped into the roadway; the man survived but was injured and later tried to sue.

To help his friend, Tofte had to gain permission to provide Capt. Benson with a witness statement, since the former's presence in Norway was a secret. Meanwhile, Marlys continued to push Hans to leave the military and get a civilian job instead, which Tofte was willing to do; however, as he was wont to do, Maj. Gen. Donovan proved persuasive and cajoled him into remaining in uniform for another four months, as head of American intelligence activities in Scandinavia and as acting head of the SI "rump" in Europe. The inevitable paper trail authorizing this assignment explained, "Major Tofte is required for services as Head of the Scandinavian Section and as Acting Head of the Central European Section, SI Branch, during the absence of the Section Head."[24]

While visiting family, he also had an unexpected opportunity to visit friends—on Constitution Day, September 17, he was invited by the Danish consul general in Toronto—a former Scout comrade from *2. Vesterbro Trop*—to speak at a gathering for Danish-Canadians. Tofte, expecting to address some 300 people, was surprised to find himself instead speaking to an audience of 3,000 assembled in a local park.[25]

An October 1945 memo that on its surface seems routine and a normal part of the responsibility that comes with military rank actually provides an interesting look back to the activities in which Tofte, his men, and his agents were involved some two years prior. The subject of the memo concerns 14 missing Elgin watches, for which Tofte had signed as the property accountability officer for the European Division. In this memo, addressed to the OSS Property Board, Tofte describes the missing timepieces as "part of operational equipment collected at that time for a mission to the Balkans." He added that to the best of his knowledge, none of the watches were in the possession of any mission members. "All members of the mission," Tofte wrote, "operated for a long period of time in enemy occupied Yugoslavia where much equipment was lost during operations and other equipment was used occasionally as 'escape currency' for similar purposes in order to enhance the efficiency of military work of a secret nature." Apparently, the Property Board was satisfied with such an explanation, and the matter was closed without further action.[26]

Back in Washington after the end of the war, Whitney Shephardson provided a general letter of reference for Tofte, attesting to his wartime accomplishments and overall character. In a letter on Strategic Services Unit (SSU) stationery, Shepardson wrote the following on November 29, 1945:

> To whom it may concern:
> Major Hans Tofte has worked under my supervision during the last two years. His assignments were directly related to the war effort and in these assignments he acquitted himself with honor and distinction. He had charge of difficult and delicate operations which required working quickly, smoothly and effectively with officers under him and over him. He often had to act at short notice and under pressure of events, but he always kept a singularly cool head which contributed immeasurably to his success.
>
> He has good judgment, his work was superior both in broad planning and in detailed execution. He has high standards of work and a strong sense of duty. He has the capacity for handling a multitude of details in his mind without impairing his ability to think and act broadly. He has an attractive personality.
>
> I commend him to any company or person requiring such a man in their business.
>
> (signed)
> Whitney H. Shephardson

Attached to the letter was a single-page summary of Tofte's wartime activities, at least in broad-brush, obviously unclassified terms:

1. Denmark 1940
   Engaged in initial underground activities after Nazi invasion of Denmark April 1940. Escaped via Germany, France, Spain and Portugal to USA a year later in 1941. Volunteered for special service in the far East with secret British agency and proceeded by air from USA via Australia to Malaya.

2. Singapore 1941
   Training in British commando warfare, jungle fighting and sabotage. Organized special units for operations in Burma and China and assumed command of same with rank of Major after Japanese attack on Singapore. Proceeded to Burma.

3. Burma 1942
   Operated supply line from Rangoon to Lashio and further via the Burma Road into China. Action at Rangoon, later organized guerrilla force of Gurkhas and Shan tribesmen near Lashio. Met and worked with General Orde Wingate and later operated in China near Hongkong. Returned to USA.

4. Middle East 1943–44
   Joined U.S. Army, commissioned as Captain after 5 months service with OSS. Training officer, assistant to Major "Dangerous Dan" Fairbairn (chief instructor of original British Commandos, author of handbook "Get Tough").

   Transferred to Cairo. Operations in the Balkans, blockade running in the Adriatic in command of 42 Yugoslav ships and 600 Partizans. Parachutings to Marshal Tito. Action with PT boats and similar naval craft. Landed 6,000 tons of supplies on enemy controlled coast of Dalmatia.

5. ETO 1944–45
In charge of extensive secret intelligence operations on the European continent. (Secret agents & underground contacts).

Washington, DC, Nov., 1945[27]

In December 1945, Tofte was assigned to the Secret Intelligence (SI) Central Europe Regional Desk in Washington, DC, replacing Howard M. Chapin, the former head of Secret Intelligence Central Europe and head of OSS Austria. Tofte wrote to Alfred C. Ulmer, Jr., Austrian mission, OSS/SSU/CIG/CIA, "We wish to emphasize again that everybody here [in Washington] is admiring the effort of SSU Austria in the face of the present serious handicaps, and we want to assure you that we are becoming increasingly convinced that the part played by your mission in the general program of keeping the SSU alive and in the picture during this period of uncertainty will bear fruit in the not too distant future." However, after only a brief three-month stay on the desk in Washington, Tofte was replaced on short notice by future DCI, Maj. Helms, who had resigned from the SSU the previous month but was almost immediately rehired to fill the sudden vacancy.[28]

While the reason for Tofte's sudden removal from the OSS/SSU Austria desk in Washington after a tenure of only three months is obscure, one writer sees the immediate postwar years as critical for both Tofte and Lt. Cmdr. Wisner. Author Annie Jacobsen explains it by simply saying that "like Wisner, something happened to Tofte between the end of World War II and the outbreak of the Korean War." She savagely characterizes Tofte as a "liar and a thief" and ponders whether to attribute the alleged development to a forerunner of PTSD, excessive hubris, or simply too much alcohol. As she writes, "The danger of covert-action operations, and the plausible deniability construct in which they exist, was that it made possible for ignoble actions to be easily concealed…Like Frank Wisner, Tofte would ultimately experience a tragic downfall…He would die impoverished, his reputation in ruins."[29]

A pair of historians who have written about the experiences of OSS/SSU in Austria during 1945 and 1946 have assessed that "a unique intelligence culture…emerged among American officers in Austria," notably different from the structure emerging for such organizations in the Washington, DC, metropolitan area. They contend that OSS and SSU Austria generally directed their own affairs, including "targeting priorities, structure, operations, [and]…reporting style." Most of the US personnel assigned to OSS/SSU Austria had spent months, if not years, out of the United States; thus, it was not surprising that German words and phrases snuck into English reports, that outdated administrative memos were simply ignored, and even that inter-office romances were common. It is also worth noting, however, that the office enjoyed several successes, including several against the hardest target of all, the USSR. Also, as the two authors stress, perhaps never before or since has US intelligence in Austria operated with fewer personnel or less resources than between September 1945–October 1946.[30]

At the end of January 1946, a request to transfer Maj. Tofte to the position of head of the Central Europe-Scandinavia Section, SI, noted that his duties had been performed in a "superior" manner, which meant he was eligible for a discharge from the OSS follow-on, the Strategic Services Unit (SSU); his separation occurred at Fort Dix, New Jersey, and was dated February 16, 1946, though he was on terminal leave from February 11–March 30, 1946, inclusive; thus, his date of relief from active duty was actually March 30, 1946. His Certificate of Service attested that: "Major Hans V. Tofte 0525313 AUS honorably served in active Federal Service in the Army of the United States from 15 June 1943 to 30 March 1946." His discharge orders noted that he had entered active duty on June 15, 1943, that he had graduated from the Royal Air Force Parachute School at Ramat David, Palestine, and that he had had two different Military Occupational Specialties (MOS) during the war—Training Officer 2520, Special Assignments Officer OSS, and Intelligence Officer 9307. The document also noted his various military awards, among them the European African Middle Eastern Campaign Medal with one Bronze Battle Star, the American Campaign Medal, and the World War II Victory Medal.[31]

But it was the other two awards that Tofte received that, justifiably, garnered all the attention. While Tofte had not always made friends and positively influenced people during his World War II service, his accomplishments had not gone unnoticed. As early as July 1944, Maj. Coon had recommended Tofte for the Distinguished Service Medal (DSM) or an alternative decoration for his activities between October 1943–January 1944, i.e., his stalwart support to the Yugoslav partisan forces. One month before Tofte was appointed chief of the US-controlled maritime supply route from Italy to Yugoslavia in early November 1943, he and Coon had traveled together to Bari, Italy. In his recommendation, Coon wrote:

> It is my impression that Captain Hans Tofte not only carried out the duties assigned to him in a highly conscientious and sincere manner as a representative of the U.S. Armed Forces, but also that he went beyond the call of regular duty whenever the exigencies of war called for it in or near his station. He held the unanimous respect of the entire Yugoslav force

> with which he operated as well as the respect of his subordinate American officers directly engaged in the operations referred to.[32]

Although he was never awarded the DSM, Tofte did receive both the Bronze Star and the Legion of Merit from Maj. Gen. Donovan in a joint ceremony simultaneously with his March 30, 1946, discharge in New York. The citation for the former explained that it was for

> meritorious service in connection with military operations while serving with the Office of Strategic Services, from 4 August 1944 to 8 May 1945. Because of the unusual skill and the tact which he displayed in the handling of delicate situations involving authorities of other nations, by reason of his rare organizational talents, his infinite care and vision in guiding a series of highly complex operations Major Tofte was instrumental in achieving the over-all operational efficiency maintained by that organization. Major Tofte's services and leadership were exemplary and reflect high credit upon himself and the armed forces of the United States.

The award citation for the Legion of Merit explained that it was being presented for "exceptionally meritorious conduct in the performance of outstanding services to the Government of the United States," and noted that he and

> two other American officers conceived and developed a plan for the establishment of a sea supply line from Bari, Italy to Marshal Tito's Partisan forces in Yugoslavia. Under the direction of Major Tofte, an operations base was established at Bari and a constant flow of vital supplies…was maintained to Yugoslavia despite increasing enemy activity during the months of November and December. In addition, a brigade of more than 2,000 troops, recruited among Yugoslavs in internment camps in Italy was transported across the Adriatic to join the fighting Partisans. Thousands of refugees were evacuated to Italy and over 800 wounded Partisans were shipped to Italy for hospitalization. In November 1943, when the Germans initiated a drive to destroy the shipping operation, Major Tofte reconnoitered the Yugoslav coast, determined Partisan needs to stave off the attack and personally directed the shipment of these supplies…On 2 December 1943, Major Tofte displayed outstanding courage while directing and participating in voluntary rescue work in the port of Bari after a disastrous German bombing attack. The initiative, perseverance, ingenuity and personal courage displayed by Major Tofte throughout his entire assignment were an inspiration to all who worked with him. His sound judgment, imagination and foresight in the planning stages of the operation were responsible for the successful supply of thousands of Partisan forces thus enabling them to divert strong German divisions from the Western front thereby facilitating the rapid advance of the Allied Armies.[33]

The end of the war convinced a number of influential individuals that there was no need for OSS in peacetime America. As one authority noted, "OSS may have won its battles in the field, but it lost its final campaign—in Washington. It was better prepared to fight armed enemies overseas than bureaucratic enemies in the nation's capital." Ironically, the rapid demise of OSS had much to do with its creator and chief, Maj. Gen. Donovan. Much more of a frontline fighter than an adroit and savvy agency head, Maj. Gen. Donovan was frequently absent from Washington during the war, "Inattentive as an administrator and uncompromising as a bureaucrat." He had always hated office and paperwork and often left such menial and undesirable tasks to subordinates, as he was used to doing at his New York City law firm. Thus, OSS was always a model of organizational chaos, which provided ready ammunition for critics, of which there were many.

The very existence of OSS threatened the War and Navy Departments, the State Department, and FBI, all of whom had been engaged in intelligence work, broadly defined, for many years. Significantly, the chief executive, President Harry Truman, was also not a fan—he didn't care for the freewheeling, overspending spy chief personally—nor did his highly regarded Bureau of the Budget director, Harold B. Smith, whom President Truman considered an honest public servant opposed to empire-building and inflated government spending. Thus, in many circles in Washington, few tears were shed when President Truman issued Executive Order 9621 on September 20, 1945, directing the formal dissolution of OSS on October 1. Some former OSS elements transferred to the State Department, but some remained with its successor, the Strategic Services Unit (SSU)—which would soon transition into the Central Intelligence Group (CIG) at President Truman's behest, and, shortly thereafter, into the Central Intelligence Agency.[34]

Many of Tofte's former OSS colleagues had been given top positions in CIA, and they encouraged him to join them. Tofte had clearly proven his capabilities as an intelligence officer and irregular warfare operator, and was invited to stay within the ranks of whatever intelligence agency everyone expected to arise in the immediate postwar period. However, somewhat surprisingly, Tofte declined, indicating his lack of desire to spend any further time in a quasi-military organization such as OSS. He did, however, agree to talk with Lt. Cmdr. Frank Wisner, head of the semi-independent Office of Policy Coordination (OPC), many of whose employees were former OSS officers like Tofte, men described as "enterprising, arrogant, adventurous, restless and strongly anti-Communist."

Lieutenant Commander Wisner routinely referred to the OPC as "the great Wurlitzer," a reference to the great cinema organ, the keys of which were all either black or white, and to himself as the "virtuoso keyboard player." But for the time being, Tofte left his cloak and dagger behind and instead joined American Overseas Airlines (AOA) in New York, serving as the director of the Danish branch in Copenhagen during the build-up of commercial aviation in Europe between 1946–48. Marlys and her daughter Teresa joined him there in

July 1946, shortly after his appointment. They moved into a large apartment near Copenhagen Central Station, and he turned his attention to commercial airline development in postwar Europe. However, AOA planes often couriered mail between United States and Danish intelligence agencies, which allowed Tofte to keep in touch with former OSS colleagues.[35]

Thus, the Toftes entered what was, comparatively speaking, an idyllic period. Hans was out of uniform, save as a reservist, with a good job, living in a comfortable environment in his birthplace, with the women of his dreams: his wife and stepdaughter. Yet, it was during this pleasant interlude that Marlys began to not only notice some negative personality traits in Hans's behavior, but also to hear disquieting things about her husband, especially his relations with other women. Although Marlys knew Hans had a number of close personal friends, she also began to notice that he "could also seem cold towards people he didn't care for or who simply didn't interest him," such as subordinates at AOA who claimed he had no concern for their working conditions. Similarly, he never again visited Thor and Sonja Ibsen, despite the fact they had been close once and Tofte had aided Sonja in getting her US visa. As Sonja recalled, "He [Hans] easily entered the lives of people who then never heard from him again…he lived so much in the moment that everything else was pushed aside. Later, in quiet moments, he could bitterly regret and apologize for his behavior."

Furthermore, Marlys was "accustomed to economic abundance and order" and was having an increasingly hard time coming to grips with the ups and downs of their life together. She was also coming to grips with Hans's odd relationship with his father, and with the penchant for flirtation with women other than their wives that both seemed to share. In this regard Ludvig made excuses for Hans, noting that it was the nomadic lifestyle the latter led that prevented him from bringing more to their marriage. Though, Ludvig also warned Marlys about his son's relationship with women. The one positive familial development for Marlys was her ability to develop a good relationship with Finn, which grew stronger over the years.[36]

Tofte's duties at AOA involved negotiating flight rights for the airline, which meant working closely with Foreign Minister Gustav Rasmussen, whom Tofte knew from his days in London. One day, Rasmussen asked Tofte to come to the ministry, where he informed him that he was to receive the Knight's Cross for his work for the Danish resistance in the final year of the war. Shortly thereafter, he, Marlys, and Teresa were invited to Christiansborg Castle in Copenhagen in 1947 for a ceremony in which Tofte received the award and a knighthood for his wartime service from King Frederik IX.

During his audience, the king asked Tofte what it was like to be an American—Tofte replied that he was comfortable as an American, but happy with his Danish origins and loved his fatherland. But after two years in Copenhagen, the man of action was growing restless again, eager to prove himself in his new homeland. So, it proved fortuitous when Marlys inherited the majority of the shares in textbook publisher Klipto Loose Leaf Company, in Mason City, Iowa. Marlys then bought out her uncle, John Corsaut, and in December 1948, the family moved to Mason City and Hans started a new life as a Midwest publishing director, a job at which he excelled, since he had long since demonstrated strong oratorical skills. He did, however, maintain his status as a US Army officer in the Reserves and was promoted to lieutenant colonel, with an effective date of 1947.

For a man who preferred and was used to non-stop action, Tofte adjusted surprisingly well to suburban life in Iowa—he became a member of the Rotary Club and the Parish Council of the Episcopal Church, as well as a Boy Scout leader. Not surprisingly, he made many important friends, perhaps the most significant former general Hanford MacNider, a truly outstanding Iowa native, a highly decorated veteran of both world wars, a founder and later national commander of the American Legion, the assistant secretary of war, and candidate for US vice president. General MacNider would prove to be a valuable ally in Tofte's future. Tofte also was quite successful in his new occupation and proved to be a dynamic speaker, though his 120 employees received neither guidance nor support from their restless boss. Yet, as his original biographer notes, "Nevertheless, strongly encouraged by Marlys, he was determined to live a quiet and comfortable existence, even as old friends urged him to resume the agent career."[37]

CHAPTER 5

The Korean War

Over Christmas 1949, Tofte visited Washington, DC, where he was heavily recruited by two wartime friends now working for Central Intelligence Agency, the OSS/CIG/SSU follow-on whose formal existence dated to the National Security Act of 1947. Over lunch at the swanky Sulgrave Club, Tofte politely but firmly rejected the pleas of Deputy Director for Plans (DDP)/Covert Operations Chief Desmond FitzGerald and Major General Richard Stillwell, chief of Far East operations, to join the Langley crowd. He explained to his friends that he was happy living his middle-class life in Iowa—it may not have been as exciting as directing paramilitary operations in Italy and Yugoslavia had been during the war, but he was content.

Nevertheless, Tofte did agree to talk again to another wartime colleague now in the Agency's employ, OPC Chief Lt. Cmdr. Frank Wisner. The sorry state of the meeting site between Lt. Cmdr. Wisner and Tofte was a stark reminder of the orphan status of CIA during its early days—a series of low-slung, quasi-derelict wooden buildings around the Reflecting Pool. Lieutenant Commander Wisner pulled no punches with his friend, telling Tofte, "We sure need you." Tofte again declined to join CIA, however—in an ironic bit of foreshadowing—told Lt. Cmdr. Wisner, "But if there is another war, you can count on me." As events would soon demonstrate, while Hans had plenty of challenges in his new job in Mason City, they proved to be "not the type of challenges that suited his temperament," leaving the door open.[1]

Six months later, Tofte, a lieutenant colonel in Military Intelligence in the US Army Reserves, was attending three weeks of active-duty infantry training, which normally occurred at Fort Riley, Kansas. However, this time Tofte was slated to attend a June 12–23 Counterintelligence Corps officers advanced course at Camp Holabird, Maryland. On Sunday morning, June 25, 1950, after graduating from the two-week course, he heard of the North

Korean invasion of South Korea, beginning the Korean War. Just as he feared, Lt. Cmdr. Wisner called him the next morning and asked, "Is this enough of an emergency for you?" When Tofte replied that it was, Lt. Cmdr. Wisner asked the "mercurial" Tofte to come to Washington right away, and by Tuesday morning, he was at Agency headquarters in DC, such as it was. He was fully aware that the combination of his experience in the Far East plus his knowledge of (now) six foreign languages made him the ideal recruit for Korea, so it likely came as little surprise when he was informed that he had been selected to lead CIA's covert operations in the Korean War, based in southern Japan. Lieutenant Commander Wisner and Maj. Gen. Stillwell arranged for briefings to get Tofte up to speed but it proved too early in the game for formal orders; as had sometimes been the case in OSS, he was given broad missions but essentially left on his own. As Tofte recalled, "There was no book to go by. This was the first time that CIA was to function in a hot war."[2]

There was, however, general guidance concerning the functions of CIA. The first such foundational document was National Security Council (NSC) 4-A, the subject of which was "Psychological Operations." The initial paragraph of the directive read, "The National Security Council, taking cognizance of the vicious psychological efforts of the USSR, its satellite countries and Communist groups to discredit and defeat the aims and activities of the United States and other Western powers, has determined that, in the interests of world peace and U.S. national security, the foreign information activities of the U.S. Government must be supplemented by covert psychological operations."

The document also determined that "the Central Intelligence Agency [is] the logical agency to conduct such operations." Thus, "The National Security Council directs the Director of Central Intelligence to initiate and conduct, within the limits of available funds, covert psychological operations designed to counteract Soviet and Soviet-inspired activities which constitute a threat to world peace and security or are designed to discredit and defeat the United States in its endeavors to promote world peace and security." Finally, on the off chance that there was any confusion on the matter, "Nothing contained herein shall be construed to require the Central Intelligence Agency to disclose operational details concerning its secret techniques, sources or contacts."[3]

The other seminal document was NSC 10/2, the NSC Directive on the Office of Special Projects, dated June 18, 1948. As Section 5 read:

> As used in this directive, "covert operations" are understood to be "all activities (except as noted herein) which are conducted or sponsored by this Government against hostile foreign states or groups or in support of friendly foreign states or groups but which are so planned and executed that any US Government responsibility for them is not evident to unauthorized persons and that if uncovered the US Government can plausibly disclaim any responsibility for

> them. Specifically, such operations shall includer any covert activities related to: propaganda; economic warfare; preventive direct action, including sabotage, anti-sabotage, demolition and evacuation measures; subversion against hostile states, including assistance to underground resistance movements, guerrillas and refugee liberations groups, and support of indigenous anti-communist elements in threatened countries of the free world. Such operations shall not include armed conflict by recognized military forces, espionage, counter-espionage, and cover and deception for military operations.

NSC 10/2 also explained that given the "vicious covert activities" of the USSR, the NSC had determined that "in the interests of world peace and US national security, the overt foreign activities of the US Government must be supplemented by covert operations." To that end, the NSC also authorized the creation of a new office of "Special Projects" within CIA, which would operate independently of "other components of Central Intelligence Agency" and whose chief would report directly to the director of Central Intelligence (DCI). Predictably, such an arrangement did not sit well with other federal entities, to the extent that on October 11, 1950, a meeting was held between CIA and representatives from the State Department, the Department of Defense, and the Joint Chiefs of Staff on that very issue. Lieutenant Commander Wisner informed the other attendees that the DCI saw no compelling reason at the time to revise NSC 10/2 to formally integrate the OPC into CIA. He reiterated that the OPC would remain open to the receipt of advice and policy guidance from these offices, but not to the extent of giving orders or direction to the OPC. According to Lt. Cmdr. Wisner's meeting memo, the office representatives were in agreement and indicated they would inform their superiors.[4]

In addition to dealing with the emerging US intelligence community, Lt. Cmdr. Wisner also had the responsibility of bringing his boss up to speed. At the end of October 1948, Lt. Cmdr. Wisner, assistant director for policy coordination, had written a progress memo to the first-ever DCI, Rear Admiral Sidney W. Souers, to brief him on OPC planning activities. Lieutenant Commander Wisner informed the DCI that the OPC had been holding a series of meetings of the Advisory Council, a select group of senior, security-cleared individuals from the Army, Navy, Air Force, Joint Chiefs of Staff, and the State Department. He shared with Rear Admr. Souers the five emerging areas of clandestine activity within CIA:

1. Functional Group 1—Psychological Warfare, with Press, Radio, and Miscellaneous sub-sets;
2. Functional Group 2—Political Warfare, with sub-sets for Support of Resistance (i.e., Underground), Support of DPs and Refugees, Support of anti-Communists in Free Countries, Encouragement of Defection;
3. Functional Group 3—Economic Warfare [additional information redacted];

4. Functional Group 4—Preventive Direct Action, with sub-sets for Support of Guerrillas; Sabotage, Counter-Sabotage and Demolition; Evacuation; Stay-Behind;
5. Functional Group 5—Miscellaneous, with sub-sets for Front Organizations; War Plans; Administration; and Miscellaneous.[5]

If efficient organization had anything to do with mission accomplishment, ultimate success seemed guaranteed. The other factor that made success in launching such an ambitious venture more likely was the experience level of the personnel involved. Tofte, Lt. Cmdr. Wisner, and Maj. Gen. Stillwell were all veterans of the vaunted OSS and Tofte was intimately familiar with the operating environment, having spent many years in Manchuria and northern Korea.[6]

As Tofte explained his charge, "Basically, I was told to choose a site and build an operations base outside Tokyo, big enough to handle one thousand people, with our own comms. Whatever else happened, I was on my own." He called his wife who was in Mason City and asked her to meet him during a brief layover in Minneapolis on his way to Tokyo. She brought him two suitcases of clothes—as Tofte put it, "I never went home." But he did take care of one other detail before leaving the United States. Because he was well aware of how things worked in General Douglas MacArthur's headquarters in Tokyo and of the "martinet" qualities of Major General Charles Willoughby, the theater G-2, with whom he would have to work intimately, Tofte refused to go with his reserve rank of lieutenant colonel; rather, he insisted that he would go to Tokyo only with Agency rank equivalent to Gen. MacArthur's "trusted squire," to which the Agency agreed—meaning that Tofte now carried himself as a major general, just as Maj. Gen. Willoughby was.

Tofte's insistence was well-founded, as it was only the previous month that Maj. Gen. Stillwell had gotten Gen. MacArthur's permission for CIA to operate in-theater, a concession leveraged only with "immense pressures" from Washington. The rushed nature of affairs also meant that Tofte had little time to adapt to CIA and new ways of doing things, which meant in practice that he fell back on the ways he got things done in OSS, oblivious to the reality that the international situation was radically different in 1950 from what it had been in 1943. As his original biographer put it, Tofte "still played by his own rules, and this quickly earned him enemies within the ranks of the CIA."[7]

Tofte arrived in Tokyo with several letters of introduction, written by close friend and fellow Mason City resident Gen. MacNider, described as "one of the most distinguished citizens of northeast Iowa." One of the letters that Gen. MacNider wrote, dated July 28, 1950, on the stationery of the Northwestern

States Portland Cement Company of Mason City, was addressed to Gen. MacArthur. It opened:

> Dear General MacArthur:
> This will be presented by my good friend and fellow townsman, Lieutenant Colonel Hans V. Tofte, presently at your headquarters. Colonel Tofte can tell you in his own story of some rather remarkable service in World War II, a good part of which was spent in the O.S.S. under our mutual friend, Bill Donovan, who considered him one of his ablest and most valuable operatives.
>
> Colonel Tofte has spent a good part of his adult life in the Far East, particularly in Manchuria and China, and would seem to have all the necessary background to be of definite service to you in the present emergency. I have faith in his abilities, his loyalty and his resourcefulness, and I commend him to your consideration for any tasks for which you may feel his experience qualifies him.
>
> Very respectfully,
> Hanford MacNider

McNider penned a similar letter to Gen. MacArthur's G-2, Maj. Gen. Willoughby, and commented "Tofte did some outstanding work in the last big fracas for Bill Donovan, who told me only a few days ago that he considers him one of the best in almost any capacity for which his experience qualifies him."[8]

When Tofte arrived in Tokyo, it was as the head of a department named "Historical Research Section V," a cover name for Lt. Cmdr. Wisner's OPC. He found that CIA presence consisted of what he referred to as "six poor lost souls working out of a hotel room." This intimate little group focused on collection and espionage as part of CIA Special Operations (OSO) in Japan and maintained an uneasy truce with what Tofte called "the tight little island" of Gen. MacArthur's staff. The OSO chief, George Aurell, was the former consul in Yokohama, had been born and raised in Kobe, Japan, and was a Southwest Pacific Area (SWPA) veteran, ensuring his acceptance into the group of "Bataan Boys" surrounding Gen. MacArthur. But Aurell was based in Tokyo, with an office in the Far East Command's *Dai Ichi* building in Tokyo, along with Gen. MacArthur and his staff; thus, everyday operations for the OSO element were left to Aurell's deputy, OSS China veteran

Mr. and Mrs. Hanford MacNider, 1930. (Library of Congress)

William Duggan. There was, however, a more well-defined Agency footprint at Yokosuka Naval Base, near the port city of Yokohama, where Tofte's unit, focused on covert operations, constituted the Office of Policy Coordination (OPC) element.[9]

With his physical and mental marching orders at hand, Tofte took to researching the best location for a new OPC presence in Japan, technically subordinated to the "Joint Advisory Commission Korea," or JACK. Described as a World War II veteran with "extensive experience in para-military activities," Tofte was, according to a pair of historians, "able to identify vital border crossings along the little-known northern frontier [Manchuria]," and could "place his units in position to cause maximum damage." In this task, he came to rely heavily on his able deputy, Colwell Beers, a US Naval Academy graduate and experienced bureaucrat who had worked for the Civilian Conservation Corps, the US Forest Service, and the Hoover Commission, which had focused on government efficiency. As Tofte commented, "Beers was a hell of a good bureaucrat. He kept me out of jail because he knew his way around government and how to handle the paperwork and details. We became a formidable team."[10]

The pairing with Beers was undoubtedly a good thing—as Kruger notes, "Tofte had been given a fairly free hand financially to build up his network, a disposition that his bosses probably quickly regretted, because the Dane was not a man who chose the cheapest solutions. He did as he saw fit, passing the bills without squinting at the number of zeros." The duo spent their first week in Tokyo in July 1950 driving around in search of the ideal site. It was while they were walking around eating lunch at Atsugi Air Force Base—a former Japanese naval air station 47 miles south of Tokyo, with a view of Mount Fuji—that they discovered an isolated area of some 50 acres along the Sagami River, between Atsugi and the factory town of Chigasaki on Sagami Bay. As Tofte recalled, "I had a beer in one hand and chicken sandwich in the other, and I pronounced, 'This is where the base will be.'" They began walking off areas for specific buildings and within the week engineers and construction units were at work on the site.[11]

The next obvious need was manpower, but Tofte was astute enough to realize that there was opposition to the mere presence of CIA in Japan, much less to the "lending" of military personnel to support Agency operations. Aware of the hostility, especially within the senior ranks of the military, Tofte focused on lower-echelon staff officers. The military in general, and the US Air Force in particular, had stressed the critical need for a well-developed, highly effective escape-and-evasion (E&E) program for US military personnel who found themselves downed behind enemy lines. Predictably, the Air Force, the Navy, and even the Army were willing to provide Tofte with bodies for the conduct of this mission. Tofte essentially sequestered two each officers from these three services and ordered them to develop a viable E&E plan. As Tofte noted, "If a pilot was hit up around the Yalu River, in MiG Alley, and he had twenty minutes' flying time before going down, it made a colossal difference if he knew where he had to head for."[12]

To properly focus the mission, Tofte provided his guidance for an E&E plan:

1. The main E&E locations for downed airmen would be two islands off the east and west coasts of Korea, which would be manned by CIA and communications personnel.
2. A strip across the Korean peninsula would be occupied by trained guerrillas working as guides, whose fixed inland positions would be provided to pilots during flight briefings.
3. There would be covert agents and E&E observation points on both the east and west coasts of the Korean peninsula, just below MiG Alley, at 20-mile intervals, equipped with communications gear.
4. Two CIA-controlled indigenous "fishing fleets" would patrol the coasts looking for downed fliers, using black market operations as cover.
5. CIA agents would pre-brief pilots on E&E techniques and debrief rescued airmen once the system became operational.
6. A supply of $700,000 worth of 1-ounce gold bars imprinted with the old Bank of China logo, so that each pilot could carry three or four on his person, to pay Koreans for help. [Tofte knew there was an ample supply of gold on Formosa (Taiwan).]

After some discussion and the inevitable revisions, the Air Force and Army accepted the plan, though Maj. Gen. Willoughby objected, arguing that currency restrictions meant Formosan gold could not be brought into Japan. Rather than argue with his nemesis, Tofte flew to Formosa that night, made a private deal with the exiled Bank of China, and returned to Japan with the $700,000 in gold. As Henrik Kruger assessed the situation, "Typical of Tofte, he didn't bother waiting for things to follow the slow chain of command, especially when the outcome was usually negative. When he had made a decision, he carried it out without waiting for permission from anyone. This made him extremely effective, but at the same time it made him powerful enemies." But his enemies notably did not include the then-commander in chief, Far East, General Matthew Ridgway—who had replaced Gen. MacArthur after President Truman relieved him—at whose direction Tofte received a Commendation for Meritorious Civilian Service in 1951. The document announced that "Mr. Hans V. Tofte, Department of the Army Civilian Has Received Official Commendation for Outstanding Performance of Duty." The citation read:

> As Chief of the Historical Research Section V, G-2 Section, General Headquarters, Far East Command, Mr. Tofte distinguished himself by performing meritorious service from

> July to November 1950. Through his unusual initiative, ingenuity and determination Mr. Tofte rendered maximum assistance to the Military Intelligence Section in the collection of vital intelligence on Korea. Based on his specialized knowledge of unconventional warfare, he made important, basic recommendations for plans to rescue airmen downed behind enemy lines. Mr. Tofte's efforts contributed immeasurably to inter-service unity, troop morale and the United Nations' success in combat and reflect great credit on himself and the Department of the Army.
>
> (signed) Matthew Ridgway
> Commander-in-Chief, Far East

CIA Director General Walter Bedell ("Beetle") Smith also expressed his support for the concept, writing a note on March 3, 1951, to Gen. Ridgway, which read:

> Dear Matt:
> I have asked Mr. Tofte who is one of my key men in Tokyo, to see you or Lev. Allen [Maj. Gen. Leven Cooper Allen, 8th Army Chief of Staff] personally. I think that the escape and evasion work that he has been organizing to help the air force primarily, might also be helpful to the ground forces if and when any of your people get lost or taken prisoner. If so, I would be very happy.[13]

In terms of operations, Tofte was astute enough to realize that Korean refugees and POWs could render far more in the way of service than simply assisting in E&E missions—carefully screened Koreans could also provide manpower for sabotage and paramilitary operations. Largely based on his operations in China and Yugoslavia, Tofte decided early on to find and train agents and guerrillas, mostly North Korean refugees, and infiltrate them into North Korea, Manchuria, and northern China. Thus, CIA interrogation teams routinely screened Koreans in refugee and POW camps and paid special attention to refugees and their reasons for leaving the country—those who expressed an interest in liberating the North from the communists were chosen for guerrilla missions.

In the first six months of the Korean War, CIA screened and recruited hundreds of the North Korean civilians crowding the refugee camps around Pusan. Tofte was savvy enough to realize the actual motivations of some refugees, such as food, clothing, and medicine, but still believed the refugees could be of value. As he described them, "The refugees were down-in-the-mouth, bored with nothing to do. Joining the guerrillas would give them a chance to get out, to eat three meals a day, to have something to do. They would be buddies with a purpose, rather than shuffle around the camp." The screening process yielded enough experienced radio and telegraph operators—primarily from the South Korean Telephone Company—to flesh out the communications units for the guerrillas.

Those Koreans selected were taken to an Agency training base, a tent city on a 20-acre site on Yong-do Island, 90 miles south-southwest of Pusan. Tofte chose CIA Officer Maurice Curry for the daily management of affairs at Yong-do, while the guerrillas, who ultimately numbered some 1,200, were trained by a small CIA detachment under Major Vincent R. "Dutch" Kramer, USMC, in weapons use, ambushing truck convoys, sabotaging trains, interrupting of the supply flow from Manchuria and eastern Siberia, and small rubber boat operations (used for the nighttime insertions of small teams ashore).

Major Kramer was selected for this mission rather than a US Army member because CIA had a more congenial working relationship with the Navy and the Air Force. Assisting Maj. Kramer was North Korean refugee Captain Han Chul Min, who had escaped from North Korea to the United States in 1945 and for a short time had been a staffer to South Korean exiled leader, Dr. Syngman Rhee. Trained in the United States as a military officer, Min had been sent to combat as soon as war broke out and gotten wounded; Tofte contacted and recruited him while he was recuperating. Min took up his position at Yong-do in September 1950 and set about selecting suitable North Korean agents—once he had some 200, training began. The trainees were unpaid, so that they could not be considered CIA mercenaries; instead, they were given clothing, food, and sometimes small rewards, though never money.[14]

Tofte expanded an old Japanese training camp on Yong-do to include five shooting ranges, a parachute training area, a close-combat training course, and a maritime training facility. Surface assets available to Tofte included the USS *Bass*, a Navy destroyer, for operations in the Yellow Sea and Korea Bay (on the west coast of the peninsula), and a former submarine supply ship, the USS *Perch*, for operations in the Sea of Japan (off the east coast of Korea). He also had a large number of smaller boats from the Hoyum unit at Song-do, near Pusan. This unit had started with six fishing boats (*Sea Dragon*, *Sea Horse*, *Sea Gull*, *Sea Rang*, and others), all twin-engined for speed. The crew usually consisted of a captain, two crewmen, a mechanic, another officer, five agents, and a Chinese interpreter, all South Koreans. Hijacked ships

CIA paramilitary operations chief in Korea, Captain Hans Tofte, USA; ROK Major Han Chul Min; and Major Vincent R. "Dutch" Kramer, USMC, Atsugi Airbase, Japan, 1950. (US Army)

became part of the Hoyum unit, which usually engaged in landing agents, conducting E&E missions, and attacks on North Korean and Chinese islets and ships.[15]

Armed with Browning automatic rifles (BARs), light machine guns, mortars, and hand grenades, the non-maritime guerrillas learned map-reading, intelligence techniques, and psychological warfare measures. They would be deployed from airbases around the neighboring islands to be dropped over the mainland; others were sent directly into action from Yong-do, from headquarters in Chigasaki, or from Song-do. Tofte—caustically described by one author as "an OSS veteran with a greater talent for deceiving his superiors than enemies"—organized the guerrillas at Yong-do into the "Y-unit," which was then divided into four brigades, colorfully known as White Tiger, Yellow Dragon, Blue Dragon, and Owl, broken down into 44 teams. The brigade names were also code for the geographic areas in which each would operate.

The rubber boat training was led by the Navy's Underwater Demolitions Team (UDT) personnel; they also took their Korean charges with them on death-defying missions. The small landing craft would deploy near the horizon while the infiltration and sabotage teams inflated their rubber boats and rowed to the beach. As Tofte commented, "I wanted it known [by the Koreans] that the Americans [UDT] took the guerrillas in by hand. This gave the Koreans respect for us and the military services also." Potential leaders among the guerrilla recruits were screened and transferred for more intensive training at a base at Chigasaki, Japan, approximately 10 miles from Atsugi, on the beach of Sagami Bay. Training here continued throughout fall 1950 and the early months of 1951, with personnel periodically pulled out for E&E missions in the North.

Eventually, Tofte had more than 1,000 personnel living in a secure compound at Atsugi, ready for CIA covert operations missions without having to be beholden to the US military for transportation thanks to Civil Air Transport, support which Tofte characterized as "absolutely invaluable." Such operational latitude meant Tofte could also ignore the embargo on bringing indigenous peoples in and out of Japan, instead moving hundreds of guerrillas and agents in and out of Agency training compounds, both in the war zone and throughout occupied Japan.[16]

Unfortunately, two early operations were not promising—in both August and October 1950, the OPC launched missions which cost men and materiel and suggested to some that perhaps Tofte had tried to do too much, too soon. The October operation, launched on the 15th, involved 150 Agency-trained guerrillas and 20 agents at Paengyong (Pyongyang), led by US Navy Lieutenant

Eugene F. Clark. Outfitted with weapons, food, gold bars, and radio equipment, the guerrillas had boarded a South Korean naval vessel and four fishing boats seized by CIA, intent upon locating and destroying a North Korean radar station on the Yalu River. But along the way, Lt. Clark lost two of the fishing boats and 75 men, and the guerrillas never found the radar station. Only a handful of the original mission members returned, with the disturbing news that there were 300,000 Chinese soldiers deployed near the Yalu. Many of the guerrillas were captured or killed by the North Koreans, with some shot, and some hanged in public. In a masterful understatement, Henrik Kruger wrote, "There was much evidence that Major General Hans V. Tofte and CIA had underestimated the North Koreans." It soon became obvious that in the Korean War, the United States faced a very different foe than it had in World War II—the Germans had routinely taken POWs, while the North Koreans rarely did; furthermore, the latter "fought in their own country, where they knew every blade of grass."[17]

In addition to selecting, training, and deploying guerrillas on various missions during the Korean War, Tofte also found himself in a familiar place—the aviation industry. Besides the fleet he had collected, his transportation empire also came to include 40 aircraft that had been transferred to Japan and Korea for his use. They were collectively known as Civil Air Transport (CAT). The aircraft now displayed both CAT and Nationalist Chinese livery and the pilots and ground crew were on the CIA payroll. Perhaps predictably, Tofte reserved for himself a comfortable C-47—tail number XT-854—so that he could conduct personal inspections of the six CIA training stations in Japan and others in Korea.

Always a fan of pampering, he also appropriated for himself a luxurious villa on Yong-do island, overlooking Pusan Harbor, which he used as a retreat and a conference planning facility. "This was one of the best views in Asia," Tofte explained, "and getting down there away from all the clamor in Tokyo enabled us to work better and faster." He also had a retinue of servants—one of the North Korean guerrillas who served as a waiter for a time at Yong-do recalled, "Most CIA officers wore civilian clothes or uniforms without insignia. There was a thin Japanese-American known only as Captain Tanaka; 'Mr. Smith,' a fat old man in civilian clothes, who was actually Maj. 'Dutch' Kramer. And there was 'Colonel Johnson,' who was actually Maj. Gen. Hans Tofte, the boss, who was a very cold guy. He loved to party with the Red Cross nurses. It was my job to bring food and drinks to these parties, which often lasted well into the night. We had to stand and watch them dance and caress, until the officers either scored or gave up their sexual pursuit." The nurses may have been from the Danish hospital ship *Jutlandia*, which docked in Pusan in October 1950. Tofte often visited the ship, whose captain, Kai Hammerich, was a friend.[18]

Tofte's sweeping mandate also gave him responsibility for covert operations far beyond the boundaries of the Korean Peninsula. His potential area of operations included eastern Siberia as far inland as Lake Baikal; all of Mongolia and northern China, including Manchuria; and the Kurile and Ryukyu islands, the former under Soviet control. Little wonder then, that by July 1950, less than a month after the beginning of the Korean War, Tofte was referring to his creation as a "paramilitary empire," known by the cover-name Joint Technical Advisory Group (JTAG). On other occasions, he used the term "belt" to describe his proliferation of guerrillas across Korea, "A belt across the peninsula to be saturated with trained guerrillas as guides, working from fixed inland positions that would be given [to] pilots as part of their combat briefings." In keeping with the free-wheeling style that had characterized his World War II activities, Tofte clearly demonstrated that as long as the end was achieved, he wasn't concerned about the means. In a series of interviews with historian Joseph Goulden, Tofte remarked, "We were never asked for military orders in Japan or Korea, but wrote our own to look like the official papers without which nobody could move."[19]

In the rich target set Tofte had at his ready access, the sprawling Soviet naval base at Vladivostok, Siberia, was key—the Russians compelled many Chinese and Korean laborers to work on the base, a situation which enabled the insertion of CIA operators post 1950. At one point, CIA had a half-dozen agents on the base, reporting generally on Soviet naval activities and specifically on any indications of a decision to intervene in Korea. Compounding agent operations was the fact that the base was heavily guarded, which made radio communications too risky, prompting the decision to use carrier pigeons instead. As Tofte commented, it was "damnably dangerous work, but necessary." By air and by sea, Tofte's agent teams penetrated Manchuria and eastern Siberia, while other specially trained units from the Atsugi CIA facility were inserted into the Shantung Peninsula and the Tientsin area of north China. Since political restraints precluded CAT missions over Russia and China, Tofte was compelled to rely on the pilots and planes of General Earl E. Partridge's Fifth Air Force instead, gratefully volunteered to the Agency given the latter's rescuing of so many downed airmen.[20]

***

By the end of 1950, the E&E contingent operated by the OPC numbered some 1,000 personnel, and eventually reached 1,200, un-harassed by Gen.

MacArthur and Maj. Gen. Willoughby because such covert activity did not infringe on G-2 activities. Within six months, the Korean War which, to date, had been characterized by wide-ranging movement, stagnated, and the focus shifted to guerrilla warfare—operating behind enemy lines, sabotaging trains, ambushing truck convoys, and generally disrupting the flow of supplies from Manchuria and eastern Siberia to communist forces in Korea.

From April to December 1951, the OPC sent 44 guerrilla teams and intelligence units into North Korea, some by air, most by sea. These teams operated over a wide area, from Antung in the west to Rashin and Yuki in the northeast, harassing enemy lines of communications (LOC). Tofte was proud of his guerrillas, whose presence and operations prompted an assessment by the Chinese that the force likely numbered 50,000, an accomplishment which Tofte justifiably regarded as "highly successful," though FECOM guerrilla forces, which numbered up to 20,000 in strength, likely contributed to the Chinese assessment figure. Tofte later claimed that these operations were a "tremendous success," though in more measured terms he added, "there is some evidence that the enemy felt some very small stings."[21]

However, several observers have concluded that CIA's infiltration of guerrillas into North Korea was more "smoke and mirrors" than verifiable success. One author characterized the effort as "only slightly better" than similar operations into China and Maj. Gen. Bissell, DCI in the late 1960s and early 1970s, candidly noted that "the CIA's contribution to the Korean War was minimal." Lieutenant Commander Wisner had sent Tofte—described as "an OSS veteran with a genius for self-promotion"—specifically to the Far East to run guerrilla operations there, though this author concluded that "Tofte's early efforts were not auspicious." For example, a once-classified CIA history of operations in Korea noted that the guerrillas wore "captured army uniforms and Korean civilian clothing, but unfortunately wore self-incriminating U.S. Army issue underwear," the sort of strategic glitch that doomed missions and got men killed.[22]

In late April/early May 1951, 171 White Tigers and 158 Blue Dragons had been inserted into North Korea, dropped by parachute, about four months prior to Tofte's departure from Korea. Despite several supply drops and the glowing reports he had made about their accomplishments, by early November most of the White Tigers had been killed, captured, or were missing; most of the other Blue and Yellow Dragon team members suffered a similar fate, and those who survived did so only because they either fled to the mountains or agreed to be turned, at the threat of death. Ultimately, none of the guerrilla members survived and most of the E&E team members were lost or killed. Such cases were examples of "the many CIA ops in China and North Korea that Hans Tofte and from the end of 1951 his successors launched without achieving great results."[23]

Similarly, the number of guerrillas actually dropped has been subject to much debate and dispute; since Agency records on the subject are still sealed, extant figures tend to come either from Tofte himself or his trainees. While some say the total number is 9,000—a figure likely supplied by Tofte himself—others claim a more modest number of 3,000 throughout the war, with 1,500 to 2,000 of those deployed during Tofte's tenure. What *is* known, however, is that of the 1,200 dispatched from Yong-do, fewer than 300 returned—the rest were killed, disappeared, or defected.[24]

***

In the stand-up of Agency operations in Japan, Tofte also met and worked with the illustrious—or notorious, depending upon one's viewpoint—Dr. Sidney Gottlieb, the CIA chemist who was the chief of the Chemical Division, Technical Services Staff. In circa June 1950, Gottlieb visited the secret CIA facility at Atsugi Naval Air Station, near Yokohama. From this 50-acre site, CIA was running covert operations into North Korea. As an OSS veteran who claimed to know "every inch of the countryside" from past days hunting big game in the region, Tofte was in charge of this operation—as he put it, "I am, I suppose, the classic gun for hire."

Upon their meeting, Gottlieb tasked Tofte with a bizarre mission—gathering a selection of Korea's insect life and small animals, like jungle rats and voles. Such a task seemed more appropriate for an entomology or zoology graduate student than a seasoned clandestine intelligence operative. However, Gottlieb delivered the same shopping list to US Army Captain Henry Alderholt, an accomplished special operator who operated his own independent fleet of "sheep-dipped" (i.e., devoid of US military markings) C-47 cargo planes. Captain Alderholt's trademark was dropping into a jungle clearing in the middle of the night and creating havoc behind enemy lines. The ultimate goal was to find suitable hosts that could be injected with germs in an attempt to develop feasible biological warfare agents, bringing back fresh, disturbing memories of Japan's infamous Unit 731.[25]

Tofte also had access to a special chemical section at Yokosuka, where a group of Japanese scientists—allied with the Noborito Research Institute—worked. Although Japan had fought on the Allied side during World War I, Japanese Army leaders soon realized that they were at a serious disadvantage, especially in terms of chemical warfare. As a response, in 1919 Tokyo reorganized the

Army's explosives institute into the Army Science Research Institute; six years later, in 1925, a department for chemical warfare was added. By late 1939, a laboratory within the department devoted to covert warfare applications led by Army Captain Shinoda Ryo had grown into a branch institute at Noborito, south of Tokyo, in Kanagawa Prefecture. In 1942, the Army Science Research Institute was reorganized and Shinoda's laboratory became the 9th Army Technical Research Institute, the only one of ten Army institutes subordinate to the Army General Staff's Second Bureau (Intelligence); by 1945, Shinoda, now a lieutenant general, supervised a thousand employees.

The institute was involved in the development of poisons, biological agents to destroy crops and plants, and the balloon bombs sent over the western United States near the end of the war. However, the primary beneficiaries of the Noborito Research Institute were the covert operatives trained at the Army's Nakano School and Kempeitai counterintelligence officers. A veteran of the 9th Institute, Ban Shigeo, left a written record of his work there, which clearly implicated the institute in the horrific biomedical experiments inflicted on Allied POWs during World War II by Unit 731. With the end of the war, however, the US Army quietly recruited former members of Noborito in its efforts to thwart communist plans in the early Cold War years—researcher Ariga Tsutao, who worked with Ban's widow on his memoirs, noted that Ban led the chemical section of a US clandestine unit buried deep within the structure of the Yokosuka naval base during the Korean War. Not one to be troubled by official rules and regulations, Tofte commented, "We ignored the embargo on bringing indigenous personnel in and out of Japan and moved hundreds of guerrillas and agents in and out of our own training and staging camps both in the war zone and throughout occupied Japan."[26]

But Tofte's paramilitary operations chief, Maj. Kramer, a veteran of the fighting on Guadalcanal and the US Naval Group China, was convinced of the futility of guerrilla operations deep behind enemy lines after experiencing little success with the proposed and highly touted E&E corridor. Rather, Maj. Kramer proposed the creation of a standing CIA guerrilla force, dubbed Special Mission Group (SMG), to be dedicated to intelligence collection and special operations. He and Tofte both saw the need to isolate SMG from the other guerrilla and agent training occurring on Yong-do Island as they planned and conducted their compartmented, "need to know" missions, and so established a more isolated base for SMG on Kadok-do, a small island northeast of Koje-do and west/southwest of the port city of Pusan. The first two SMG missions with full teams involved the use of trawlers *K-333* and *K-444* to land and extract JACK teams, rescue downed airmen, support SMG coastal raids, and direct naval gunfire along the coast. Although these missions "proved disappointing," one knowledgeable authority has assessed that of all the CIA covert operations against North Korea, the paramilitary and intelligence collection missions of the JACK maritime element were most successful.[27]

Less successful, at least for a time, was Tofte's relationship with Maj. Gen. Willoughby, Gen. MacArthur's chief intelligence officer. At the nadir of the relationship, Maj. Gen. Willoughby ordered Japanese counterintelligence agents to surveil Tofte's operatives as they conducted their missions; one such surveillant so vexed Tofte that he admitted considering "drowning" the individual. At one point, Tofte bitterly remarked, "MacArthur has three enemies: the Russians, the Chinese, and the North Koreans. I have four, those three plus MacArthur!" Major General Willoughby periodically threatened to throw CIA out of the Far East, but Tofte ignored the threat, which Maj. Gen. Willoughby proved unable to back up. Not helping was the fact that, true to his combative nature, Tofte was always ready to assert his importance. For example, shortly after his arrival, Tofte insisted on a suite at the Imperial Hotel, the jewel of lodging in downtown Tokyo. Major General Willoughby indignantly huffed that such was impossible—the Imperial was only for flag officers and other "top military men of special importance." However, when Tofte reminded Maj. Gen. Willoughby of his two-star "rank," he got his suite.

Similarly, Tofte demanded that the US military supply him with a two-star flag for his car; when authorities balked at such an audacious request, Tofte simply had one made for himself. As for his dealings with the over-sized, over-bearing G-2, he noted, "I decided that the only way to deal effectively with Willoughby was to kick him in the pants every chance I got, to let him know I was tough as he was, or tougher." Thus, when Maj. Gen. Willoughby made his near-monthly threat to throw Tofte and CIA out of Japan, Tofte would reply, "Shut up, you work for me, I'm an American citizen and a taxpayer, and you can't order me around." Clearly, not everyone in theater was intimidated by Maj. Gen. Willoughby, understood by most to be fully representative of the near-deified Gen. MacArthur. The irony was that the two eventually developed a somewhat even-keeled relationship, based in part on their mutual affinity for foreign languages. Tofte would call Maj. Gen. Willoughby one day and speak in Chinese, the next in Russian, but there was one unchangeable proviso, in Tofte's words—"I will not speak with you in your goddamned German," due to his days in the Danish underground, fighting Maj. Gen. Willoughby's former countrymen.[28]

These two overweening personalities also came to terms due to the exigencies of the situation—post-World War II cuts in defense spending had left the Truman administration with meager intelligence assets in the Far East, meaning that Maj. Gen. Willoughby actually needed the support Tofte and the Agency could provide. To somewhat maintain the illusion of liaison, Maj. Gen. Willoughby did allow the OPC to have an office in Gen. MacArthur's headquarters, with the cover name "Documents Research Section V."[29] Tofte's running battle of words with Maj. Gen. Willoughby generally lasted only until May 1951—by which time Maj. Gen. Willoughby had retired and returned to the United States—and never actually inhibited the growth of CIA in the Far East.[30]

Part of the grudging cooperation between Maj. Gen. Willoughby and Tofte concerned collaboration in the September 1950 Operation *Trudy Jackson*, the reconnaissance campaign in advance of Operation *Chromite*, Gen. MacArthur's bold amphibious landing at Inchon. Major General Willoughby, with US Navy assistance, used his own G-2 joint special operations branch to conduct *Trudy Jackson*. Organized by Major Stephen A. B. Norberg, the operation also benefitted from the assistance of the CIA covert operations chief in Japan—Tofte. Besides the Army and CIA, the US Navy also played a significant role in the lead-up to the amphibious operation. Lieutenant Clark, a 39-year-old Navy officer, had previously conducted a terrain study of Inchon and the immediate area and was ready when US Navy Captain Edward "Eddie" Pierce asked him to lead an intelligence team to the area, adding, "We need additional information from up there." Lieutenant Clark not only accepted the intelligence-gathering mission, but also used a group of Korean agents—secured in part by working closely with Tofte—who were dispatched on a daily basis to discover any indications that North Korea was planning to actively repel the amphibious assault. Lieutenant Clark's Korean guerrillas also conducted active raids on both land and sea and specifically collected critical intelligence on the approaches and seawalls at Inchon, as well as information on the tides and current, and accomplished—albeit at heavy cost—the critical task of turning on the lighthouse at Palmi-do to help the invasion fleet navigate. On August 28, 1950, Tofte arranged for a CIA flight for Lt. Clark and two of his aides to Sasebo, the US Navy base on the island of Kyushu, in southern Japan, where Lt. Clark met his three-man communications team.[31]

But even though Gen. MacArthur could justifiably bask in the success of Operation *Chromite*, he was still irritated by the success and significance of Tofte's Office of Policy Coordination (OPC). On October 25, 1950, Gen. MacArthur cabled the Joint Chiefs of Staff (JCS) and charged that the OPC, "which [was] operating under special agreements, had been intermittently violating these agreements." General MacArthur's generic complaint referred to the recent airdrop of an agent into Soviet territory from a FEAF aircraft, an incident which had taken on what the FECOM commander characterized as "serious proportions." General MacArthur therefore advised the JCS that he was suspending such operations and ordered subordinate commands not to engage in similar projects without his approval. The Joint Chiefs responded two days later, reinforcing the Civil War-era precedent of not interfering with the prerogatives of a theater commander and reiterating that "no responsible official in Washington questioned [MacArthur's] command authority over the operations of the CIA, in his theater or in areas projected therefrom." They did add, however, that they "hoped he would afford such support to authorized intelligence and covert operations of CIA as would be consistent with CINCFE responsibilities."[32]

Aside from collaborating with the Army and the Navy, Tofte also received from Lt. Cmdr. Wisner an unusual and very sensitive mission in the early days of the Korean War—the infiltration of an agent into Pyongyang to assassinate North Korean dictator Kim Il-Sung, whose real name was Kim Sung-ju. Not long after, Tofte received a cable indicating that an assassin had been selected—Tofte was to receive him in Tokyo and then smuggle him into Pyongyang. The curious individual who volunteered to do the dirty deed—with great pride—was a Cherokee Native American code-named "Buffalo." When Washington asked him, "How would you like to kill [North Korean Premier] Kim Il Sung?" Buffalo reportedly replied, "I'll start today," and immediately left for the Far East. While eager, Buffalo also proved to be somewhat paranoid—he refused to meet at covert CIA sites, insisting instead upon meeting Tofte and other officers "at sunset near the wall of the Imperial Palace." Tofte complied with the request, met with Buffalo, and offered him what Tofte referred to as "a grand prize of a considerable amount of money," paying him an initial amount in cash and promising the remainder of the agreed-upon payment upon completion. And then…nothing… The mission failed and Buffalo was never heard from again.[33]

The bizarre tale of Buffalo brought to center focus another aspect of psychological warfare that increasingly concerned both Tofte and CIA—namely, brainwashing. The return of agents deployed to Manchuria brought persistent questions of why none of them could recall their passage through a particular zone in Manchuria. The agents' memories were completely and uniformly blank, leading to fears that the Russians and the Chinese might be actively using successful brainwashing techniques against their enemies. Edward Hunter, an OSS veteran who served in the SSU and then joined CIA under journalistic cover, wrote a book in 1951 entitled *Brainwashing in Red China: The Calculated Destruction of Men's Minds*, which garnered a great deal of attention (though later it was criticized for its questionable conclusions). The conundrum faced by Tofte and CIA also inspired Richard Condon's *The Manchurian Candidate*, about an American agent brainwashed into becoming an enemy-controlled assassin.

Inspired by German experiments during World War II, CIA had begun secretly researching brainwashing in 1947, notably by investigating the properties of lysergic acid diethylamide (LSD), first discovered in 1943 by Swiss researcher Albert Hoffmann. By the advent of the Korean War, CIA's Office of Scientific Intelligence (OSI) had been engaged in Project Bluebird for more than a year, focused on changing people's nature so much that they could be used to conduct assassinations. By July 1951, the effort, now joined by the military, became known as Project Artichoke, and later morphed into the infamous Agency program MK-ULTRA. Extant information suggests that as early as October 1950, Tofte's headquarters in Japan was conducting such experiments on North Korean POWs, and it is possible that the intended assassin Buffalo was a subject. The Agency steadfastly denied its involvement in such activities, but in 1978 was pressured into releasing documents which indicated that it had been going on for 25 years, from 1949–74.[34]

Thanks to a serendipitous opportunity, Tofte had another chance to further hone his psychological warfare skills. American officials and CIA had watched with concern as the Soviets encouraged leftist groups in Japan, warning of the potential consequences of overly close ties between Japan and the United States, not the least of which was the prospect of destruction in a nuclear confrontation between the two superpowers. In late 1950, the Soviets began releasing hundreds of Japanese POWs conveniently "lost" in Siberia. Tofte feared that the released POWs, combined with an aggressive Soviet psyops campaign, would provide the Soviet Union with an undue advantage. Though both Tofte and Beers were eager to forestall this potential development, they proved unable to come up with any viable ideas to blunt the threat.[35]

Ironically, it was Maj. Gen. Willoughby who provided them with the solution. A Willoughby staffer had come into possession of a diary kept by a Japanese colonel and former Soviet POW, which predictably made for grim reading. Uncertain what to do with the diary, Maj. Gen. Willoughby passed it off to CIA, somewhat as a joke. Tofte had the diary translated and told Beers, "We're going into the movie business. We are going to make a movie about how it is to be a prisoner of war in Russia." As if the storyline were not dramatic enough already, the producers inserted a love story into the tragic tale—a Russian nurse at the prison camp falls in love with a Japanese POW, and when he is tortured to death at the end of the film, she commits suicide. To produce and market the film, Tofte urged Gen. MacArthur to lift the postwar ban on the Japanese film industry and requested both a writer and a director from CIA. Working with Japanese technicians, under Agency oversight, they built a replica Soviet prison camp on snow-covered Hokkaido, Japan's northernmost island. Among the bizarre items Tofte ordered were four railcars full of tomato ketchup. When Beers asked why, Tofte replied, "Because this is going to be the bloodiest movie ever," which, according to some observers, it proved to be. As Tofte described the venture:

> I knew we were on the right track when Communists tried to sabotage the set. The movie was a dreadful exposure of the Soviets. The Japanese film industry loved it because it put actors and technicians back to work after a long layoff. Audiences loved it because it was a damned good film. We opened at twenty Japanese theaters simultaneously, and it ran for weeks, a smash hit at the box office. Eventually it played at more than seven hundred theaters. It created tremendous indignation and anti-Soviet feeling. And when we added up the figures, CIA took out a profit of a hundred four thousand dollars, which was turned over to the US government.[36]

The film was purportedly based entirely on the POW diary passed on by Maj. Gen. Willoughby, and Tofte hoped it might run in 100 Japanese theaters and create some anti-Soviet publicity. However, "he had not in his wildest imagination imagined that the film would cause the huge stir that it did." Tens of thousands who had seen the film demonstrated outside the Soviet Embassy in Tokyo and consulates around the country, smashing windows and setting cars on fire. Predictably, Russian officials objected to the film, which claimed—accurately—that the plot was "pure fabrication." Nevertheless, the film made the US government $234,000, before accounting for expenses.[37]

Inspired by the success of his directorial debut, Tofte created another movie that claimed to include "actual combat footage" of CIA guerrillas operating in North Korea. Predictably, this film was shown widely in government circles, to rave reviews, and redounded to Tofte's credit. That is, until Lt. Cmdr. Wisner's aide, Arthur Jacobs, noticed a discrepancy during its showing at the Pentagon—did CIA really send its paramilitary teams ashore behind enemy lines in *broad daylight*? After many pained looks around the room, Tofte later confessed that the film was…simulated, and the film portrayed a *training* mission rather than an *actual* mission. "Tofte had to confess. He had deceived his superiors and put Lt. Cmdr. Wisner in an embarrassing situation." In a larger context, the unfortunate incident provided ammunition for the US military to use against CIA in general and Tofte in particular.[38]

The continuing focus on guerrilla warfare presented Tofte with another opportunity to direct guerrilla operations in a different area of the Far East, specifically mainland China. This opportunity, known as Operation *Tropic* or *Third Force*, was CIA's covert support to third-force Chinese guerrillas—i.e., anti-communist Chinese guerrillas not affiliated with nationalist leader Chiang Kai-Shek. The goal was to recruit and train a network of Chinese expatriates who could infiltrate China, set up a guerrilla force, and identify disaffected Chinese generals who could destabilize the People's Republic from within.

A more immediate goal was to deter China from any further involvement in the Korean War. The offensive operated from a small cluster of whitewashed buildings surrounded by barbed wire at a clandestine CIA base in Japan. CAT pilots flying at night used C-47 or DC-4 cargo planes or World War II-vintage B-17 bombers to deliver the guerrillas, in return for an extra $10 per hour as an incentive; even with such an enticement, one-third of CAT pilots refused to fly these dangerous missions. Specially trained personnel were dropped to guide downed pilots or stranded agents to shore, where they could be picked up by helicopter or boat.

However, due to no fault of Tofte, Operation *Tropic* ultimately proved ineffective and was plagued with various missteps. For example, on February 7, 1951, one of Tofte's CIA officers, Lieutenant Naylor-Foote, and a pilot, Duane Thorin, took off in a helicopter to retrieve a wounded pilot, a Lieutenant Junior Grade Harry Ettinger, who had been shot down over North Korea. CIA had already dispatched three of its Korean personnel to assist Lt. JG Ettinger and two of them, aboard the rescue chopper, spotted the pre-arranged pickup signal and saw Lt. JG Ettinger standing alone in a clearing. However, the helicopter was damaged upon landing and when Lt. Naylor-Foote contacted the CIA Korean assets using the proper code, three North Korean soldiers suddenly appeared. They disarmed Lt. Naylor-Foote and Thorin, and led them to a building where they were greeted by a North Korean general—whom Lt. JG Ettinger recognized as the "CIA agent" who had arranged his "rescue." The bona fide CIA personnel had been secured, and the would-be rescuers had been lured into a trap; the three Americans spent the rest of the war in a POW camp. It was little wonder that by 1952, Operation *Tropic* had been set aside in favor of more successful future guerrilla operations. As CIA historian Nick Dujmovic characterized it, "The whole program smacked of amateurism."[39]

A more traditional intelligence operation in which Tofte was involved came at the behest of the Armed Forces Security Agency (AFSA), the signals intelligence forerunner to the National Security Agency (NSA). In the early months of the Korean War, AFSA analysts were struggling with decoding North

Korean and Chinese messages—the Chinese used an underwater telephonic cable running from various commands in Manchuria, across the Yellow Sea, to Peking, an asset that was obviously untappable, the traditional means of intercepting enemy cable communications. So the AFSA queried whether the Agency could somehow disable the cable, thereby forcing the Chinese to rely on radio broadcasts, which were more susceptible to monitoring. Tofte received this query one day in his early morning cable traffic, quipping, "It was always fun opening the mail, for one received the oddest things." As luck would have it, Tofte was quite familiar with the cable in question—prior to World War II, he had often vacationed in a home close by. As Tofte noted, "The cable went into the water about six hundred yards from my garden fence. Further, it was owned by a Danish company, the Great Northern Telegraph Company [*Det Store Nordiske Telegrafselskab A/S*]." With the aid of sources inside the company, Tofte was able to get the positions and depth of the cable in the Yellow Sea.

Several days later, a fleet of CIA small boats, ostensibly Korean fishing boats, sailed out of Song-do to a position from which they could most readily grab the cable. Wires with hooks were lowered to raise and then cut the cable. Separate vessels then took the ends of the severed cables and headed in opposite directions. AFSA analysts soon were listening to radio traffic between deployed Chinese forces in Manchuria and North Korea and the Chinese Defense Ministry in Peking. While an assessment of the effectiveness of this operation is best left to insiders, Tofte nevertheless was pleased by a translated intercept: "The High Command in Peking warned the field commands that fifty thousand guerrillas were loose between the lines. Actually, we had about twelve hundred men in the field, no more."[40]

In January 1951, Tofte's contributions to the war effort were temporarily placed on hold, due to serious illness. Tofte fell into a coma from, as he put it, "intestinal fever and malaria," telling Marlys that he would be in the hospital for a few more weeks. Medical experts in the years since have surmised that Tofte actually might have had Songo fever, studied and weaponized by Kitano Misaji during World War II, a malady better known today as Korean hemorrhagic fever. Kitano had graduated as a physician from Tokyo Imperial University and then joined the army as a lieutenant and surgeon. Just prior to the Sino-Japanese War (1937), he had taught microbiology at the Manchu School of Medicine in Manchuria, but by 1942 he was second in command of the infamous Unit 731. Following the Japanese surrender he was placed in a POW camp in Shanghai, but struck a deal with the Allies and was released in exchange for biological weapons research material. Repatriated to Japan in 1946, he became the chief director of the Japanese pharmaceutical company Green Cross.[41]

As Tofte was recuperating, a high-level face-to-face meeting was occurring that would force a bargain of sorts between CIA, in the person of Director Walter Bedell Smith, and the Army, in the formidable person of Gen. MacArthur. In mid-January 1951, DCI Smith and Gen. MacArthur came to a compromise, the result of a trip that knowledgeable insiders believed was made at the behest of President Truman, in an attempt to compel greater cooperation by Gen. MacArthur in particular. The compromise committed Gen. MacArthur's Far East Command (FEC) to stop interfering with CIA operations in the theater as long as CIA established an E&E network for downed airmen, which was already extant by that time. Prior to his trip to Tokyo, DCI Smith had told the Army and the Joint Chiefs of Staff that the Agency would provide tactical intelligence for the duration of hostilities in return for freedom of action in Korea—although Gen. MacArthur's watchdog, Maj. Gen. Willoughby, continued to keep close tabs on CIA, at least until Gen. MacArthur was relieved by President Truman that spring and Maj. Gen. Willoughby retired shortly thereafter.[42]

***

By late March 1951, Tofte found himself not in Tokyo or in Korea, but back in Mason City, Iowa, having been sent home, now talking to reporters about the war. In his chats with the media, he conveniently forgot to mention his CIA employment, instead telling the press and others that he worked at Gen. MacArthur's headquarters in Tokyo. He also reminded his countrymen that the Russians were working overtime to destroy the United States and urged them to "get ready for the big showdown just as surely and urgently as we got ready after Pearl Harbor."[43] While in retrospect such statements may seem overblown, they reflected the majority of public opinion in 1950s America, and the myth of the Soviet monolith would die only a slow and lingering death.

With his return to the United States in 1951, Tofte returned to his comparatively idyllic life in north-central Iowa. He became a member of the Rotary Club, a congregant of the Episcopal Church, and a Boy Scout commissioner. He and his Iowa-born wife Marlys had also become entrepreneurs, having purchased the controlling interest in the publisher Klipto Loose Leaf Company in Mason City from Mrs. Tofte's uncle, a solid vote in favor of spending the rest of their days in the small town. According to a professional business publication, the Klipto Loose Leaf Company was located at 15–17 Delaware Avenue, Mason City, Iowa, and its officers were Hans V. Tofte, president; Marlys L. Tofte, treasurer; and Ralph McCarron, assistant treasurer. The Klipto firm produced binders, legal blanks, school forms, and related products.[44]

Back in the world of international intrigue, the renewed emphasis on guerrilla warfare that dated to mid-1951 was complicated by an entity created at the behest of President Truman and DCI Smith—who had become DCI in October 1950—namely, the Psychological Strategy Board (PSB); coincidentally, the Board stood up on April 4, 1951, Tofte's 40th birthday. The stated purpose of the PSB was to "authorize and provide for the more effective planning, coordination, and conduct within the framework of approved national policies, of psychological operations"; in the minds of virtually everyone, the unwritten purpose of the Board was to prevent interagency rivalries among organizations involved in psychological operations, which had been an issue during World War II and which remained largely unresolved. The successor to the State-War-Navy Coordinating Committee, established during World War II, the Board consisted of the undersecretary of state, the deputy secretary of defense, and the director of central intelligence, who were collectively charged with reporting to the National Security Council (NSC); the first director of the PSB was Gordon Gray, an Army veteran, attorney, and politician, whose tenure was from June 1951–January 1952.[45]

Predictably, neither Lt. Cmdr. Wisner nor his "tough guy Hans Tofte" were keen on putting down on paper operational details about OPC projects to satisfy the Psychological Strategy Board; however, while they *did* have to comply, they didn't have to do such expeditiously—and they didn't. As one author characterized their compliance, Tofte and colleague Charles Tracy Barnes—who went by Tracy—proceeded "with extreme slowness" to gather the necessary materials. Lieutenant Commander Wisner described the project as "an acute security problem," though the greater reality was likely that compliance would reveal issues of which he didn't want President Truman or DCI Smith to be aware.[46] Besides, it was clear that critics of the "Mighty Wurlitzer" did not recognize the entity for the successful creation that it was—using musical terms derived from its organ counterpart, Lt. Cmdr. Wisner noted that the OPC "could play military and diplomatic tunes; it could mount operations, control newspapers, influence opinion." By mid-1953, when the OPC and the Office of Special Operations (OSO) merged into the Directorate of Plans, the new entity was spending $200 million on global operations—adjusted for inflation, that amount is equivalent to nearly $2.3 trillion at time of publication, a substantial sum.[47]

***

Meanwhile, back at the war, in early 1951, Gen. Ridgway was trying to revitalize his battered forces fighting on the front lines, a challenging task given that his enemy outnumbered him by at least a four-to-one ratio. He was able to secure assistance from several quarters, however, one of which was the Danish-American spymaster Hans Tofte. Tofte's assistance came about as the indirect result of an urgent message from CIA headquarters, sent in January 1951 to all station chiefs throughout the Far East. A CIA agent, placed high within the Indian government, had reported early in the year that the Nehru government was planning to clandestinely ship critically needed medical supplies to Chinese forces fighting in Korea. The agent reported that the medical supplies amounted to more than three field hospitals' worth of equipment, along with tons of drugs, and a full staff of physicians, nurses, and technicians.

The message pointedly noted that "at any cost," the Norwegian freighter charted by the People's Republic of China (PRC) and sitting in the port city of Bombay, India, had to be stopped. As an indication of the importance of the mission, the Agency authorized $1 million, with no strings attached, to conduct the critical operation. Tofte could not fail to notice this abrupt departure from the historically tight purse strings at CIA, which convinced him that stopping the ship was "definitely an 'act-first-and-talk-later' proposition." The only proviso given was that, whatever action was taken to ensure the cargo never arrived, it would not embarrass the US government. Thus began Operation TP-STOLE, described by one author as the "successful piracy of an international vessel on the high seas without guilt, explanation, or apology" and by another as the most significant single CIA operation in terms of the US/UN effort in the Korean War.[48]

Predictably, the mission seemed fraught with as much opportunity for disaster as success. Military entities in Tokyo were especially skittish about seizing a civilian vessel or otherwise interfering with its mission. Confronted with a potential diplomatic nightmare, the US Navy said its hands were tied and the US Air Force was unwilling to risk a covert bombing mission, accurately assessing that it would be all too easy to identify the source of the action. However, Tofte was able to work his magic yet again and persuade the two services to track the vessel so that in Japan he could get regular radio updates on the ship's location.[49]

A CIA headquarters message soon landed on the Atsugi desk of Tofte—described as "a handsome Danish-American with thinning blonde hair and a touch of his native Scandinavia in his voice," though being an individual "virtually unknown outside the insular intelligence community." Regardless, Tofte had an established reputation amongst his peers as "one of the more remarkable operatives of the twentieth century." Tofte met with CIA station chiefs throughout East Asia to brainstorm ideas for stopping the ship. At one point, it appeared it might stop in Hong Kong for supplies, so Al Cox, station chief there, operating under the very noses of the British, requisitioned explosives and other supplies from CIA Atsugi, only to have the vessel head northward without stopping. Sidestepping the neutrality of Norway, Fifth Air Force was willing to bomb the ship if it put into a North Korean port, but such was unlikely given UN control of the waters off Korea.[50]

Perusing a map and realizing time was growing short, Tofte hopped onto a plane that belonged to CAT and flew to Formosa for a conference with Jiang Jieshi, better known as Nationalist Chinese leader "Generalissimo" Chiang Kai-Shek; Tofte had lived in China for eight years and had made Chiang's acquaintance as a Burma Road guerrilla in early World War II. Needless to say, the Chinese Nationalist leader could provide access to resources on Taiwan that Tofte could never hope to receive through official US channels. Fortunately, Chiang remembered Tofte and did not bat an eye when Tofte requested his assistance; rather, he summoned the Nationalist Chinese Coast Guard commander and ordered him to "give Mr. Tofte what he wants." Once again, Tofte's in-theater experience and his extensive circle of contacts paid significant dividends. Soon, a flotilla of Chinese gunboats—with Al Cox and other CIA personnel ensconced below decks—deployed, guided to the location of the freighter, just north of Formosa, by US Navy communications. When they reached the freighter, armed Chinese boarding parties held the crew incommunicado and transferred the cargo to their own vessels. Tofte allowed the Nationalists to keep the medical supplies as a war trophy. As far as the mobile hospitals' labor force, "The nurses, doctors, and other medical personnel were never heard of again, and he [Tofte] does not speculate as to their fate." The now-empty freighter was allowed to proceed on its way, the crew knowing only that they had been raided by Asian pirates on the high seas. In a masterful understatement, Tofte referred to the operation as "fairly discreet piracy under CIA supervision."[51]

Thus, the risky operation proved to be a success—as Tofte characterized it, "The operation justified the entire CIA budget for the next three to five years. By delaying the enemy's spring offensive for three months, it probably saved seventy-five thousand American lives, for when the Chinese came, Gen. Ridgway had had time to organize his artillery positions. The Chinese were mowed down by the thousands when they launched their attack." The OPC's successful interception of this cargo served as a direct force multiplier for UN forces in Korea. As one observer noted, "This non-delivery resulted in literally thousands of Chinese casualties."[52] General Ridgway credited Tofte with "the collection of vital intelligence on Korea, based on his specialized knowledge of unconventional warfare."[53]

It was as unheard of for the non-profit US government to make money on an operation as to have funds released for an operation returned to the government in toto—Tofte returned the $1 million that had been authorized. As he put it, "I didn't need a penny of it; Chiang Kai-Shek did everything." Years later, when Tofte was dining at the exclusive India Club, a private restaurant for shipping executives in Manhattan, he overheard two maritime lawyers discussing a claim about a mysterious incident in the Far East—he soon realized they were talking about TP-STOLE and simply smiled to himself, saying nothing.[54]

Tofte's operational successes also contributed to a larger goal, namely increasing the power and prestige of an organization that had been anemic just a few years prior, an upstart unwelcomed by most already on the "block." Especially to several senior US military officers, CIA's presence on what they regarded as their "turf" was both unnecessary and unwelcome. For example, early in the Korean conflict, CIA officer Al Cox had sent a telegram to FECOM commander Gen. MacArthur offering him the use of facilities that belonged to the Agency's CAT on Taiwan as a logistical training ground. Cox, a former OG member during the days of OSS, was involved—along with Conrad La Geux, former 90th Infantry Division Commander John Mason, and Tofte—in providing CIA assistance to CAT operations designed to rescue US military pilots shot down behind enemy lines in Korea. However, Gen. MacArthur turned down the assistance, reiterating that the US military had sufficient logistical capabilities to deal with war on the Korean Peninsula.[55]

The origins of CAT—and its later, more famous iteration, Air America—lay in the swirling dust of World War II-era China in the form of Gen. Chennault's American Volunteer Group (AVG). General Chennault, an old China hand, had been given approximately 100 P-40 Warhawk fighters to blunt the Japanese invasion and to conduct air raids on the Japanese mainland (though the raids never actually occurred). The aircraft were shipped to Rangoon, Burma, on the freighter of a neutral country, and then distributed in China. The AVG became an official Army Air Force unit in 1942, better known by its nickname, the "Flying Tigers," due to the distinctive shark nose art of the P-40 fighters the pilots flew. After the end of World War II, this ragtag air force still had an important mission—namely, the provision of reliable air transportation from Chinese coastal cities to the interior, especially to deliver United Nations relief supplies to the suffering Chinese. Renamed CAT in October 1946, by the following year, the organization boasted five C-47 transport planes and over 150 employees.

With the 1949 fall of China to the communists and the flight of the Nationalists to Taiwan, CAT followed but faced serious problems—previous routes had dried up, the number of available aircraft dwindled, and the organization was soon facing bankruptcy. At just the same time, CIA realized that it needed covert air power in order to conduct "deniable, cheap, and effective missions in Southeast Asia." In June 1950, CIA queried co-founders Gen. Chennault and Whiting Willauer concerning the potential sale of CAT; they agreed to the sale and CIA purchased CAT for $950,000. That same month, OPC senior Lt. Cmdr. Wisner communicated the sale to the departments of State, Defense, and the Joint Chiefs of Staff and received the approval of the then-CIA director for the purchase that same month. The timing could not have been more fortuitous, given the outbreak of the Korean War in June 1950. Notably, the changed circumstances on the peninsula that summer prompted Gen. MacArthur to accept the assistance he had spurned earlier and on August 25, 1950—after the Air Force approved the contract—CAT began airlifting supplies into the Korean Theater.[56]

***

In 1949, the OPC had a staff of 302 and a budget of $4.7 million and operated from seven foreign stations; by 1952, the office had 2,812 direct hires, plus an additional 3,142 "overseas contract personnel" of varying definitions, a budget of $82 million, and was working out of 47 foreign stations. The growing clout of CIA was also attributable to the forward-leaning leadership of DCI Smith, who ascended to the top spot in the Agency on October 7, 1950. Though physically small, DCI Smith had a "powerful aura" and was reportedly "a man who got things done." To his way of thinking, covert operations were "CIA's most important task and best weapon in the Cold War."

Lieutenant General Walter Bedell Smith, USA, 1945. (Truman Library)

Angered that the OPC/OSO could operate independently and report directly to the State Department, bypassing CIA, DCI Smith pressured President Truman to act, charging that the OPC's failure to warn of the North Korean attack on the South in June 1950 had cost many lives. Once the president relented, DCI Smith was able to implement his reform plan, which not only brought the OPC/OSO under the CIA umbrella, but also made Allen Dulles his deputy, and divided the Agency into four sub-directorates—Intelligence, Science and Technology (S&T), Administration/Training/Personnel, and Plans, or "clan ops" or, more commonly, the "dirty tricks" department. As one unnamed observer put it, Lt. Cmdr. Wisner's large Wurlitzer was now "exchanged for a slightly smaller one which, however, came to play better."[57]

Major Helms expected to be Lt. Cmdr. Wisner's second, but Lyman Kirkpatrick was selected instead, and Maj. Helms was shunted aside for the time being. On the strategic level, DCI Smith also was able to use the dramatic Chinese intervention in Korea in November 1950 to compel Gen. MacArthur to come to grips with the presence and growing influence of CIA in Far East Command (FECOM), highlighted by DCI Smith's January 1951 visit with Gen. MacArthur, at the behest of President Truman—though Gen. MacArthur and Maj. Gen. Willoughby denied it, the unstated purpose of the visit appeared to be to ensure there would be no further FECOM interference in CIA business and operations in the Far East.[58]

The recall and subsequent retirement of Gen. MacArthur by President Truman in April 1951 and Maj. Gen. Willoughby's retirement in September that year understandably gave Tofte and CIA reason to believe that Agency-military relations would improve, especially since Gen. Ridgway and Tofte got along well. However, neither Tofte nor the Agency were aware of Gen. Ridgway's hidden agenda, which did not come to light immediately. Predictably, the previous Agency-military conflict had resulted in conflicting reports from agents operating in enemy territory, an issue Gen. Ridgway sought to address at a meeting, held against a backdrop of early peace negotiations in Korea. Since all parties involved expected a quick ceasefire, DCI Smith agreed that all unconventional activities should now be under Gen. Ridgway's command, but with Tofte and the Agency retaining their continued latitude when it came to operations. But in October, Gen. Ridgway announced the creation of the Combined Command for Reconnaissance Activities Korea (CCRAK), staffed with military intelligence officers who would now make the decisions that previously had been CIA's—this change meant that Tofte's position became untenable overnight and he soon returned home.

In retrospect, a number of observers concluded that CIA operations in Korea had constituted a failure that came at too high a cost in dollars and lives, and the legacy of this perceived failure would serve as an albatross around the neck of the Agency for the rest of the war. Despite this development, Gen. Ridgway did nominate Tofte for a medal for "outstanding performance of duty" during the war. Despite this recognition, Tofte was already planning to leave the Agency, at Marlys's request, and return to his prewar life in Mason City. But DCI Smith, who thoroughly appreciated Tofte and was well aware of his accomplishments during World War II, persuaded him to continue as his personal assistant and troubleshooter; besides that, the two got along well. But Tofte acceded to DCI Smith's wishes, bought a house in Georgetown, and alternated between staying either in Washington or overseas, while Marlys remained in Mason City to run the family publishing house—as one observer described the situation, "Marlys was looking forward to a normal family life, but it was not to be."[59]

Tofte's return from Japan prompted CIA Deputy Director Allen Dulles to pen a letter on April 14 to the Agency's on-again, off-again nemesis, Maj. Gen. Willoughby, Gen. MacArthur's G-2. Deputy Director Dulles wrote:

> Dear General:
> I am taking the occasion of Colonel Tofte's return to send you my very kindest personal greetings and best wishes. I wish to assure you how much the Director and I appreciate the cordial and effective cooperation we have been receiving from you and which I feel has been advancing our mutual interests.
>
> Tofte will be bringing you a few of the recent publications which were thought were of interest here. Maybe you already have them but I know how anxious you are to keep abreast with everything that is going on in the field of writing.
>
> Sincerely,
> Allen W. Dulles
> Deputy Director[60]

Approximately 10 days later, Tofte sent a letter to his new boss expressing his concerns about a colleague being considered for a leading position in the Far East. Speaking of this individual, whose name has been redacted, Tofte said:

> I learned that he is fed up with the Far East in general. This attitude coincides with that of many other old china-hands. It also became clear to me that ______ is very happy

> in Sanfrancisco [*sic*], where he married a very photogenic wife two years ago. In view of __________ lack of a genuine interest in the Orient and oriental people I would feel inclined to question his eligibility for the number one job in the area.

Although the identity of the individual is not provided, the significance of this letter is that Tofte was a senior and a sufficiently well-respected figure to be asked for his assessment of a candidate for a senior position in a foreign environment in the Agency.[61]

While we have little information about Tofte's activities during his first year back from the Far East, he was clearly involved in Operation *Mockingbird*, which Lt. Cmdr. Wisner had started two years previously. The purpose of the operation was to persuade or compel American journalists and media personnel to serve the Agency by acting as spies or propagandists. As one CIA officer boasted, "We could buy a journalist cheaper than a call girl, for a few hundred dollars a month." Operation *Mockingbird* was considered a huge success for the Agency—400 journalists were put on the Agency's payroll, including at *The Washington Post* and *The New York Times*; at the magazines *Time* and *Newsweek*; and at the CBS, ABC, and NBC networks. The operation stayed in the minds of the American public into the late 1970s, and in 1978 Tofte noted:

> When it is claimed in the last year that the CIA has supported or directly self-published magazines and newspapers around the world that advocated for the United States and turned against the Soviet Union and Communism, then I can only confirm it. I myself have helped start lots of such magazines in several countries—well, I've actually written quite a few of their flaming anti-Communist leaders...sometimes our fight was more direct. We did not go so far as to directly kill Russian agents or their aides. But we did everything we could to embarrass, sabotage, compromise and blame these people so much that they chose to die themselves. I actually became very good at this tactic, and I have had the satisfaction of seeing several Russians and their henchmen shoot themselves in the forehead or go out and hang themselves from a tree—it was now part of my job.[62]

In terms of combat operations, it soon became apparent—at least to some—that the covert-action missions being planned and conducted by the United States under the rubric of Operation *Aviary*, often involving multi-national paramilitary teams, had a serious problem: infiltrators who were sabotaging the missions and costing lives. For example, during one such mission, early on the morning of February 19, 1952, a C-47 was intended to drop US, Korean, and Chinese paramilitaries behind enemy lines; however, things went tragically wrong. Rather than jumping out of the plane like his colleagues, one parachutist instead pulled the pin on a grenade and dropped it inside the plane before hurtling out the door. The resulting explosion killed five instantly—the rest bailed out but were all captured by the North Korean army and either died immediately or were executed later at POW camps in the North. The CIA station chief in Hong Kong, Peter Sichel, described such operations as "suicide missions," and Annie Jacobsen, an author who was familiar with the incident, concluded it was "but one of dozens of disastrous operations which amounted to a tragic intelligence failure."[63]

The paramilitary drops into Korea that the OPC conducted during the war—which were praised and documented by those who had planned the missions initially—were subject to increasingly bitter criticism in the years that followed. For example, in 2016, the 96-year-old former OSS Jedburgh and CIA deputy chief of station in Seoul in 1951—who was in overall charge of the drops—recalled, "One of the impossible imperatives of war in Asia was that Westerners could never simply disappear behind enemy lines into the civilian populations as we had in Nazi-occupied Europe. This was a tremendous challenge in Korea and an equally difficult problem in Vietnam."[64]

Such mission fiascos hit close to home, as it was Tofte, Lt. Cmdr. Wisner, and Colonel Albert Haney who were actively planning the missions—while they were not initially aware of traitors within, documents declassified somewhat later made it clear that within the first eight months of the Korean War, the reality had become common knowledge to insiders. Jacobsen charges that even considering the "thin, spurious, or feigned" intelligence which purportedly undergirded these operations, the trio of covert operators continued to plan and conduct such missions, reporting "mission success instead of abject failure." In the words of this author, "the result was the death of what the CIA now concedes amounted to hundreds, perhaps thousands, of men and women."[65] Others have attributed the doctored figures as to the number of guerrillas killed by double agents who infiltrated the groups to the CIA station chief in Seoul, Col. Haney, rather than to Tofte, charging that Col. Haney purposely altered the reports to hide the fate of the doomed agents.[66]

At the Pentagon, the focus predictably switched to damage control; as part of that effort, Tofte was replaced in Korea by fellow CIA career officer John Limond Hart. When he reviewed the operational documents Tofte had accumulated, Hart was so outraged that he immediately informed DCI Smith, advising him that "the results of our investigation surpassed our most pessimistic expectations" and that numerous intelligence reports had been "fabricated by people living in Seoul." Director Smith dispatched deputy Loftus Becker to Seoul to inform Hart that the Agency could not afford a scandal, since its reputation was "not yet established," nor could CIA "simply…admit to other branches of government—least of all to the highly competitive U.S. military intelligence services—its inability to collect intelligence on North

Korea." Predictably, Hart's reports were classified, as were the staggering losses suffered during Operation *Aviary*. Stunned by what he had learned, Becker soon resigned, and the disastrous covert actions in North Korea during the war remained hidden for decades.[67]

***

Given Tofte's significance within the Agency and the secret and sensitive nature of his work for CIA, it is not surprising that he would benefit from various cover arrangements with select private firms. In the 1950s, for example, Tofte was provided company credentials from the Wall Street investment firm of Wood, Struthers & Winthrop, designating him one of their "vice-presidents." On one occasion, Lt. Cmdr. Wisner called Tofte in and asked him to go to Argentina, where the firm had numerous investments, and sort out a troublesome situation. As Lt. Cmdr. Wisner told Tofte, "Things usually get going when you show up."

But one notable observer was concerned about what the two operators were up to—Marlys noted, "Hans didn't tell me about his work in detail, but there is no doubt that over the years he came up with some scary tasks as a troubleshooter for Frank Wisner. I could tell it was taking a toll on him, even if he wouldn't admit it." The use of cover arrangements was not surprising given that Allen Dulles, DCI from 1951–61, was a product of the New York law firm of Sullivan & Cromwell, which extensively used his former legal and business colleagues to accomplish Agency missions during the decade. Similarly, Tofte for a time pretended to work for the Rubicon Foundation, a New York family foundation used as a secret conduit for CIA funds. The firm's treasurer, Morris Hadley, had served as assistant secretary of war during World War II and in the early 1950s was the American high commissioner for occupied Germany, negotiating the size of the US troop commitment in Europe.[68]

A clear indication that CIA was still in its infancy with regard to having a monopoly on conducting and controlling covert operations was its continuing tug-of-war with the US Army. Although the larger institution was often critical of or even hostile to proposed Agency ops, the Army did have at least two proponents of covert action, both in high places—General Robert A. McClure, the former director of the Psychological Warfare Division during World War II, and Colonel Russell W. Volckmann, the former US Army captain who had led the only non-OSS guerrilla ops group during World War II, in the Philippines. General McClure informed his superior, General

Charles Bolte, that CIA was planning to "take command of military forces designed for guerrilla warfare in time of war"; predictably, Gen. McClure was displeased—"Needless to say, I am very unhappy about it both because I question the ability of CIA and second, because I have never believed the Joint Chiefs intended to abrogate their responsibilities for the active command of military operations in time of war."

Also concerned, somewhat ironically, was Army Gen. Walter Bedell Smith, the director of CIA. In a letter to his advisor on the National Security Council staff, Ludwig Lee Montague, Gen. Smith expressed his fear that DCI Dulles and Lt. Cmdr. Wisner could drag the Agency into "some ill conceived and disastrous misadventure." But Pandora's box was already open, with critics noting that the amount of actionable intelligence likely to emerge from such a closed society as North Korea was negligible. As Lt. Cmdr. Wisner's deputy and future DCI, Maj. Helms, characterized the situation, "The possibility of recruiting and running any such sources was as improbable as placing resident spies on the planet Mars." Furthermore, by the early 1950s CIA's covert action budget was three times that of the intelligence and espionage budgets combined, a clear indication of priorities on the Agency's to-do list and a rank-ordering not likely to be quickly turned around.[69]

Yet, DCI Smith was highly protective of CIA, so it is not surprising that analysis of its operations in Korea remained under wraps for 50 years. When such analysis was released, the conclusion was that the Agency's paramilitary operations in Korea were "not only ineffective but probably morally reprehensible in the number of lives lost." The report admitted that *Aviary* missions were doomed from the start, in large measure because it proved impossible to tell friends from enemies—given the take, "The amount of time and treasure expended was enormously disproportionate." In summer/fall 1952, John Limond Hart replaced Col. Haney as the CIA station chief in Seoul; Col. Haney had deployed some 1,500 agents into North Korea during spring and summer that year. Suspicious of the positive reports Col. Haney had been sending to Washington over the past several years, Hart investigated and discovered that Col. Haney had used 200 American agents, none of whom spoke Korean, to recruit and manage the operatives; the agents then hired South Korean contractors to do the work of writing the reports, which ensured that they were glowing in terms of accomplishments. Hart concluded that "nearly every Korean agent he had inherited had either invented his reports or worked in secret for the Communists. Every dispatch the station had sent to CIA Headquarters from the front for the past eighteen months was a calculated deception."[70]

CHAPTER 6

The "Dynamic Dane" and Regime Change

In the postwar world, the United States came to rely upon covert "psychological warfare" measures—i.e., propaganda—as well as such overt measures as the Truman Doctrine and the Marshall Plan in order to blunt the Soviet threat. As author Gregory Treverton has put it, propaganda was "a way to respond to the Soviet Union by means that were less than war but more than nothing."[1]

The origins of CIA's two attempts to effect regime change in Guatemala in the early 1950s can be found in a noteworthy predecessor—TP-AJAX, the Agency's successful overthrow of Iranian leader Mohammed Mossadegh in favor of Shah Mohammed Reza Pahlavi. On August 21, 1953, following a week of rioting in Tehran, Prime Minister Mossadegh, who had nationalized the oil industry, surrendered to General Fazlollah Zahedi; three weeks later, the Shah returned to power. A few days afterwards, he toasted the CIA officer who had engineered the downfall of Mossadegh—Kermit "Kim" Roosevelt, Jr., who was not only the CIA's Near Eastern and Africa Division chief, but also the grandson of former US president Theodore "Teddy" Roosevelt. The Shah gushed, "I owe my throne to God, my people, my army—and you!"[2]

As TP-AJAX was winding down, most observers were convinced that the results had proven the viability of covert action as a tool in the Cold War. Thus it was hardly surprising that those who worked for the CIA Western Hemisphere chief, Colonel Joseph Caldwell King, were eager to prove the concept again, this time in South America, specifically in Guatemala.[3]

Even before a plan for regime change emerged, there was political turmoil in Guatemala, often surrounding the actions and intentions of United Fruit Company, headquartered in Boston. United Fruit was the creation of Sam Zemurray, who had spent 60 years virtually cornering the supply and distribution of bananas to the United States and Europe, with his fleet of 50 white Liberty ships constantly on the move. In the words of one author,

"With bribes and threats, the company controlled virtually all politics in the banana states, whose cheap labor was exploited to the limit." United Fruit's lawyer and paid lobbyist was Tommy "The Cork" Corcoran who, in spring 1950, warned Zemurray that former officer and trained economist Jacobo Arbenz Guzman might become the next president of Guatemala, potentially bringing labor unions and nationalization of United Fruit assets, threatening the US company's bottom line.

By some accounts, Arbenz had saved democracy in the country in 1949 by killing General Francisco Javier Arana, who had waged a coup, supported by landowners and United Fruit. Concerned, Corcoran went to see the director of the State Department's Office of Inter-American Affairs, Thomas C. Mann, to ask if there were any plans to prevent Arbenz from becoming president; Director Mann replied, "That is for the people of that country to decide." A dissatisfied Corcoran then paid a call on DCI Dulles, who was more favorably disposed to the idea, having represented United Fruit in the 1930s. Director of Central Intelligence Dulles told Corcoran that although CIA was sympathetic, it could not act without the approval of the State Department. In the same breath, however, he assured Corcoran that whoever won the presidential election in Guatemala, he would not be allowed to nationalize United Fruit operations in the country.[4]

The shadowy threat took on solid form when, in the 1950 election, Arbenz won 65 percent of the popular vote and took office as the next president of Guatemala on March 15, 1951. In stark political and economic terms, Arbenz was far from a card-carrying communist or a future Castro in training; in reality, Arbenz was a democratically elected land reformer who had indeed accepted communists into minor positions in his ruling coalition. However, bona fide communists were excluded from the cabinet, the national police force, and most government departments. But the United Fruit board of directors feared that he might introduce such unwelcome concepts as labor unions, land reforms, even nationalization.

More significantly for CIA and President Dwight Eisenhower—elected in November 1952 and a stalwart believer in the Soviet monolith and the dangers that it presented to the United States and the rest of the Free World—President Arbenz exhibited enough red streaks to make the question not whether, but how, to remove him from power. Corcoran, meanwhile, worked to persuade others, notably including members of Congress, that President Arbenz was not just a liberal, but rather a dangerous left-wing radical who needed to be stopped. The strategy worked, as Congress was alarmed by President Arbenz's June 1952 agrarian reform program, Decree 900, despite the fact that it was later assessed to be "moderate, capitalist reform" similar to measures supported by the United States in Japan and Taiwan. But both the United Fruit board of directors and dictators in surrounding countries viewed such developments with alarm.

In February 1953, DCI Smith was appointed deputy secretary of state in the new Eisenhower administration, with John Foster Dulles as secretary of state and Allen Dulles as DCI; the two Dulles brothers were determined to do something about Guatemala. In March 1953, the Guatemalan government nationalized nearly 210,000 acres of uncultivated United Fruit Company land and offered them $525,000 as compensation; United Fruit wanted $16,000,000 for the land, clearly a serious disconnect. On March 29, 1953, 200 rebels captured the provincial town of Salama, but government forces crushed the revolt, killing some and capturing others. It was at this point that TP-AJAX came to mind in terms of regime change, but President Eisenhower and the National Security Council were convinced that a covert operation was what was needed in Guatemala.[5]

Predictably, events transpiring in Guatemala were a concern to that nation's neighbors as well. Even prior to the 1950 election, United Fruit representatives had contacted President Arbenz's bitterest rival, Carlos Castillo Armas—one of Gen. Arana's officers—who was attempting to assemble a small rebel army in Nicaragua, with the support of dictator Anastasio Somoza Garcia. Co-conspirators included Rafael Leonidas Trujillo, and Marcos Perez Jimenez, the US-backed dictators of the Dominican Republic and Venezuela, respectively. The Agency's stake in what happened in Guatemala was at least in part due to the close ties that DCI Smith had to the United Fruit Company's board; thus, he was favorably inclined to have CIA support a coup targeting Castillo.

The rub was that the Guatemalan minister of foreign affairs asserted that President Arbenz had been democratically elected and posed no perceivable threat. But by 1952, President Arbenz had allowed some unions, even communist ones, and the feared nationalization of some of the United Fruit plantations had begun. He had also tried to implement gradual land reforms, but United Fruit had leaned on the United States and the World Bank to reject such requests. Corcoran contacted President Somoza and warned him that potential revolution in Guatemala might spill over into Nicaragua. In April 1952, President Somoza visited Washington and met with some of President Truman's advisors—he told them that with US arms, he and Armas could solve the problems in Guatemala. President Truman's military advisor, Major General Harry Vaughn, persuaded the president to agree to President

Appendix B

PBSUCCESS Organizational Chart

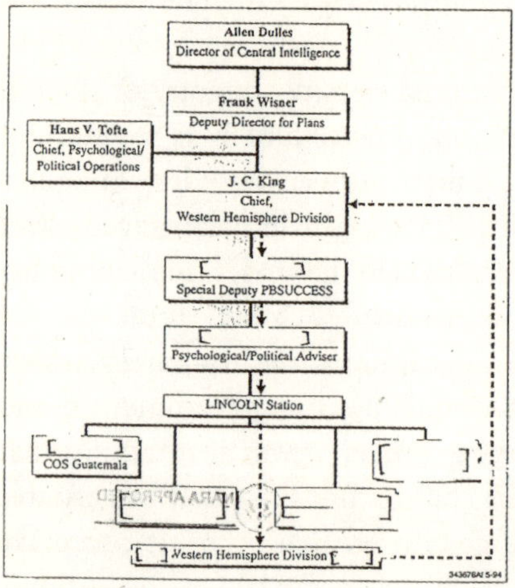

Organizational Chart for PBSUCCESS, as drawn up by Col. King, Latin American division chief, in a memo to DCI Dulles, September 11, 1953. (NARA)

Somoza's proposal. Then, without consulting the State Department, President Truman gave the green light to DCI Smith, who embarked on regime change in Guatemala.[6]

The first such attempt was codenamed PBFORTUNE and was largely the responsibility of CIA Latin American division chief, Col. King, who was to coordinate the operation with Lt. Cmdr. Wisner's Directorate of Plans, in which Tofte was the leading luminary. United Fruit's lawyer and one of America's leading lobbyists, Tommy Corcoran, was designated the liaison between CIA and United Fruit's board of directors. Corcoran was well-known to Tofte and was a major figure in the "China Lobby," with close links to Chinese Nationalist leader Chiang Kai-Shek. Corcoran had already proven his value to CIA as the man who brokered the deal for the Agency to acquire CAT, whose aircraft Tofte had used in Korea.[7]

On July 14, 1952, Tofte, Lt. Cmdr. Wisner, and Col. Haney were briefed on the decision made by US authorities to provide weapons to Castillo Armas and President Somoza. Unlike the doomed operations in Korea, this one was pre-emptive rather than reactive in nature and would become a familiar concept, formally yet innocuously known as "regime change." The weapons were shipped in large boxes marked "Agricultural Machinery" and loaded onto a United Fruit ship bound for Nicaragua. Among the weapons were 1,500 Danish Madsen submachine guns with ammo. Tofte had close connections to Madsen via his long-time friend Lt. Col. Nyholm and when both were in China Commando Group during early World War II, Tofte had worked undercover for Madsen in Chongqing. As part of the operation, Armas helped the Agency compile a list of 58 names of people considered "dangerous" communists to be assassinated before or during the coup and 72 others to be imprisoned.

The United Fruit ship was on its way to Guatemala when Deputy Secretary of State David Bruce received a tip about the secret CIA activity and informed his boss, an enraged Secretary of State Dean Acheson. The secretary of state was concerned about the promise of non-intervention in South American affairs that the United States had committed to in the 1947 Rio Treaty—and covert regime change hardly met the definition of "non-intervention." Even Tofte had misgivings about the operation as envisioned—in a September 4, 1952, memo, he pointed out that "the current situation in the target country would have to undergo a considerable change before it would be favorable and suitable for the implementation of PBFORTUNE." The practical effect of these concerns was that PBFORTUNE, formally approved on September 9, 1952, was cancelled as of October 8.[8]

Despite this development, planning continued with an eye to ousting Arbenz as the president of Guatemala, an effort which required much subterfuge and sleight of hand, not only to make President Arbenz appear a much greater threat than he truly was, but also to make Armas's army much more capable than it actually was. Not only did several of the principals continue to make the necessary preparations, likely believing that the operation would continue, but President Arbenz also continued taking what senior US figures considered "provocative" actions, such as promoting the perceived growing influence of communists in the government and the purchase of weapons from the USSR.[9]

On August 12, 1953, the National Security Council determined that the Guatemalan government of President Arbenz "posed a threat to the national security sufficient to warrant covert action against it." This time, however, Col. King, behind the failure at Salama, was sidelined in favor of Lt. Cmdr. Wisner, who appointed Tofte the head of the Psychological and Paramilitary Operations Staff and his best friend in the Agency, Tracy Barnes, as the supervisor of several aspects of the undertaking, optimistically named PBSUCCESS. Given Tofte's past service in Burma, China, and Yugoslavia, he had a reputation for planning and conducting "behind the lines" operations and this assignment within the CIA's Directorate of Plans (DDP) meant he was ideally placed for such work. Part of the plan was to win over Guatemalan military officers and civil servants, a challenging goal since CIA had few reliable contacts in-country. Lieutenant Commander Wisner also warned that the operation might take longer than TP-AJAX's six weeks and that the allotted budget of $2.7 million might prove inadequate.[10]

On September 1, 1953, CIA produced a memo on the subject, "PBFORTUNE, Essential Elements," which more explicitly laid out the rationale for prompt action, listing 11 specific courses of action that would comprise the operation. The introduction discussed "the urgency for effecting a change in the Government of Guatemala, while effective opposition still exists and before the cancer of Communism has spread and established itself still more firmly in this Hemisphere." It also stressed that "while other action will be necessary, it is recognized that only through military action can a new and stable government, friendly to the United States, be established promptly. It is agreed that RUFUS [Castillo Armas] is the only individual with the background, ideals, following and organization who can satisfactorily effect this change through armed action." The intended savior of Guatemala, Armas was viewed in his country as a folk hero, had been wounded in a previous coup, and reportedly had escaped from prison by digging a tunnel with his bare hands. In a closing statement that would serve as an ominous conclusion, the memo emphasized that "all action taken must be carefully planned in detail, timed to perfection, and faultlessly executed. Support of all interested groups must be prompt and complete."[11]

Two days later, as the attempt at regime change in Guatemala progressed, Col. King and Tofte met with the Agency's principal field case officer assigned to PBFORTUNE, who had 15 months' experience with the principal indigenous agent—RUFUS (also known by the code names CALLIGERIS and PANCHO), aka Castillo Armas. To this point, Armas had been operating under the assumption that "the Company" would provide "relatively limited support." However, in his memorandum for the record, Tofte reiterated that Armas believed strongly in PBFORTUNE, the principal agent and his overt and covert organization, but did note "that there is no tangible proof to date as to the scope and potential of the covert setup inside the country." But since the operation was now US government-sponsored vice Agency-sponsored, Armas would assist in evaluating the guerrillas' capabilities, especially inside Guatemala.

Tofte also noted that Armas had approximately 250 to 300 men ready to assist in Honduras, a number of whom were officers with professional military backgrounds. He also mentioned that Nicaragua had pledged the use of a military installation to Armas for the training and staging of his forces, an offer which the unnamed principal agent thought should be taken advantage of immediately, for reasons of morale and expediency. Perhaps of greatest concern was the issue of timing—the principal agent indicated that the population of the target country—Guatemala—was exhibiting "increasing soft spots," i.e., that the spirit of opposition to the current regime was rapidly declining; to that point, the principal agent indicated "that unless the operation were completed within 90 to 120 days, it would be too late."[12]

On September 11, 1953, Lt. Cmdr. Wisner, Tofte, and Barnes outlined a six-stage operation, a step-by-step primer to effect regime change:

1. Selection of suitable staff for the various parts of the operation; briefing of participants in Central America; assessment of friends and enemies in Guatemala; preparation of detailed action plans.
2. The establishing of a headquarters for OP Lincoln [the forward operating base for PBSUCCESS, in Florida]; character assassination of Arbenz and supporters; anti-Arbenz propaganda; creation of military agreements with Nicaragua, Honduras, El Salvador; beginning financial pressure; begin training Armas' paramilitary force in exile.
3. Increasing economic and political pressure on the Arbenz government; generate diplomatic pressure from other Latin American countries; military build-up in neighboring countries; strengthening of paramilitary units with training in sabotage.
4. Maximum financial pressure; intensive rumor campaign about impending military attack to draw enemy forces away from capital; rumor campaign about popular support for Armas' rebel force; paramilitary units ready; CIA Headquarters approval.
5. Sabotage against important targets; Armas declaration of sufficient force to overthrow Arbenz and take power; subsequent ultimatum to government to surrender to avoid unnecessary bloodshed; if ultimatum rejected, paramilitary attack launched and rebellion begun by friendly anti-Communists in country; Armas takes power.
6. Arrest of Communists and sympathizers; dramatic proclamations, new government formed; long-term domestic and foreign policy announced; United States and Latin American countries declare diplomatic recognition of, support for new government; US Government promises financial support; PBSUCCESS ends.[13]

The planning for Operation PBSUCCESS went on for more than a year, known only to President Eisenhower, the Dulles brothers (one the secretary of state at the time, the other CIA director), and a restricted circle of senior figures at the White House, State Department, and CIA. Tofte and his colleagues perceived that the Guatemalan economy was vulnerable and therefore decided to target oil supplies, shipping, and coffee exports. The plan was to have a group of pre-cleared New York City businessmen put covert economic pressure on Guatemala by creating shortages of vital imports and by cutting export earnings. These efforts would be supplemented by overt multilateral action, possibly by the Organization of American States (OAS), against Guatemalan coffee exports. Mission planners believed that economic pressure could be surgically used to "damage the Arbenz government and its supporters without seriously affecting anti-Communist elements."[14]

The planning process also included the shuffling around of personnel and duties—much to his irritation, one of those "shuffled around" was Col. King, who was "very upset" at being ousted by Frank Wisner, the deputy director for plans, from running the operation; in short, "PBSUCCESS became Wisner's project." On September 15, Lt. Cmdr. Wisner convened a meeting in his office with Col. King and Tofte and informed them that both DCI Dulles and DDCI General Charles P. Cabell had read the action plan for Guatemala and had approved it; the requisite details would be discussed in a meeting three days later in the DCI's office. Tofte had just returned from Korea to become chief of operations for Tracy Barnes, chief of the DDP's Political and Psychological Staff. Lieutenant Commander Wisner had been tasked with choosing a field commander for PBSUCCESS, *parte deux* of the plan for regime change in Guatemala. Once Kermit Roosevelt turned the job down, Lt. Cmdr. Wisner persuaded DCI Dulles to recall the station chief in Korea, former US Army Col. Haney; Tofte, a Barnes protégé at CIA, had worked for Col. Haney in Korea and may have roped him in for this mission.

In late October 1953, once Col. Haney had been briefed on the operation, he accepted on the spot and moved to Opa Locka, Florida, where he began setting up the forward base known as LINCOLN on the site of an abandoned US Marine Corps airbase. Here, in a group of offices over a nursery, Maj. Gen. Bissell and Tracy Barnes began setting the operation in motion. It is noteworthy that neither man was DCI Dulles's first choice to run this delicate operation—DCI Dulles had first queried Kermit "Kim" Roosevelt, Jr., who had just waged the successful TP-AJAX operation in Iran, ousting President Mossadegh in favor of the Shah. But Kermit begged off, telling DCI Dulles that for a coup in Guatemala to be successful, the army and the people would have to want what the United States wanted, and he sincerely doubted that Guatemalan peasants wanted what the United Fruit Company wanted. Colonel Haney had control of Agency station chiefs in the nations surrounding Guatemala, as well as direct control of the forces assembled for PBSUCCESS. Haney adopted the pseudonym "Jerome B. Dunbar" and DCI Dulles soon stipulated that all operational cable traffic be sent to LINCOLN for Dunbar, vice to headquarters, and then repeated to Opa Locka.[15]

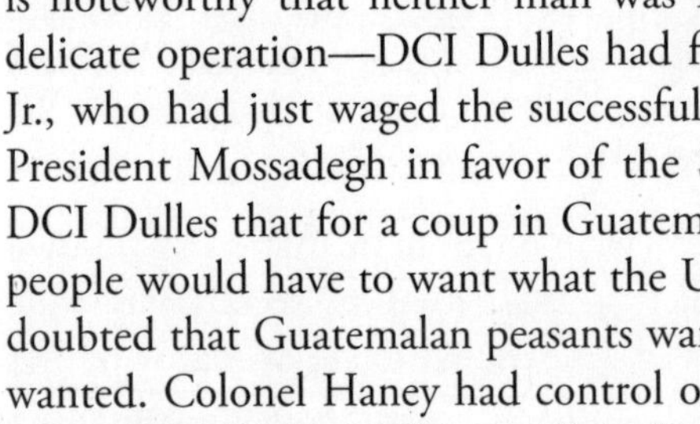

CIA identification card of DCI Dulles. (CIA)

For all the ensuing excitement and anticipation about the operation, those most intimately involved realized the complexity and the stakes involved and urged some measure of caution. In follow-on discussions on the afternoon of September 18, 1953, "Messrs. Wisner, Tofte, and Roosevelt pointed out that PBSUCCESS is an extremely difficult and sensitive operation requiring the utmost care in preparation and execution. It was agreed that any ultimate military action must be preceded by thorough exploitation of all other capabilities and that a preparatory campaign of eight months duration, or more, is deemed advisable."[16] Nevertheless, in a November 11, 1953, memo, Tofte noted that the DCI had secured the $3 million in funding for the operation from the Bureau of the Budget and that the DCI had directed Deputy Director for Administration Lawrence K. "Red" White to handle the details in securing the funds "without undue delay." Tofte also recommended that a general briefing on PBSUCCESS be prepared for the DCI, DDCI, DDP, and COP sometime during the week of November 16, 1953.[17]

In December 1953, Armas boldly announced that he would be returning to Guatemala as head of the "National Liberation Movement"—supported by CIA, operating from a base in Honduras, with substantial funds, and mercenaries from throughout South America. He then embarked on a leisurely six-month preparation period.[18] That same month, on December 23, CIA took formal possession of the site code-named LINCOLN. One of the men who worked out of that building was future Bay of Pigs and Watergate alumnus E. Howard Hunt, who recalled, "Our field headquarters occupied a two-story barracks on the partly closed-down Marine airbase at Opa-locka, Florida. We slept and worked in the same building and ate at the base mess hall not far away. Several project officers with reserve status wore uniforms in order to lessen interest in our building." The presence of a day-care center on-site also helped with cover.[19]

Many parts of the plan dealt with psychological and paramilitary operations, which meant Tofte was responsible for those aspects. Part of what Tofte was planning included "a war of nerves against selected persons"—CIA personnel sent small coffins, nooses, and fake bombs to select communists and trade unionists in Guatemala. Helpers inside the country painted such slogans as "Here Lives a Spy" and "You Have Only 5 Days" on the walls of houses. Letters with death threats were sent nearly daily, and Tofte already had a detailed proposal for sending "poison pen" letters to select persons in Guatemala. His place was clearly at headquarters, while Col. Haney's—as plans and policy chief of operations in the field—was at Operation *LINCOLN*. To safeguard the participants, all Agency employees subordinate to Lt. Cmdr. Wisner had code names assigned. Lieutenant Commander Wisner was "Harold S. Whiting," Barnes was "William D. Playdon," E. Howard Hunt was "Walther C. Twicker," and lead character Armas was either "John H. Calligeris" or "RUFUS." It is highly likely that Tofte had one as well, but it has not been divulged.[20]

On June 15, 1954, President Eisenhower authorized CIA to conduct PBSUCCESS, telling DCI Dulles, "I want you all to be damn good and sure you succeed. When you commit the flag, you commit to win." Somewhat ironically, President Eisenhower intended to use CIA rather than the military to blunt the perceived Soviet threat. As historian Arthur Schlesinger, Jr. explained, "Eisenhower didn't trust the military. He knew too much about it." He preferred CIA because it was "small, relatively cheap, elite, nonbureaucratic and, best of all for a political leader, deniable." The problem, as some observers pointed out, was that the men of CIA "knew almost nothing about the 'Developing World.'"[21]

One of the aspects of PBSUCCESS that received less attention, at the time or since, was that the plan always included the potential need for assassinations, either of President Arbenz himself, if he proved uncooperative, or his stalwart supporters, or both. On January 11, 1954, coup planners sent 20 silencers to a K-team (an assassination team from Armas's paramilitary forces) in Honduras, and Tofte was the erstwhile POC for the shipment. That same month, CIA field operatives and potential assassins were sent a special manual for assassinations. The 19-page manual began, perhaps ironically, with a discussion of the moral aspects of assassination and stressed that such should only be carried out by people with the proper training.

It then turned to more specific information, such as the helpful observation that:

> The essential thing about an assassination is the death of the victim. A person can be killed in many ways, but efficiency and safety are often overlooked by assassins who are emotionally affected by the gravity of the act they are about to carry out. The particular technique used depends on many factors, but the focus must be one hundred percent on one thing—the fatal exit must be completely safe.

In an interesting historical reference, the manual noted that the reason that all of the various attempts on the life of Adolf Hitler during World War II failed was because this one factor was not taken into account.[22]

The "how-to" guide continued by describing, in some detail, recommended manual assassination techniques. "It is possible to kill a man," the manual stated, "with the bare hands, but very few are skilled enough to do so safely." Instead, it advised that "simple nearby tools are often the best," such as a hammer, an ax, a wrench, or a screwdriver, "or anything else hard, heavy and handy will suffice." Predictably, knives were described as "some of the best weapons," though "rope, wire, or belt can be used if the assassin is sufficiently strong." An additional advantage of all these weapons is that they are all "immediately available and seem innocent." Generally, an improvised versus a manufactured weapon is better, as it avoids detection. To drive home the point, the manual also noted that attempts to kill Stalin's enemy Leon Trotsky with a machine gun failed, while that with a stage prop (a pickaxe) succeeded.[23]

As an alternative to manual procedures, a planned and controlled accident was also a viable means of assassination. As the guide noted, "When done effectively, it attracts little attention and is only superficially investigated." In this regard, the "most effective" such measure is a fall of 20 meters or more onto a hard surface—elevator shafts, steep stairs, open windows or bridges (not over water) were especially recommended. "Falling in front of trains is usually effective, but requires precise timing and can rarely be done without witnesses." Not recommended were car accidents, which were "not particularly useful for assassinations."

After manual means and controlled accidents, the third possibility was the use of chemical and pharmaceutical agents, "which can be very effective"—for example, "an overdose of morphine will cause death quietly and without much risk of detection." While more exotic agents might come to mind, they were not recommended: "Special poisons, such as arsenic and strychnine, are effective, but acquisition are incriminating, and the exact dosage is problematic." Another category that might come to mind would be sharp and pointed weapons, but as the guide noted sagely, "a minimum of anatomical knowledge is necessary to achieve certainty of outcome." While the manual stated matter-of-factly that it was not easy to either locate or hit the heart with a pointed weapon, cutting the spinal cord in the neck region was "absolutely fatal," as was cutting the throat, as long as the assassin ensured that both the artery and the vein on both sides of the trachea were severed.

The final category of more "primitive" assassination means includes blunt weapons—a hammer, a baseball bat, a large branch, a heavy rock, or an iron rod. To prove fatal, the assassin should aim the blow at the temple, the area just behind or below an ear, or on the back of the skull. The "shopping guide" for assassinations concluded with a chapter on firearms, silencers, and explosives suitable for the purpose—the Madsen submachine gun, familiar to Tofte, was rated highly as "particularly useful and reliable," jokingly referred to in the text as "The Danish Madman."[24]

In late summer 1953, President Arbenz had suspicions that something was up, but he underestimated the opposition; while he had a 6,000-man army, it was hampered by obsolete weaponry. That fall, he was contacted by the Panamanian commercial attaché in Managua, Nicaragua, Jorge Isaac Delgado, who offered to keep him up to date on what Armas was doing. Delgado was a courier between the CIA station in Mexico City and PBSUCCESS training camps in Nicaragua and Honduras. In January 1954, Delgado photographed several PBSUCCESS documents, which revealed CIA's complicity in the planned regime change. On Saturday, January 31, 1954, the Arbenz government published a white paper on the conspiracy, and the media in Guatemala ran the story throughout Latin America and the United States.

Predictably, PBSUCCESS planners viewed this development as "almost catastrophic" in nature. Lieutenant Commander Wisner and Col. King met on February 2 and decided that at that point the operation had to go forward but that some damage control was necessary, particularly removing from the active planning of the operation those who had been compromised—one of whom was Tofte, either because he was now exposed or simply because as head of paramilitary operations, he was deemed responsible for the security lapse; either way, he was compelled to step back and watch the operation unfold from the sidelines.[25]

In addition to security concerns, CIA planners also had a "perception management" problem to deal with—to more convincingly "sell" the communist threat, the Agency needed to support its claims of heavy Soviet influence in Guatemala. Since no such influence existed, Lt. Cmdr. Wisner and his colleagues resorted to Operation *Washtub*, the objective of which was to place and then expose Soviet weapons in the country. On February 19, 1954, agents placed a container of Soviet weapons, along with paperwork indicating Guatemala as the final destination, and Guatemalan cigarettes. This container was conveniently placed on a beach in Nicaragua, where it was "found" by fishermen, paid by dictator Anastasio Somoza. These same fishermen also claimed they had seen a Soviet submarine in the area. Though no one actually believed these claims, they accomplished the desired purpose by placing an additional strain on the Arbenz government. In mid-May, Col. Haney, using his cover name, messaged the chief of station in Guatemala and LINCOLN about the operation and the subsequent publicity:

1. We understand that the story of the unidentified submarine which landed in Nicaragua, caching arms of Communist origin at the shore, did not receive much, if any, publicity in the Guatemalan press. This story however should not only interest Guatemalan newspapers because it concerns a rather ominous event in a neighboring country, but most specifically since certain communications implicate Guatemala directly. The most specific of these clues were the cigarettes of Guatemalan origin found together with the weapons; this has received ample publicity in Nicaragua…
2. We suggest, therefore that you make a cautious effort to obtain added publicity for this story in the Guatemalan press and public opinion. We would consider it particularly apt if

you could induce one of the oppositional members of the Guatemalan congress to address a letter to the President, expressing concern about these clues, pointing at Guatemalan complicity in this arms smuggling affair and demanding a full, public investigation…

3. If you should find it impossible to utilize a member of congress for the above purpose, we suggest that you try using any of your available press contacts. It might perhaps be possible to arrange for an interview of any suitable traveler who happened to have been in Managua on the day of President Somoza's press conference on the subject and to tie the questions relative to the Guatemalan cigarettes to that interview…
4. Please advise as soon as you have been able to take action along either of the above lines.

JEROME C. DUNBAR[26]

On March 1, at the Organization of American States (OAS) conference in Caracas, Venezuela, US Secretary of State John Foster Dulles delivered a fiery speech about the communist threat in Guatemala. However, the recipients were more concerned about US encroachments on the continent than communists. Furthermore, as Secretary Dulles well knew, the communist threat in Guatemala was greatly overblown—the Communist Party had only 4,000 members in a country of over 3 million people and minimal electoral support. In the decades since, "The CIA's own historians have acknowledged that the Communist threat was wildly exaggerated." To further heighten the temperature, that same month the Arbenz government confiscated 70,000 hectares (173,000 acres) of land as part of Decree 900, implemented two years earlier.[27]

On April 10, Deputy Secretary of State Henry Holland briefed Lt. Cmdr. Wisner, who was shocked by how poor PBSUCCESS operational security still was, due in large part to the continuing penetration of Armas's paramilitary forces and also to the discovery of hidden microphones in the US Embassy in Guatemala City. Since this discovery implicated Ambassador John Peurifoy, JMBLUG in Agency message traffic, that was a significant problem—each passing day seemed to uncover more and more of the Agency's originally somewhat hidden hand.

The Dutch government demanded a high-level review of the entire operation; Lt. Cmdr. Wisner wrote the report in response, which estimated that there were 35,000 reliable supporters of regime change in Guatemala. He recommended that the operation continue full-speed ahead and Secretary Dulles agreed. Thus, PBSUCCESS moved into its final phase, which included a tailored radio/tape propaganda program, Operation *Sherwood*, aimed at the Guatemalan populace. It was under the supervision of David Atlee Philips, described as a "clever and enterprising contract employee" and a one-time actor and newspaper editor in Chile. Operation *Sherwood* involved the transmission into Guatemala of anti-communist propaganda messages, interspersed with music, and supporting regime change, delivered by four Guatemalan men and two women, first from a radio station in Miami and then from a dairy farm in an undisclosed location. The operation was considered a success—as Philips recalled, "When we started, everything was calm, both in Guatemala City and in the countryside, and in a few weeks we created unrest everywhere."[28]

In mid-May, the date was set for the invasion. Even at this juncture, the White House and the State Department used the occasion as the opportunity for one last propaganda push to gain world approval for the invasion of Guatemala. The alleged Soviet weapons were portrayed as the classic example of Soviet influence in the country, with President Eisenhower warning that they could lead to a communist takeover and resulting dictatorship in Guatemala.

While the Soviet weapons in question were mythical, the Arbenz government, unwilling to simply roll over and play dead, had indeed purchased 2,000 tons of quite real weapons and ammunition from the Czech Socialist Republic in the spring of 1954, to be transported to Guatemala by the Swedish-owned and flagged freighter SS *Alfhem*, whose captain believed he was transporting a cargo of glassware and "optical goods." The weapons were loaded in the Baltic seaport of Szczecin (Stettin), Poland, and the ship then zig-zagged towards Dakar, West Africa (now Senegal). It then headed west across the Atlantic, supposedly bound for Curacao, in the Dutch West Indies, only to later be redirected to Puerto Cortes, Honduras.

However, it was a radio message to the ship's master that betrayed the vessel's true final destination—Puerto Barrios, Guatemala, 185 miles northeast of Guatemala City. Although CIA and the State Department made several attempts to stop the ship, it arrived safely in Puerto Barrios on May 15; according to the crew, two additional ships were heading to Guatemala from Stettin. The next day, a summit meeting between the DCI and officials from the Pentagon and the State Department agreed on a plan to sabotage the rail transport of the weapons from Puerto Barrios to Guatemala City; however, a sudden rainstorm altered the plan, which then devolved into an anemic armed assault against the guards on the train as it made its way southwest. From the perspective of US planners, the bad news was that the weapons arrived unscathed; the good news was that since the weapons load was a package deal, many of them proved useless. For example, there were numerous antitank weapons in the package—which might have proven useful had any nation in Central America had tanks at the time. As *The New York Times* described it, the Arbenz government had bought a shipload of "white elephants."[29]

Despite the imminence of the rebel invasion, one critical factor was still missing—air support. In a bid for air dominance, the Agency had scraped together the "Liberation Air Force," a Heinz 57 hodgepodge of some 30 aircraft, flown by CAT pilots brought from Asia; US military pilots could not participate in the operation since the United States was not officially involved, and there were no pilots among Armas's paramilitary force. In addition, CIA also hired six private pilots with previous combat experience and an in-depth knowledge of Central America; they were paid $2,000 per month and $250 for every mission. The contingent included Cessna 140 and 180 aircraft, a PBY Catalina flying boat, two C-47 Dakota cargo planes from CAT, and P-38, F-51, and P-47 fighters, primarily from the Texas and Puerto Rico Air National Guard.

While the transport aircraft operated from Managua to ferry supplies from the United States via Nicaragua to Honduras, the fighter aircraft operated from Las Flores airbase in Honduras. The military aircraft were brought to Honduras and Nicaragua under the guise of military aid to these countries. On May 26, the Liberation Air Force flew over Guatemala City and dropped leaflets urging the populace to turn against the Arbenz government. Many Guatemalan military officers were frightened—some had already left the country, and some were actively conspiring against President Arbenz; on-the-ground observers characterized the situation, there was "widespread confusion and anxiety" in the general populace.[30]

There are conflicting accounts of the numbers of foot soldiers engaged in the actual ground assault portion of the operation—a widely used figure suggests that there were some 480 rebel troops facing off against 6,000 men of the Guatemalan Army, meaning the former were outnumbered at least 12 to 1, hardly a recipe for victory. But Tofte's original biographer claimed that the foot soldiers of PBSUCCESS consisted of 150 to 200 men who were training on one of the plantations that belonged to the Nicaraguan president/dictator, Anastasio Somoza. The weapons they were to use included some Israeli weapons, delivered by former CIA operative Samuel Cummings, who had founded the company International Armament Corporation (Interarms) and had opened several offices in Europe, including in Copenhagen.

The primary trainer for CIA was a US mercenary named William "Rip" Robertson, Jr., who was not at all impressed with "the Liberator," Armas. Robertson, a USMC officer and World War II and Korean War veteran, had been a CIA officer since 1947. In Guatemala, he and others engaged in loud but non-lethal demonstrations of force to expedite the coup. His efforts, combined with false news reports from secret transmitters on Swan Island, off the coast of Honduras, convinced President Arbenz that he was facing a large, well-equipped army able to take the capital at any time.

Such tactics, combined with a flyover and a few bombs dropped, convinced President Arbenz to flee. Tracy Barnes was equally unimpressed with Armas, but tried to put a good face on a less-than-ideal situation anyway. On June 18, 1954, Armas led a ragtag group of 200 revolutionaries—whom he had just met the week before—from several locations in Honduras 6 miles across the Honduran border into Guatemala and established a camp at the Church of the Black Christ of Esquipulas. He demanded President Arbenz's immediate surrender, and then...waited. Early that morning, Secretary Dulles had phoned the White House with the news that PBSUCCESS was underway—White House Press Secretary Jim Hagerty responded, "Officially, we don't know anything about it," an early example of "plausible deniability." Major General Bissell and Barnes were back at Langley when the operation occurred but remained absolutely convinced that South America was in real danger of falling to the communists unless they acted in Guatemala. Major General Bissell later commented, "Tracy and I were not concerned with an ideological debate over whether to do it, just how to do it." Barnes's wife added, "Tracy was so relieved he could actually do something."[31]

Although a number of observers took the name "PBSUCCESS" at face value, there were concerns within some quarters at Langley that the entire operation could easily turn into a fiasco. As late as mid-November, CIA planning for the covert action was still being fleshed out; others felt that the promises made by Nicaraguan dictator Anastasio Somoza to help bring down the Guatemalan government were untrustworthy; and a plan to use US military assistance officers from several Central American countries ran into serious opposition from the Pentagon. An assistant to the secretary of defense for special operations refused to allow CIA to draw the US military into the morass—Tofte was so frustrated with the lack of cooperation and commitment that he complained to Tracy Barnes, but even the policy and plans (PP) staff chief could do no better.[32]

Director of Central Intelligence Dulles sought to give the operation a shot-in-the-arm by creating "the impression of very substantial military strength," and told President Eisenhower that the illusion of such was the product of a huge media disinformation campaign run by CIA, State, and the US Information Agency, as well as by the "Liberation Air Force." Despite such measures, however, the rebel offensive did not go well initially—four days after his small force crossed the border, Armas told CIA that unless it could undertake a heavy bombardment to support the offensive, he would be compelled to surrender. In response to this crisis, the "Liberation Air Force" launched a bombing mission on June 25, which allowed Armas's forces to capture the town of Chiquimula and jump-start the resistance offensive.

President Arbenz found himself deserted by his air force and his army, the latter of which refused his order to arm the workers and peasants. On June 27, after some twists and turns, President Arbenz agreed to leave office gracefully—after a radio address in which he denounced Armas's betrayal and the US attack on his democracy. After some debate, Armas became president of Guatemala and all resistance ceased over the next two days, though he was not formally declared president until September 1. President Arbenz fled to Mexico City, along with his foreign minister, while several hundred of his followers were captured and executed by Armas's CIA-trained assassins.

When the coup was complete, President Eisenhower shook DCI Dulles's hand and said, "Thanks, Allen, and thanks to all of you. You've averted a Soviet beachhead in our hemisphere." It was party time at Langley, where DCI Dulles went around clapping colleagues on the shoulders enthusiastically, shouting "Bully, bully, we did it!" The party continued at the White House, where President Eisenhower congratulated all concerned. Later that night, Lt. Cmdr. Wisner paid a visit to Tracy Barnes's house where, according to an eyewitness, the "two men danced around like silly teenagers." The success of the operation freed Lt. Cmdr. Wisner's hands, both fiscally and operationally, and also augured well for Tofte, Lt. Cmdr. Wisner's personal assistant, though Hans faced both internal critics and Marlys, "who wanted him to stop playing cowboys and Indians and come home to Mason City to be a husband and businessman."[33]

Ironically, several developments in the coming years and decades would cast a bit of a pall over the victory. First, in 1955, a Panamanian right-wing group attempted a coup in Costa Rica. An indirect participant was CIA arms dealer Samuel Cummings, of Interarms, who delivered a batch of Madsen light machine guns to Anastasio Somoza in Nicaragua, who supplied them to the rebels in Costa Rica. However, the coup failed, and the incriminating Madsen weapons were found throughout Latin America for many years thereafter, most recently in the civil war that occurred in El Salvador in the 1980s.

Second, in the wake of the regime change, the US Department of Justice accused United Fruit Company of violating anti-trust laws; in a 1958 compromise, UFC was compelled to cede some of its land and properties in Guatemala to local businessmen.

Third, and more significantly, things went badly for the Armas government once installed in power. Widespread dissent led to demonstrations and student unrest and on July 27, 1957, Armas was assassinated by one of his military guards, who then committed suicide. His predecessor Arbenz moved from Mexico to Switzerland (where his family originated), to Paris, and then to Cuba, where Fidel Castro offered him asylum. But he was not a communist and was generally unwelcome in Cuba, opting instead to retire to Mexico City, where he was found drowned in his bathtub in 1971. Some believe he had a fatal heart attack in the bathtub, others that he committed suicide.[34]

While PBSUCCESS was anything but flawless, CIA certainly considered the Guatemalan coup one of its greatest successes; more importantly, for good or for ill, it set the pattern for future operations in Latin America. In the words of one knowledgeable authority, the course and results of TP-AJAX and PBFORTUNE/SUCCESS "made the Agency's reputation and set the pattern for covert action in the years ahead. Small, cheap, fast and tolerably secret, they encouraged Washington to think other covert actions could be likewise." Thanks to men like Tofte and their exploits, supplemented by the growing working relationship between CIA and the military during the Korean War, the influence and standing of the covert-action side of the Agency rose throughout the 1950s.

In retrospect, however, historians studying and writing about the regime change in Guatemala have been increasingly critical—Nick Cullather, who spent more than a year writing his definitive history using declassified documents, wrote, "The overthrown Arbenz government was not a Communist regime, but a reform government that was perhaps the last chance for a progressive, democratic development in the region." A 1999 United Nations report, *Guatemala—Memory of Silence*, investigated almost 43,000 human rights violations committed during the operation, including 626 massacres; according to the report, 93 percent of these crimes had been committed by the Agency-trained paramilitary death squads in the country. As for Tofte, though he was compelled to sit out a portion of the operation, he nevertheless "had his share in this historic misstep, and it was not to be the last time he appeared on the Latin American stage."[35]

In the late 1950s, political upheaval broke out in several nations in Central and South America. Of all those nations, the one clearly of greatest strategic concern to the United States was geographically the closest—Cuba where, in 1959, revolutionary Fidel Castro gained power in the Caribbean nation, located only 90 miles from Key West, Florida. The potential specter of a communist nation that close to the United States and the possibility of communism spreading throughout Latin America in the electric geopolitical environment of the 1950s sent a shock wave through the Agency. Yet, at least for the next few years, it was the South American nation of Colombia, some 2,400 miles to the south, which seemed most likely to adopt the teachings of Marx and Lenin. Given Colombia's strategic location, US national interests mandated that the nation not be allowed to fall into revolution, thereby creating a government hostile to the United States. For the preceding decade, Colombia had been plagued by "La Violencia," the conflict between the country's conservative and liberal parties, sparked by the assassination of reform presidential candidate Jorge Elicier Gaitan.

President Alberto Lleras Camargo had managed to craft a truce between the Conservatives and the Liberals, to form a National Front, dedicated to ending the violence and bloodshed in Colombia. But the unrest had cost the lives of 250,000 people and had left 1,500,000 homeless. Gangs controlled parts of the five richest provinces and fears were widespread that the communists could take advantage of a bad situation, especially after the formation of the Fuerzas Armadas Revolucionarias de Colombia (FARC).

In contrast to the gangs of "La Violencia," FARC's greatest support was in the rural areas of Colombia. President Camargo, backed by the right wing and a close friend of Nelson Rockefeller, repeatedly asked the United States for internal security assistance in 1959. In response to this request, the US Department of State, in concert with the Department of Defense, asked CIA for a team of experts in unconventional warfare in Europe, whose expertise they could use in South America. In November–December 1959, the so-called Asia-Survey Team Mission, also referred to as the Joint Survey Mission, was dispatched to Colombia to study the "National Emergency Issue," a euphemism for the widespread violence in the country. The purpose of the mission was to make recommendations to the White House prior to President Camargo's official state visit to the United States in April 1960. Care had to be taken, however, as the Mutual Security Act of 1954 made overt US military support to regime change illegal.[36]

Due to his paramilitary ops experience in Korea and Guatemala, and because of his negotiating skills, Tofte was designated the leader of the six-man team. Of all the team members, the most impressive—aside from Tofte himself—was Colonel Napoleon Valeriano, a veteran of both the Philippine and US armies. Colonel Valeriano had escaped from a Japanese prison camp and joined Gen. MacArthur's forces in Australia, and post-Philippine independence (July 4, 1946) led operations for former advertising executive Edward Lansdale's hunter-killer guerrilla unit against the Hukbalajaps ("Huks," pronounced "hooks"), quasi-communist guerrillas in the Philippines. A veteran of the Philippine Constabulary and the former police chief in Manila, Col. Valeriano was considered "the most successful anti-guerrilla fighter in the military campaigns against the Huks." In 1954, he had traveled to Vietnam to conduct operations against the Viet Minh. He later visited the School of the Americas in the occupied portion of the Panama Canal Zone and later Colombia, on a mission led by Tofte, and also trained one of the two groups involved in the Bay of Pigs assault.[37]

Other team members included Major Charles T. R. Bohanan, a former World War II guerrilla leader in the Philippines and advisor to the government during the Huk uprising; Lieutenant Colonel Joseph T. Koontz, the military attaché in Colombia in 1952–56; Colonel Berkeley Lewis, a retired officer and ordnance expert with logistics experience and a tour as a military attaché in Argentina; and former US Marine Corps Lieutenant Bruce Walker, who had undertaken foreign service tours in Ecuador and Honduras. All of these men were Spanish-speakers and had cut their teeth on counterinsurgency as veterans of Edward Lansdale's group.[38]

Though the team's mission was top secret, a Colombian newspaper, *La Gaceta*, was convinced something was up—no sooner had the survey team landed on October 26, 1959, than the paper wrote, "Silent, as befits a secret agent, Colonel Hans Tofte, Danish by birth, but on a special mission for the Americans, got into the waiting car and drove towards the Hotel Tequendama." Predictably, other national papers hopped onto the bandwagon, speculating that the government was entering into some sort of secret military pact with the United States. That speculation, of course, was spot on, but the damage control efforts of Tofte and Col. Lewis prompted the Colombian Ministry of Defense to tell the press that it was a special FBI mission that was going on, an attempt "to clarify some technical problems in connection with a recently concluded agreement on the fight against drugs." The press—all except *La Gaceta*—accepted the explanation, but the matter soon died down, leaving the team free to do its work out of the prying eyes of the press.[39]

The survey team traveled more than 14,000 miles, meeting with political and labor leaders, military commanders, and jailed bandit and guerrilla fighters and chiefs. On January 27, 1960, the team completed its preliminary report, which summarized the basic problems of bandit and communist guerrilla violence. It was very critical of the government's anti-guerrilla training center, Escuela de Lanceros, which had been established just four years prior and was staffed by US Army Rangers serving as instructors. Team members faulted the school for training too many individuals vice mobile teams in anti-guerrilla warfare, a critique of the method, rather than the goal, of the center. Instead, the team proposed the creation of a special, secret counter-guerrilla squad, i.e., a "death squad," known as "*Force X*," whose activities would be codenamed Operation *Able*.

The basic idea was to form fake guerrilla groups whose massacres would be attributed to the real guerrillas; simultaneously, *Force X* members would infiltrate the real guerrilla groups to provide intelligence for the regular anti-guerrilla forces. *Force X* became a reality shortly after President John F. Kennedy took office in January 1961. President Camargo had asked the United States for helicopters to fight the guerrillas but efforts to train the Colombians were disastrous and proved to be a waste of both money and equipment.[40]

The Joint Survey Team Report also recommended the use of third-country nationals, hired by the Colombian government, as advisors to the counter-insurgency forces, with undercover contracts but under covert US control; the use of covert psychological warfare methods; and new counterintelligence operations and the establishment of civil affairs programs. The purpose of these suggestions was to "rehabilitate the public image of the Washington-aligned military and police" in Colombia.[41] This recommendation then would be forwarded to the White House prior to President Camargo's official state visit to Washington, DC, scheduled for April 1960.[42]

While the helicopter experiment never got off the ground, other parts of the program proved more successful. In the summer of 1962, the first GIL (hunter/killer) teams were created, each consisting of 25 men, a mix of civilians, military officers, and policemen. The 1963 Colombian military manual explained, "Any person who in one way or another supports the enemy's objective must be considered a traitor and treated as such." The practical effect of such a policy was that peasants forced to help the guerrillas were thus considered traitors and executed as a result. The chairman of the Colombian Human Rights Committee, former foreign minister Alfredo Vasquez Carrizosa, noted:

> During the Kennedy administration, Washington went to great lengths to transform our regular military into anti-guerrilla units that accepted and applied the new death-squad strategy. These initiatives, implied in what is known in Latin America as the National Security Doctrine, is not in defense against an outside enemy…but it is the right to fight and exterminate trade unionists and social workers, men and women who do not support the system and are therefore presumed to be Communists.

Tofte biographer Henrik Kruger blames the Tofte team's reports and recommendations for "a significant part of the atrocities that have plagued Colombia ever since."[43]

It is perhaps predictable that sometimes the same individuals who demonstrate risk-taking and acts of derring-do and have such success in the field have trouble with the more mundane aspects of an intelligence career, such as playing by the rules, especially those concerning the handling of classified documents. Several examples of such behavior can be found in Tofte's career, the first of which came in December 1964, when FBI documents disclosed that a single document classified "Secret" had been found at Tofte's former residence in Sterling, Virginia. Subsequent Bureau reporting made it clear that the document concerned Tofte's work as the chief of the "survey team," an oblique but unmistakable reference to the covert action plan for Colombia circa 1959–60. As FBI reporting explained, the document apparently had been prepared in May 1959, and was a fulsome description of the finance and accounting issues and problems faced by CIA officers in the field. Tofte had classified it as "Secret" due to the use of such terms as "deep cover agent" and "indigenous operations" in the document.

Tofte had immediately informed the authorities of the loss, explaining that he had crafted the document at his residence but had then lost it the same day on his way to a restaurant—though the fact it was found in his residence suggests that it never left his house. The discovery of the missing classified document prompted the Washington Field Office (WFO) of FBI to check with CIA, to determine if the document were actually classified; if it could be declassified in case of prosecution; and what effect the disclosure of the information in the document would have upon the national defense. However, William Osborn, head of the Agency's Personnel Security Division at the time, said that the only individual who could further speak to the nature of the missing document and determine if it were actually classified was the Western hemisphere division chief, Col. King, Tofte's superior at the time, who was out of the area on Company business until January 6, 1965. He did, however, confirm that from 1957–60, Tofte had been a supervisor of clandestine operations in Latin America and had a "Top Secret" clearance. He added that Tofte would have had the authority to both classify and declassify the document he had created. He told the Bureau agents that there was no information to suggest that Tofte represented a security risk, though he noted the allegations made against Tofte in the mid-1950s that had been investigated and dismissed both by CIA and FBI.

Interestingly, Director of Security Osborn told the Bureau that CIA had no strict control of documents classified below "Top Secret." When Col. King returned to work in early January, the Bureau queried him about the document—he noted that while Tofte had the authority to take the document to his home given the circumstances, leaving it at his former residence indicated "considerable negligence." But Col. King added that he had found Tofte to be a "capable and reliable staff officer, and he had no reason to doubt his loyalty." As to the offending document, Col. King described it as "obsolete" and "of no value" and could be declassified. Following this interview, the Bureau wrote, "In view of the information furnished by KING, it is felt that this is an administrative matter which more properly should be handled within CIA. Also it is noted that both KING and OSBORNE [*sic*] indicated subject has held some extremely sensitive positions with CIA, the nature of which is highly restricted."[44]

Thus, the discovery of the classified document appeared to be much ado about nothing; however, the incident would leave questions, if not a black mark, on Tofte's record, in the eyes of some, especially in light of an unrelated incident in late 1963.

CHAPTER 7

Mason City Interlude

Despite the action-packed life he had lived until then, Tofte adapted quickly to a slower-paced, rural lifestyle. Thanks to the April–July 1954 bill S. 2647, a bill to create an independent Civil Aeronautics Authority and an independent Air Safety Board, Tofte became a member of the Mason City Airport Commission, a logical interest for him given his airline employment just prior to and after World War II. That same year, the Toftes contributed to the preservation of Iowa history by publishing a new history of the state. The authors thanked them in print for their "generous and unfailing assistance throughout the preparation of this book."[1]

He also developed a marked interest in public education. In 1954, he delivered a banquet address to a conference of the Missouri State Teachers Association—a contemporary account described the conference as "designed to stimulate teachers to improve classroom technics [*sic*] and become active leaders in their local associations." Similarly, in March 1955, Tofte was identified as the main speaker at the first general session of the Texas State Teachers Association meeting, due to convene at 8:00 p.m. on that particular evening. He was described as a "world traveler, former diplomat, and president of the Klipto Loose Leaf Co, Mason City, Iowa." Although there is no record of the subject of Tofte's address, the mere fact that he would be invited to be the keynote speaker is noteworthy.[2]

Unfortunately, during this same period, Tofte felt compelled to take a leave of absence—which lasted from late 1954 until early 1956—to address the potential bankruptcy of Klipto Loose Leaf Company, which seemed a distinct possibility at the end of 1954. Over the next six months, he and Marlys were able to turn the company around; however, about the same time he received a plea from DDP Frank Wisner and a letter from his subordinate Maj. Helms urging him to return to CIA as soon as possible. Tofte sent a letter to 4105

Bradley Lane, Bethesda, Maryland—Maj. Helms's personal address—explaining that he needed to get the family business in order but would then bring his family with him and live in Washington, DC, permanently. The curious part of this interlude was that Tofte claimed to have taken 14 months' leave, while Marlys claimed he was only home for six months—what was he doing during the other eight? Possibly preparing his cover at the New York finance firm Wood, Struthers & Winthrop, Inc., a cover that he used for some 11 years. The firm was responsible for huge American investments in Latin America, in close cooperation with Nelson Rockefeller and CIA. Whatever the explanation, Tofte officially returned to CIA in early 1956.[3]

At the time, the nation was gripped by McCarthyism and the fear of communists hiding under every bed in America, aided by such international developments as the discovery of the "Cambridge Five" spy ring in the United Kingdom. Within the Agency, the same period was dominated by the curious figure of James Jesus Angleton, the head of CIA Counterintelligence, referred to behind his back as "The Oracle of Delphi"; from 1956–74, he would be the McCarthy of CIA.

In order to further his own career, Maj. Helms had forged an alliance with Angleton. Given the milieu at the time, Tofte felt that he was under Angleton's microscope on the former's return to the Agency, given his still being so "Danish" despite being a US citizen of more than a decade at this point. Angleton also had his suspicions about Tofte's old communist friends in Yugoslavia from the days of Operation *Audrey*, especially since two of them were now diplomats at the Yugoslav Embassy in Washington. It was true, however, that when Tofte was abroad, he always visited the Danish Embassy before the American one and also ensured he visited the offices of the East Asiatic Company, his former employer, whenever he found them, as three directors there were among his closest friends.

Marlys confirmed that in many ways Tofte still felt like a Dane and always sought out fellow Danes when he could. So, perhaps it should have come as little surprise when in 1956 Tofte learned that some officers in CIA's Security Division had concerns about his loyalty and even considered that he might be a Soviet agent; reports from Asia that the EAC was employing communists also set off Angleton's internal alarm. Given Tofte's service to the nation in various guises over a 15-year period, such doubts bordered on the insulting, but focused on his employment with the company in Copenhagen from 1929–38. Tofte had joined the company as a young man and had spent five years in Manchuria, where he picked up three of his eight languages—Japanese, Russian, and Chinese. The Helsinki communist daily, *Kansan Uutiset*, had sniffed out the story, outlined in an article entitled, "Now, CIA Sees Hobgoblins in Denmark—Security Tangle in Washington." The Finnish paper clearly identified the EAC as a "Communist front organization" as defined by CIA. "It was said that since I was with the East Asiatic Co. and spoke Chinese that I was a Communist. That is like saying Jesus Christ must be a goat because he was born in a barn." Tofte attributed the dust-up to the "incompetence" of some security people who increasingly viewed everyone connected to the company as "a possible Communist."

As a feeler, Tofte was ordered to prepare a report on the EAC's "Communist activities." When Tofte realized the request was serious, he was enraged and refused to do it. Tofte then became the subject of an FBI investigation for 11 offenses, including murder, financial fraud, and treason, since the Bureau believed the organization was a Soviet front. He was summoned to Washington to undergo extensive questioning and, at his own insistence, a five-hour lie detector session "to clear myself and also East Asiatic Company for good." Tofte couldn't resist telling his interrogators, "If what you are hinting at is true then I am the most clever foreign agent of all times, and everybody on the top level in CIA should be fired for having me around." He passed the lie detector test without any problems and was cleared of all doubts—as the Bureau blandly put it in a memo, "Results of the…investigation available to WFO [Washington Field Office] indicate investigation failed to substantiate charges made against Tofte." He then wrote a lengthy history of the company, only to discover when he later requested it "that someone had taken out everything I had written about it. All of it was simply gone. It makes one wonder what is the condition of other files they have out there." As Marlys recalled, though Hans survived the inquisition, it was an unpleasant time.[4]

It was about this time that Marlys decided to sell the publishing house and, assuming that they were headed to the Washington, DC, suburbs for good, she and Hans purchased a house at 1667 35th Street, Georgetown. Living the luxurious lifestyle to which both had become accustomed, with important friends, the couple believed they could now live a normal family life, with Marlys's daughter Teresa and Marlys's mother, Charlotte Leister. Interestingly, both Teresa and Charlotte were quite taken with Hans and both openly flirted with him. Marlys had always been aware that Hans was somewhat of a playboy, but she was the last to learn that he had had several affairs along the way.[5]

As seemed to happen often, international events once again disturbed any sense of normalcy the Toftes had been enjoying—in late May and early June 1956, trouble broke out in Argentina. The year before, a coup had ousted the government of Juan Peron and replaced it with a provisional government headed by a general. But by mid-1956, Peronist rebels had risen up against the provisional government, which mobilized troops and arrested approximately 2,000 rebels and executed 38. The unrest brought prolonged strikes and financial losses for American investors, notably including Wood, Struthers, & Winthrop (WSW), where Tofte was a "sub-director," and fears of communist involvement and growth.

Lieutenant Commander Wisner sent Tofte to Argentina to sort out the situation—"Things usually get going when you show up," he told his troubleshooter. Tofte established a network of anti-communist organizations in the country and enlisted locals to serve the CIA's contract agents there. Interestingly, Lt. Cmdr. Wisner also asked him to keep an eye out for Hitler's former deputy, Martin Bormann, who was believed to be hiding out there. This postscript was ironic, given that Lt. Cmdr. Wisner, DCI Dulles, and CIA in general had helped many ex-Nazis escape through Operation *National Interest* and Operation *Bloodstone*. So Tofte set himself up as a director of WSW, in a 15-room luxury apartment, complete with a butler. Marlys joined him, but it proved to be only a brief visit—after only a few weeks, she returned to Washington, disgusted by the "boastful Argentine macho types" with whom she had to deal.[6]

That summer of 1956, Finn—Tofte's son from his first marriage—came to Argentina for a visit; perhaps surprisingly, Marlys came to have a good relationship with him despite her rollercoaster life with Hans. Finn was impressed with his father's luxurious lifestyle, and especially remembered the butler serving champagne every day at 5:00 p.m. and his father driving a large American car around the streets of Buenos Aires. When Finn asked about the car his dad had left at home in Washington, DC, Hans replied that he couldn't remember the name, but that it was "a smaller European car"—only when Finn traveled to DC a few weeks later to visit Marlys, did he discover that the "smaller European car" was actually a Jaguar.

At the time of Finn's visit, Hans was in the process of establishing an airline—a familiar procedure—and had bought a seaplane to fly between Buenos Aires and Montevideo, Uruguay, and other cities along the Rio Parana. The company also had within its inventory a few Helio Courier planes, intended to fly into "desolate and impassable areas." Produced in Boston, these aircraft had a top speed of 180 kilometers per hour (112 miles per hour) but could take off at only 50 kph (31 mph). They needed less than 200 feet of runway for takeoffs and landings but had a range of nearly 1,000 miles.

Such capabilities made them ideal for CIA operations in remote areas and a USAF special operations pioneer, Lieutenant Colonel Harry C. "Heinie"

Aderholt, championed their use; the Agency indeed used them in several places in Latin America, Africa, Laos, and Vietnam. Tofte had partnered with a former Luftwaffe pilot to fly the seaplane and establish the company, which had brought a cry of protest from an Argentinian parliament member. He argued that an association of former, "unreconstructed" Luftwaffe officers in Argentina posed a threat to the government, especially since they could openly advocate for a return to Nazism, since none had been charged with war crimes. The Luftwaffe association was led by two Luftwaffe legends and aces—Lieutenant Colonel Hans Ulrich Rudel, a Ju-87 Stuka dive bomber pilot on the Eastern Front, and General Adolf Galland, once head of Germany's fighter command and one of the first to fly Germany's jet fighter, the Me-262. The Argentinian parliament member claimed that at least 40 former Luftwaffe personnel had fled to Argentina via Denmark after the war.[7]

After 18 months of work, Tofte's network of contract agents in Argentina numbered 20, allowing the harried Hans to relax a bit. Marlys came for a visit, and the two vacationed in Chile. When not relaxing, Tofte was also working on several $1 million+ deals for WSW, in between forwarding to Washington reports from his agent network in southern Argentina on increasing Soviet interest in the South Pole, where the USSR had established its first base in 1956 and by 1958 had five bases. Obviously, the United States did not want the Soviet Union to use Argentina as a supply base for South Pole operations, nor did it want to allow the Soviets access to the sizable uranium deposits in Argentina. When Argentine newspapers reported in 1958 that a submarine of unknown nationality had been spotted off the coast, Tofte sensed a golden opportunity for a disinformation operation.

He told an Argentine journalist that he had been told by "an extremely reliable source at the American Embassy" that the submarine was Russian and that he had also learned a number of technical details about the vessel. Despite Tofte's private admission that this was all "pure fabrication," the story appeared in the Argentine press the next day and the Argentine navy ordered an increased level of readiness. Other papers picked up the story, leading to increased agitation in general, and to the Argentine navy firing on several whales in particular, believing them to be submarines. Readers then learned that a Soviet research vessel was scheduled to stop in Buenos Aires on its way home, which prompted Tofte to tell his journalist friend: "I told him in the deepest confidence that indeed, the Russian ship was equipped with scientific apparatus, but it was primarily designed as a mother ship for subs and was now supposed to bring supplies to the submarines that had been operating off the coast of Argentina." Alarmed, the Argentine naval leadership decided to act, and when the Soviet ship appeared off Buenos Aires, it was confronted with eight motor torpedo boats (MTB), which closely monitored its activity.

The protests of the Russian captain were ignored, and the ship's arrival was greeted with huge protests as it was "bombarded with rotten eggs and tomatoes by a crowd of thousands, who also prevented the crew from getting ashore." Demonstrations also occurred in front of the Soviet Embassy, with people throwing stones through the windows and setting fire to the cars of embassy officials. The operation was a definitive win for CIA—the ship left Buenos Aires the next day, in haste. As far as Lt. Cmdr. Wisner's other tasking—the whereabouts of Martin Bormann—Tofte could only report that the Argentine intelligence service had a file on him and that it seemed probable that he had indeed come to Argentina in 1948, under the name Eliezer Goldstein; reportedly, he had later been seen in Paraguay and Uruguay.[8]

Despite the success of this disinformation operation, 1958 proved a difficult year for Tofte. First, his father died that year, following a period of illness. He had called for Hans on his deathbed, but the son never came, leading to a rupture in the family that meant he didn't see Finn for the next 15 years. Also, in August 1958, his mentor and protector, Lt. Cmdr. Wisner, was taken from his Langley office in a straitjacket and subjected to electroshock therapy for the next six months at Shepherd Pratt Hospital, in Baltimore, Maryland. Lieutenant Commander Wisner worked for CIA for another four years post treatment, but never again as a manager. He was first dispatched to England and then to other, less demanding stations abroad, but the wily and creative ops veteran was no more—as Tofte's biographer, Henrik Kruger, put it, "With him [Wisner], one of Tofte's permanent anchors in the intelligence service was gone." Thus, when Tofte returned home in 1959, he faced a radically changed situation.[9]

Major Helms expected to succeed Lt. Cmdr. Wisner, but DCI Dulles instead gave the job to his assistant, Maj. Gen. Bissell. Since Maj. Helms had been an intelligence officer since 1943 and Maj. Gen. Bissell only since 1954, DCI Dulles expected some blowback. He then created a new position, the assistant deputy director for plans (ADD/P), and chose Tofte's friend Tracy Barnes for the post. Formally installed in January 1959, Maj. Gen. Bissell set out to do some major housecleaning in the DDP. He described Lt. Cmdr. Wisner's system as "dated and inefficient" and also shuffled aside Tofte, "whose claims were not matched by his exploits," according to author Evan Thomas. Major General Bissell knew Lt. Cmdr. Wisner and Tofte had been close and so purposely kept the latter at arm's length, although Barnes ensured that Tofte had appropriate assignments.[10]

This awkward situation unfortunately prompted Tofte to supplement his daily glass of wine with a few stiff Scotch whiskeys: "The singularly energetic radiance that had always been his image had begun to seem a little overexcited and perhaps a little nervous." He was still charming at home, but Marlys was concerned about his mental state and tried to keep his spirits up in an unusual fashion, namely by buying him houses. The Toftes bought a nice, large house right on the Atlantic Ocean at Rehoboth Beach, Delaware, about 65 miles northeast of Washington, and also a country house in Somerset, near Stanardsville, Virginia, approximately 85 miles southwest of the nation's capital. Thus, they had three houses, two of which were used extensively for socializing.

It was also during this period that Marlys began learning of more instances of Hans's infidelity—when he was out of the country, a young woman once knocked on their door and asked for him. Marlys soon learned that she was the fiancée of a CIA colleague and had had an affair with him and had fallen hard for him. To add to the bizarre nature of the situation, she learned that this woman's fiancée had been an enemy of Tofte's during Operation *Audrey*. Just a month after Marlys learned of the relationship, the man died of alcoholism; but Marlys was not the jealous type and it "would take more than sporadic infidelity" to break their bond. As his first biographer put it, Tofte "did not get emotionally involved with other women, and the affairs were always short. It was pure sex."[11]

Tofte returned home from Colombia just as DCI Dulles, Maj. Gen. Bissell, and Col. King were having their first meetings concerning action against Cuban head of state Fidel Castro. As one might expect, the idea was to do much as the Agency had done in Guatemala, using exiled Cubans for an air-supported invasion. Tofte claimed he participated in the early stages of what became the disastrous Bay of Pigs operation, but also claimed he assessed the plans as badly flawed and strongly objected to them. As far as he was concerned, the situation in Cuba was entirely different and Castro was a very different threat from Arbenz, as he was receiving military support from the USSR directly, which Arbenz never did.

He was also convinced that for any paramilitary action to succeed in Cuba, Castro had to be killed first. In the month prior to the Bay of Pigs operation, Tofte had the opportunity to brief President Kennedy on the operation—the president was planning a trip to South America later that year. However, Tofte's part in the planning was put on hold by a fiscal crisis within his team of agents in Argentina when an investigation revealed that several hundred thousand dollars were missing. The agent-in-charge had failed a lie detector test and it was clear that reorganizing the agent network was a priority. Ironically, Tofte's own spending in Argentina was also under scrutiny at the time.[12]

By the early 1960s, the negative legacy of his work in Guatemala—one author referred to it as "a failed tour of duty in South America"—and questions about his operational expenses, likely combined with other unspecified concerns, meant that Tofte was "on the outs." By 1962, Tofte had dropped out of the active part of the Covert Operations Division and had been transferred to the Office of Training in the Domestic Operations Division as a "senior officer" in charge of training foreign intelligence officers, a definite demotion. This transfer also was due to his OSS friend Tracy Barnes, also in the division—in what one author has called his "last ill-conceived idea," Barnes sought to defend and protect his friend, challenging to do if one accepted one description of Tofte at the time as "a blowhard who exaggerated his exploits in Korea and a pariah."

Although Barnes was able to defend Tofte when questions about the latter's expense accounts came up, he would prove unable to protect him four years hence, when it would really count. As Kruger noted, "The coldness Tofte now encountered from several sides in the CIA made him dive even deeper into the whiskey bottle." As Marlys put it, "Hans felt like a friend to all his colleagues, it was hard for him to discover that there were many who didn't like him."[13]

Meanwhile, the Bay of Pigs operation in Cuba had failed spectacularly and the shrapnel from the blast traveled far, enveloping Langley. President Kennedy was livid about the botched attempt to remove what he and most of the nation viewed as an imminent Soviet communist threat 90 miles from America and focused his wrath on CIA in particular for the debacle. And there was still the painful memory of the 1960 shootdown of a U-2 spy plane piloted by CIA contract employee Francis Gary Powers over the Soviet city of Sverdlovsk, the resulting collapse of the summit talks, and President Kennedy's embarrassment when Soviet leader Nikita Khrushchev exposed the official US lie that the surveillance aircraft was simply off course. Little wonder, then, that President Kennedy decided to make wholesale changes at CIA.

The president forced Dulles out as DCI, along with Maj. Gen. Bissell and others; Tofte's friend Tracy Barnes was sidelined. Tofte felt sorry for his friend, who had played an integral role in the planning of the operation as ADD/P, but was compelled to agree with CIA Inspector General Lyman Kirkpatrick that the planning had been "disastrous." The good news—for Tofte and others—was that Dulles was replaced as DCI by a very different man, outsider John McCone, a businessman, politician, and former chairman of the Atomic Energy Commission (AEC). The seeming litany of bad news cast a pall over the Agency, even as its employees walked the gleaming marble halls of their brand-new headquarters at Langley, which opened in 1961 and was located a mere 8 miles from Washington, DC. Tofte was less excited by the choice of Maj. Helms as Maj. Gen. Bissell's replacement, hoping that his friend Tracy Barnes would be tapped as the head of covert ops. Major Helms, described as "an icy and scheming bureaucrat with a great eye for what served his own career best," had been able to escape the Bay of Pigs blowback that had felled several others.[14]

Tofte, meanwhile, was frustrated at having been moved to the Office of Training, a seeming waste of federal government "supergrade" manpower. The training that was now Tofte's responsibility was conducted under Agency auspices at various locations, including International Police Services, Inc., a four-story building on R St., in Washington, DC; the International Police Academy, also in Washington; the Inter-American Police Academy in Panama; and the Federal School in Los Fresnos, Texas. Much of this training occurred under the cover of the Office of Public Safety, part of the Agency for International Development (AID). Despite this negative career development, Tofte remained "full of ambition and fighting spirit." Furthermore, he still had friends in high places at CIA, remained a member of the special club of former OSS officers in the Division of Covert Operations, and was still welcome in the seventh floor Executive Dining Room, a venue open only to the select few.[15]

By the spring of 1962, Barnes was the head of the Domestic Operations Division, and by the end of that year had made arrangements so that Tofte was permanently attached to the Department of Defense, a good cover for his work as an instructor of foreign police and security personnel. In support of the division, Tofte was tasked with establishing secret cooperative arrangements between CIA and American companies around the world. His previous work in Mason City and with Wood, Struthers, & Winthrop had prepared him well for the job, which soon involved him in an Agency-arranged coup in Brazil.

When the reformist center-left government of Joao Goulart, head of the Brazilian Labor Party and referred to as "Jango," took power on September 8, 1961, the Kennedy administration initially believed the United States could do business with the new Brazilian government, and was sympathetic to his widely touted program of basic reforms, including labor protections for rural workers, redistributive agrarian reform, and universal suffrage. In response, the US government provided economic, financial, and development aid assistance. But within a year, the relationship soured, beginning with Goulart's refusal to ban leftists from his cabinet. The United States was also disturbed by Brazil's overly independent foreign policy and her ties to the Socialist Bloc; by her economic nationalism, which threatened American companies in Brazil; and, in a larger sense, by the threat of another Cuba in the Southern Hemisphere.[16]

In early 1962, the United States concluded that it actually could not do business with the Goulart administration and embarked on a campaign to oust him from power, by means of diplomatic and financial pressure, support for opposing politicians, the threat of abandonment, and collusion with coup plotters, including the promise of immediate diplomatic recognition for a government established by the military leaders involved. Internally, Goulart and his ministers were deeply distrusted by the conservative elites and segments of the military, who considered him a dangerous leftist, especially because of his proposed agrarian reforms. On March 30, 1964, a classified CIA cable predicted that "a revolution by anti-Goulart forces will definitely get under way this week, probably within the next few days." Indeed, on the following day, March 31, 1964, a military coup occurred in Brazil, led by Marshal Castelo Branco, who represented a moderate wing of the armed forces.

The coup was supported by civilians, some clergy, conservative Catholic groups, and the US Embassy, which had played a key role in the conspiracy. To help ensure the correct outcome for the coup, the Agency and the Pentagon—in the person of Secretary of Defense Robert MacNamara, later the World Bank director who provided huge credits for investment in Brazil—launched Operation *Brother Sam*, which involved the deployment of a naval task force from Virginia headed by the carrier USS *Forrestal* (CVA-59), a helicopter carrier loaded with paratroopers, as well as six destroyers, four tankers, 26 aircraft, and several ammunition ships. However, Branco soon informed US authorities that logistical support would be unnecessary, due to the unexpected speed with which the coup advanced, and Operation *Brother Sam* was cancelled.

Although the CIA cable had been spot-on concerning the inevitability and the general timing of the coup, it had also advised that "[the] revolution will not be resolved quickly and will be bloody," two prognostications which both proved incorrect. In reality, as the coup neared its successful conclusion, Goulart and other leaders fled to Uruguay, and on April 11, 1964, the Brazilian Congress elected Branco as the first president general of the new regime. Tofte's acknowledged role in this coup was reduced to having trained some 40 British police officers to deal with the aftermath; however, it is hard to believe that Tofte played no larger role, given that WSW Chair Milbank and Vice Chair Brooks, along with Nelson Rockefeller, were among the largest investors in Brazil. Especially noteworthy was the fact that at a critical juncture in the unfolding of the military coup a fellow Dane, Henning Albert Boilesen, president of liquified petroleum gas distributor Ultragaz, provided his fleet of trucks to deliver tanks and guns to the coup plotters when faced with the government's stopping of all petroleum deliveries.[17]

If Tofte's career had somewhat plateaued by the mid-1960s, his personal life was also troubled. On February 26, 1964, Tofte was interviewed by the FBI concerning his knowing an unidentified Mason City, Iowa, businessman who had had contact with the Soviet Embassy in October 1963; though details are lacking, it was neither the first nor the last time Tofte would be questioned by the Bureau. That same year, he received a reprimand from CIA for taking classified information home—for most Agency employees and certainly for a senior executive like Tofte, the penalty was usually a symbolic hand-slap if the offending material were promptly returned, but in Tofte's case it proved to be an incident of great import.

Furthermore, his life with Marlys was evolving into a platonic one rather than a romantic one—as biographer Kruger described the relationship in 1964, "In many ways he was still a big boy, a playboy, while she was a mature and strong woman who felt she was gradually more mother than wife to him." But, as often happened, his job provided a temporary distraction—on February 27, 1965, Tofte left for Nigeria, under the guise of a trip for WSW; the real reason for the trip was that there was a sizable US investment in Nigeria and a fear that unrest in the country could balloon into civil war. But peaceful elections occurred three weeks after Tofte arrived, and he returned home a week later.

The respite proved brief, however, as his severely troubled colleague Lt. Cmdr. Wisner committed suicide on October 29 that year, leaving Tofte deeply depressed and having a predictably negative effect on his marriage as well. Never one to pull punches, Marlys told him straight up, "Now that's enough. Now you must leave the CIA!" Fed up, Marlys made it clear to Hans that if he wouldn't leave the CIA, their marriage was over. Left unsaid was the fact that Marlys already had warm feelings for a French war hero, Brigadier General Jean Charles Chatel, who with his wife had a large real estate business in Washington, DC—and who would figure prominently in the near future of both Hans and Marlys.[18]

Predictably, Hans was unwilling to leave CIA behind, even if it cost him Marlys, which it did, in somewhat gradual fashion. In this "strange half-divorce," as Kruger referred to it, Tofte kept an office and room at their house in Georgetown, but spent most of his time at the country house in Stanardsville, Virginia. Marlys, meanwhile, sold the beach house she had specifically bought for Hans—to Salvadora Debayle, the wife of Nicaraguan dictator Anastasio Somoza. In spring 1966, Tofte was at the country house when he was awakened by a noise at 2:00 a.m. one morning. He went to check on the noise, only to trip on the stairs and fall, hitting his head so hard that he lost consciousness. The married couple who lived on the farm as caretakers discovered him and took him to the hospital, where doctors determined he had suffered a concussion.

Marlys heard of Hans's accident the next morning and immediately drove to the country house, where she encountered the very excited caretakers, who showed her "two very special screws" on each side of the stairs, exactly where Hans had tripped, two screws neither recalled ever having seen before. Marlys was convinced that someone had strung a wire across the stairs at this location, in a deliberate attempt to kill him, though no evidence was forthcoming to support this allegation. Regardless, the event had spooked the caretakers who, much to the regret of Hans and Marlys, soon resigned and left.[19]

On June 30, 1966, Maj. Helms became the next director of Central Intelligence, and started ridding the Agency of some of his foes, including Inspector Gen. Kirkpatrick, who had been warning that CIA was running amok and trying to wrest power from Congress. Another critic, Directorate of Intelligence Chief Ray Cline, was dispatched overseas. Tofte and Tracey Barnes also fell into the ranks of Maj. Helms's foes, but the new DCI realized he would need a special reason to rid himself of Tofte. Major Helms believed that Tofte had secretly supported Cline's attempt to become DCI and had provided material against Maj. Helms, which led to a nasty encounter between the two. Shortly after Maj. Helms became DCI, he called Tofte in and asked him bluntly, "Don't you think you should resign?" Tofte answered just as forthrightly, "No, Dick, I think you should take your leave." According to Kruger's biography, Tofte "didn't mind Helms from the start, but they didn't become friends because Helms felt bad for the people he saw as rivals."[20] As happened repeatedly in Tofte's life, past acquaintances would loom large in his future.

OSS veteran and future DCI Richard Helms. (CIA)

CHAPTER 8

Apartment to Let

By 1966, Tofte had been with CIA for nearly 16 years and had steadily risen through the ranks. He was a GS-16, a "supergrade," making nearly $25,000 a year, and training clandestine agents, all of which indicated his senior status within the Agency. Then, in July, Marlys listed the house at 1667 NW 35th Street—a stately three-story brick home in the fashionable Washington, DC, suburb of Georgetown—with the J. C. Chatel real estate firm, the company her new heartthrob Brig. Gen. Chatel owned with his wife; the firm then advertised it for sale or rent. The Toftes had already moved out, to a more upscale house at 2362 Massachusetts Ave., NW, the former Uruguayan Embassy, on "Embassy Row," leaving behind only Marlys's mother, Charlotte Leister, who lived in an apartment on the second floor and acted as a would-be caretaker; Tofte was compelled to move to much less luxurious surroundings.[1]

On Saturday, July 23, by pre-arrangement, realtor Melita Molloy showed the basement apartment of the home as a potential rental to a Mr. and Mrs. Kenneth R. Slocum; unknown to Tofte at the time, Mr. Slocum was also a CIA employee, an electronics engineer who had moved with his wife Judy from North Hollywood, California, to the area in June. The Slocums were living temporarily at 2911 P St., NW, while they attempted to find a permanent one-bedroom apartment. Looking in the local phone directory that day, Slocum had found the Chatel realty firm and noticed they were in Georgetown, where he wanted to live, and so gave them a call, leading to their appointment at 6:00 p.m. that day with Ms. Molloy.

The Toftes were out, but Marlys's 86-year-old mother was there with the Toftes' two poodles, Bobby-Old-Boy and Brigitte. Despite virtually all reporting that suggested only the basement apartment was for rent, FBI reporting not released until many years later indicated that when the Slocums appeared to see the basement apartment, Mrs. Leister offered to show them the entire house and also informed them that there was a third-floor apartment for rent; Slocum later recalled that he went upstairs "very specifically by her direction," a statement Mrs. Leister later vehemently denied. The front room on the third floor was Tofte's study and was, in Tofte's words, "out of bounds" and that "everybody knew that"—everybody apparently except Ms. Molloy, who had never met the Toftes. She later stated that "no one suggested the third floor was out of bounds."

However, when the Slocums toured that apartment, Mr. Slocum the engineer stooped down to examine a mechanical desk calculator, one of the few items in the room. He spotted a document labelled "Secret" and other classified documents in a stack approximately 20 inches high with the CIA name and symbol on them. Per the Bureau, he took approximately four documents from the stack, slipped them into his jacket pocket, and returned to the second floor to chat with Mrs. Leister. Slocum learned that the study was her son-in-law's and that his name was Hans Tofte, a name which meant nothing to Slocum, who returned to his P Street apartment and called CIA; the Slocums were summoned to Langley, where they turned over the offending documents, were questioned, and told they would be called the next morning, Sunday, July 24. Tofte noted that these documents were indeed in a third-floor library, but reiterated that the area was off-limits, even to his wife, and claimed that they were wrapped in both a blanket and a tarpaulin, as part of the pending move. CIA security personnel agreed that they should return the following day, Sunday, July 24, which they did—in the person of Charles D. Speake, a lawyer who had been a CIA security officer for 15 years—along with the Slocums, since the latter had been told they could return to look at the apartment again. When they called, they reached Mrs. Leister, who told them it would be all right to come back and that she would leave the front door open and the dogs in her apartment so they could go directly into the house. After chatting with Mrs. Leister for a bit, the trio all went up to the third floor, to confirm the documents were still present, which they were, and to enable Speake to secure them.

While the others engaged Mrs. Leister in conversation, Mrs. Slocum drove a car around to the front of the house, where the documents—which the Bureau determined numbered 172, one-third classified "Secret" and above—were loaded into the car and driven to CIA headquarters. Speake assessed that the documents were a "compromise of major proportions," an assessment CIA later confirmed. As the case unfolded, Tofte acknowledged that he would have let CIA security personnel in to retrieve the "offending" documents had he been there and was adamant that both the front and rear doors of the house were locked. Rather, he contended they entered his home under false pretenses and violated his constitutional rights. Slocum and CIA both asserted that retrieving the documents was "impulsive and unpremeditated," denying that it was any type of "raid," as Tofte later charged.

While there was no concern that the classified materials had ever left Tofte's hands, it appeared that his having such materials at home was a violation of Agency rules. In response, Tofte pointed out that it was "customary for executives and senior personnel in key positions"—of which he was certainly one—to take papers home to work on. He added that the documents in question were part of his work on an Agency textbook concerning the training of covert agents and generally minimized the incident, adding, "There's hardly anyone who's been involved in such a long, active life, who doesn't have some small security violations…like traffic tickets." As he noted at the time, "When the security agents came for me [after finding the documents] I offered to take them to six houses [of other CIA officials who, he said, he knew had followed the same practice]," but they passed on that offer. Part of the difference this time was that Tofte had kept such documents at home for too long.[2]

On August 3, 1966, local Washington, DC, station WTOP Radio aired an interesting interview between Tofte and WTOP newsman Bill Diehl, focused on the reclaimed documents and the overall situation:

> DIEHL: "Did you feel you had done anything wrong?"
> TOFTE: "Not particularly."
> DIEHL: "There were classified documents which were reportedly in your home."
> TOFTE: "There were."
> DIEHL: "You do not feel, though, that this was any violation of any regulations at all?"
> TOFTE: "I wrote in my statements to the metropolitan police that this is customary among certain people who have certain responsibilities."
> DIEHL: "Were they left out in the open as might have been implied in some stories?"
> TOFTE: "Certainly not."
> DIEHL: "Where were they kept? Could you tell me that?"
> TOFTE: "They were on the very top floor of my house in quarters that I use as a library, that nobody has access to normally…They were wrapped up to be removed and brought back under the secure conditions where they should be kept."
> DIEHL: "At this moment, how does your job stand? Do you still have it?"
> TOFTE: "I still have my job."
> DIEHL: "Have you talked to any CIA officials?"
> TOFTE: "I have."
> DIEHL: "What have they told you?"
> TOFTE: "Not very much yet."
> DIEHL: "Have you had any difficulty talking to anyone?"
> TOFTE: "I have had difficulty in reaching the people I wanted to reach, particularly my old friend, Dick Helms."[3]

Tofte likely found it of little comfort to know that his "problem" also had attracted the attention, at least to some extent, of one of America's premier journalists at the time—Chet Huntley, of the renowned *Huntley-Brinkley Report* that aired nightly on WRC-TV, the local NBC network in Washington, DC. In the report that aired at 6:30 p.m. on August 4, 1966, Chet Huntley discussed the case:

> The CIA, the very fibers of whose being are secrecy and stealth, has an almost hypnotic propensity for publicity, usually of the wrong kind and at the wrong time. Here, as nearly as can be deciphered is the latest instance. A CIA man named Hans Tofte decided to rent his Washington house. Another CIA agent came to look it over. He didn't know Tofte was a CIA man, and vice versa. Apparently you don't have to be one to know one. But he saw some classified documents lying around. He returned with another agent and they may or may not have taken something besides the classified [laughs] material. At least, Tofte claims nineteen thousand dollars [*sic*] worth of jewelry is missing. Today, the CIA suspended Tofte; however, he'll stay on the payroll at almost twenty-five thousand dollars a year until someone decided [*sic*] who did what [laughs] to whom.[4]

Though Tofte's immediate reaction to the Huntley report is unknown, it is hard to believe that he was remotely amused or pleased at being kicked while he was down.

Meanwhile, the Bureau, sensing something was rotten in Denmark, began taking major steps to recuse itself from what increasingly appeared to be a CIA housekeeping issue. "We are instructing Washington Field Office (WFO) and Richmond," declared an August 4 FBI memo, "not to become involved in security aspects of this case since it is purely an administrative matter involving Central Intelligence Agency (CIA) employees and should be so determined by CIA…Tofte claims he had taken the material home for the purpose of homework which is customary for executives and senior personnel… Subsequently, Tofte reported to CIA and police that some jewelry…valued in excess of $18,000 was missing from his home. *The matter has created much internal controversy within CIA and has received considerable adverse publicity for CIA* [emphasis added]."

Although the WFO had sent a lead to Richmond to check with CIA to see if a security violation had occurred within the Bureau's jurisdiction, FBI remained unconvinced this was their fight—as they categorically stated in this same memo, "This is strictly an administrative squabble involving CIA personnel concerning the manner in which they control their classified material. We should not become involved in this *three-ring circus* which is not only an internal administrative matter in CIA but has been *handled by CIA in a heavy-handed manner resulting in ridicule and scorn in the press.* Consequently, we will certainly not become involved [emphasis added]." An addendum by

FBI official Alex Rosen concluded, "This whole matter smells and, therefore, no inquiries should be made concerning the alleged jewel theft, which appears to be a fabricated story, and is so closely tied in to the CIA activity that we obviously should stay clear of this entire matter in all its aspects."[5]

On Sunday, July 24, the day after the fateful apartment tour, Tofte spent the day at his farm in Stanardsville, Virginia, approximately 110 miles southwest of Georgetown. The Agency claimed it could not find him, but tracked him down that night at a friend's home in Georgetown, where he was planning to meet Marlys, swim, and have dinner. As he was about to take a dip, Mrs. Leister called and told him to call a particular number, which Tofte recognized as that of a CIA security officer, who asked Tofte to come and see him—when Tofte demurred, the Agency sent a car for him and took him first to a CIA office in downtown Washington, DC, where he talked with a security officer, and was then driven to Langley.

What followed was three days of questioning by four Agency officials. Tofte later complained on television that while at Langley he was interrogated by "underlings" who began talking of "termination, demotion and, so help me—treason," a charge CIA flatly denied. When questioned by Helm's lawyer, Laidler B. Mackall, Tofte refused to provide the names of the four officials, fearing that by so doing he might breach security laws. Mackall argued that no law barred revelation of the names, a contention upheld by District Court Judge Alexander Holtzoff; the judge instructed Tofte to provide the names if asked in a future deposition.

Meanwhile, Agency officials were sorting through the treasure trove of documents from Tofte's house, becoming increasingly alarmed by what they found. The oldest documents dated back to 1951 and while some were unclassified, some ran "all the way to the top, through 'top secret,'" according to one CIA official, though Tofte claimed none of the documents were stamped "top secret." One senior Agency figure said the papers included "recent highly sensitive 'electronic messages'" from CIA foreign operatives, and another identified recent, top-secret estimates prepared for the president by the Agency's Board of National Estimates. At this juncture, Tofte told police, "I requested to see my chief supervisor, Mr. Tracy Barnes, and later the agency's legal counsel Mr. Lawrence Houston in view of the bizarre circumstances surrounding the proceedings." He was finally able to see Barnes in a brief noontime meeting on July 28, and Houston on the afternoon of July 29.[6]

As one account noted, "So far, the Tofte affair was really banal. Over time, many CIA agents have been suspended and later fired without it ever becoming known to the public. In the intelligence service, this sort of thing is arranged internally, and absolute silence is one of the conditions to which all agents must submit. But Hans V. Tofte was not like other agents, and outwardly the jewelry theft was the final straw." It was at this point that Tofte did what shocked his friends and enemies alike—he went to the press, committing the unpardonable sin of airing the intelligence community's dirty linen in public. No sooner had several newspapers jumped on the developing story than the Agency decided to go on the offensive. On August 2, CIA issued a press release explaining that the offending documents had been discovered entirely by chance and that Tofte's reaction was evidence of his "incompetence and lack of professionalism."[7]

As the disagreement between Tofte and the Agency became more rancorous, Tofte wrote a three-page letter on August 8 to a friend, Charles E. Strickland, the retired president of the People's Gas & Electric Company in Mason City. He told his friend that he had inside information about the Bay of Pigs botched invasion, as well as operations in the Dominican Republic and Vietnam, information which could create "embarrassing issues" for the Agency. He added that his critical analyses of these operations were among the papers seized by CIA security during the July 24 raid on his home and surmised that the raid might have been motivated simply by the desire to secure the operational critiques. In his letter, Tofte also reviewed his differences with senior Agency officials since 1961, who had tried to usher him out of the Agency but failed, and asked Strickland to share with his friends the details of his squabbles with CIA. As a reporter described the situation, Tofte hoped to "force an expose and a clean-up of top personnel at the CIA and anticipate[d] a difficult and bitter fight." As Tofte put it in the letter, "All I ask is for my true friends to trust me all the way to the bitter end." He claimed to have been in a White House meeting on May 5, 1961—in the early days of the Kennedy administration—and to have spent most of the three-and-a-half-hour meeting talking with President Kennedy's top aide, Ted Sorensen, concerning how senior CIA personnel could hide their various blunders connected with the Bay of Pigs fiasco and who should lead the Agency. Sorensen noted, however, "I have no recollection of seeing Mr. Tofte in the White House, but if he was there, the Bay of Pigs did not come up, nor did the question of who should be named director of the CIA."[8]

Tofte also suggested that his Mason City friends read *The Invisible Government* to better understand his situation, adding that the Agency had tried to prevent publication of the book, that the authors—Tom Ross and David Wise—had been harassed by CIA, and that even Marlys had been subjected to surveillance in recent weeks. Throughout his letter to Strickland, Tofte made clear his impression that he was the subject of a conspiracy, a vendetta against a whistleblower. "The papers they found in my house," Tofte wrote, "represent years of study aimed at perfecting a plan, that would revolutionize the entire CIA and make it do the work it is supposed to do—better, more professionally, and without a colossal waste in regard to money and human tragedy." He denied that there had been any clean-up within the Agency in the wake of the Bay of Pigs event, adding, "The same people, who planned and executed that disastrous affair are still sitting in Langley in bigger and better jobs." He suggested that "the worst mistake any President of the United States could possibly make would be to put a CIA professional in the top spot of the Agency," adding that he was "vastly relieved when Kennedy appointed a type like [John A.] McCone" as the successor to DCI Dulles, having been especially critical of President Lyndon B. Johnson for previously appointing the career CIA officer, Maj. Helms, as director.[9]

To add further to the "bizarre" nature of events, Marlys originally reported to police that in the wake of the two visits, $29,000 worth of jewelry was missing from a purse in a first-floor closet, with no indications that anyone else had been in the house. She soon revised this figure down to $19,000 once she realized that a number of items were at a local jeweler for repairs. Regardless of the value of the jewelry, Marlys was incensed and decried the "impertinence and ruthlessness" of those who were "plowing through this house." Tofte had made a passing reference to jewelry missing from his home on Monday, July 25, but was told to report such to the local police department; on Wednesday, the 27th, he mentioned it again, but estimated the total at $50,000, and was told again to report the alleged theft to local police, which Marlys did on Thursday the 28th, a follow-up to her preliminary report of Monday, July 25.

As far as Tofte was concerned, the raid on that Sunday was "deliberately staged. Unfortunately someone over-reached and took Marlys's jewelry in the process. This I cannot prove, but if anyone has a better theory, I would like to hear it." She had reported the disappearance of her jewelry to her insurance agent, B. Powell Harrison, in Leesburg, Virginia, on Monday, July 25. Harrison had known the Toftes for more than 20 years and was "thoroughly inclined to believe they are right in everything they say," an assessment also shared by a DC lawyer, Gerhard P. Van Arkel, who had served in OSS with Tofte, whom he described as "utterly veracious."[10]

As Tofte would soon learn, it became increasingly difficult to convince officials at CIA, FBI, or the Metropolitan Police Department (MPD) that any jewelry had disappeared during the classified documents raid. The Washington police were to first to express their doubts—on August 3, an MPD officer told two FBI special agents that he did not believe the jewelry theft on July 24 was "a legitimate theft, as it appears that TOFTE caused the theft to be reported to counter CIA's possible charge against him for unauthorized possession of classified documents." The FBI summary of the MPD report noted that at 11:09 p.m. on July 25, 1966, a woman—Marlys—had phoned the police to advise them that she and her husband were in the process of moving and that a "quantity of jewelry" was missing from a first-floor closet at the residence. She did not know how many pieces of jewelry or their value and could not provide a description of them. She indicated that she would appear at the station the following day to file a report, which she did, ultimately settling on a value of $18,000 for the missing jewelry. She added that a number of "manuscripts" were also missing.

Officers conducted an investigation but were unable to determine the method of entry into the house, but assessed that the jewelry went missing sometime between 8:00 a.m. on July 24 and 11:00 p.m. July 25.[11] Interestingly, DOS Osborn informed a Bureau liaison agent that Tofte had admitted to originally leaking the story of the missing jewels to a reporter at the *Minneapolis Tribune* on August 2, 1966. The Bureau report noted that Tofte had "consistently changed the value of the missing jewels, each time lowering the value considerably. CIA is of the belief that there are no missing jewels and that the story is a fabrication on the part of Tofte to cover up the fact that he violated Agency rules in bringing classified information home."

Director Osborn added that Metropolitan Police were planning to interview the Slocums early on the morning of August 3 and anticipated calling Tofte in at 10:00 a.m. to confront him with the fact that he did violate Agency rules in bringing classified information home. Unless he could provide a satisfactory explanation, he would be suspended and a board of CIA officials would be convened to adjudicate his case, which the Agency believed did not involve any security implications.[12] The story of the jewelry, whether legitimately missing or not, grew to have a life of its own—not only did the constantly changing value and vague recollections of the pieces raise questions and concerns, but so did stories Tofte told others about them—according to one account, Tofte claimed that just a single piece of Marlys's jewelry that had been stolen was "a 130-carat half-moon sapphire, a very rare thing, that usually sits in the turban of a maharajah of India." The Toftes later claimed that the half-moon sapphire—surrounded by diamonds—was alone worth at least $75,000.[13]

During an August 3, 1966, interview on the WTOP-TV program *Newsday*, Tofte was asked by a reporter, "How do you think you're going to come out in all this?" Tofte replied, "I have no idea, but I do know that since I came over here as a refugee this business first—the OSS, then the CIA—that has sort of been my family. I know that I have many, many, many good friends. The thing that irks me is that the system has worked out in such a way that it looks as if you can be dropped as an old banana peel without seeing your best friends. So when I found out that my home was invaded—my lawyer calls it grand larceny—and my 86-year-old mother-in-law—my senior citizen—was bamboozled, I was outraged. Nobody pushes my family around and nobody pushes any senior citizen around in my presence."[14]

The next day, August 4, FBI Director Hoover sent a memo to the SACs in the Washington Field Office confirming that "the Bureau considers the reported unauthorized possession of classified CIA documents by subject to be an administrative matter to be handled by CIA and not one in which we should become involved. Discontinue all action concerning the classified documents. No action is to be taken concerning the alleged Interstate Transportation of Stolen Property violation."[15]

Several days later, there was more clarity concerning the mysterious would-be jewel robbery. On August 9, 1966, at the direction of DCI/Maj. Helms, Slocum, another CIA employee, and Slocum's wife—all of whom who were at Tofte's home when the classified documents in question were retrieved—were polygraphed concerning their involvement in the claimed jewel theft that reportedly occurred simultaneously. The polygraph results indicated that neither CIA employee had any knowledge concerning the reported theft. In an indication of what was to come, a Bureau report dated August 10 contained this assessment—"We are not becoming involved in this case from the standpoint of Interstate Transportation of Stolen Property inasmuch *as there is considerable doubt that the jewels were actually stolen* [emphasis added]." That same day, DCI Helms appointed a commission headed by Admiral Charles Melson, who was tasked with investigating the case, strictly behind closed doors.[16]

On Tuesday morning, August 13, Tofte received a call to appear at Langley the following day for what appeared to be a continuation of the inquiry into his alleged security violation. He had received a letter relieving him of his regular duties and directing him to instead report to DOS Osborn until the Agency's investigation was complete. Tofte instead hand-delivered a letter demanding an explanation for the July 24 "raid" on his home and stating that he had no intentions of submitting "to a secret kangaroo court" until he received some assurance that DCI Helms would answer questions concerning CIA's "illegal" actions in this case. In his letter to DOS Osborn, Tofte reminded him that he had walked out of a board of inquiry meeting the day prior, stating that he would fully cooperate with the Agency as soon as it answered one question—"Has the CIA now stopped entering people's homes illegally, minus a warrant, and without due process of law within the continental limits of the United States of America?"

Besides Tofte, another inveterate critic of CIA also took a personal interest in the case—Senator Joseph McCarthy (D-MN), who asked the Senate Foreign Relations Staff to "follow this up and see what happens." Some six months later, Representative H. R. Gross (R-IA) said that CIA had admitted that it had erred in dispatching its agents to search Tofte's home without a search warrant.[17] According to one account, DCI Helms later told an unspecified congressman that the raid to retrieve the classified documents was a mistake. Tofte had admitted his humiliation at realizing that "my own organization could be so careless, unprofessional and stupid" and asserted that a warrant should have been obtained. As it turned out, one senior CIA figure agreed, saying the raid showed "poor judgment"; another noted that although CIA was "recovering its own property," there were "better ways to have done it."[18]

In response to the press circus which had arisen in the wake of the Tofte case, the internal CIA commission focused on the evidence in the case and was tasked with making recommendations as to whether or not Tofte's employment should be terminated. As far as the Agency was concerned, the publicity tsunami that followed was "ultimate proof of Tofte's unprofessionalism" and one newspaper opined that "one reason the board recommended his ouster was that it was felt the publicity had reduced his value in an undercover profession"; others described CIA's activities in the case as reminiscent of "a nervous elephant beset by a fly." The panel determined that Tofte would be called in on September 14 and told that his employment was being terminated immediately. CIA informed the Bureau of this decision, which prompted the latter to observe, "It is anticipated that Tofte will attempt to fight this termination and that there will be considerable publicity in the newspapers."

An interesting footnote was that DCI Helms had directed that a photograph of Tofte be provided to WFO—"for identification purposes in the event Tofte makes some wild move, such as visiting the Soviet Embassy." As the Bureau noted, Tofte was believed likely only to resort to such a move "in a moment of desperation." The memo added that "there is no evidence that subject will make such a contact, but it is conceivable that he could make such a move following notification of his termination by CIA. In the event you [WFO] develop any information indicating subject attempts to contact or visit the Soviet Embassy, this information should be promptly furnished [to] the Bureau in order that CIA can be notified."[19] Even on his way out the door at

CIA, and more than a decade after he had explained away any such concerns, Tofte's past contacts with suspect communist influences and individuals came back to haunt him.

On October 3, local media reported that, in a twist of fitting irony, the documenting of one alleged security incident had led indirectly to another. The previous Friday, September 30, local news station WTTG (Channel 5, Washington, DC) cameraman John Landi and soundman Gene Gerlach were working on their latest assignment—filming background scenes for a WTTG report on besmirched CIA Officer Hans Tofte. Their film was intended to serve as a background to Tofte's account of being driven to Langley for questioning after offending documents were found in his home in July.

A source at Channel 5 confirmed that the station had informed CIA of the program, scheduled to air in five parts, beginning October 3, at 10:00 p.m. However, as the pair turned off the George Washington Parkway and approached CIA headquarters, Mr. Landi leaned out the window and began taking his film. At this point, a CIA security guard began running from his booth toward the car, yelling, "What are you doing with a camera around here? Don't you know you can't take pictures in here?" Landi reminded the guard that the sign on the metal chain-link fence surrounding Langley warned only that photographs were not to be taken inside the fence. The guard then ordered them to pull inside the gate and remain in the car while he conferred with security. After a 20-minute wait, the guard reappeared and told the pair they were free to leave.[20]

One commentator noted that the entire Tofte incident has "upset the CIA, where it is known that Tofte was one of the high ranking officials on some of the most sensitive special projects in recent years in Africa, Asia, and Central America." He added that Tofte was one of the few to object to the disastrous 1961 Bay of Pigs invasion in Cuba, due to inadequate preparation and poor morale. This reporter also accurately predicted that "although Tofte has lived with danger for more than 25 years, it is unlikely that he ever dealt with anything as explosive as the present controversy, and from long experience the men at the top of CIA know that Hans Tofte is capable of creating great problems for them." In closing his article, the writer noted that the following day, a Monday, Tofte would be meeting with the chief of security at CIA in a conference "that probably will determine whether the Tofte matter is settled quietly or whether it erupts into a major expose of the nation's big spy agency."[21]

Tofte was fired due to the compound effect of "going public" (a board of inquiry assessed that the negative publicity attached to the incident "damaged his future value to the agency"), the documents found at his home in July, and his subsequent $25,000 lawsuit against DCI Helms (as a private individual), CIA Officer Slocum and his wife Judy, an employee of the Air Force Aid Society, and CIA Security Officer Speake. His intent in filing the suit was not only to prove his innocence but also to secure his pension rights after 16 years' service as a senior Agency official. (It would take seven years, but he would eventually prevail and have his full pension restored.)[22] When it became clear that Tofte would not be allowed to speak with his former bosses, he responded, "Now my bosses won't see me, so I decided I'll go to my real bosses, the American people. I'm not just a Government servant, you know, but an American citizen. I've tried the regular way too many times, the official way, and failed. So now, to hell with the house rules." A day later, Tofte addressed his perceived threat to release embarrassing information about the Agency, should his case not come out as planned—which it hadn't. "I'm fed up to the teeth with the Agency," he explained, "but I'm not holding a gun at anyone's throat. I'm not staging a holdup. I just don't want to be squeezed out and disgraced. And I want my wife's jewels back."[23]

A key figure in the unfolding drama and unwelcome media attention was, of course, DCI Helms, a proclaimed friend of Tofte yet named as a party in the lawsuit. In a deposition taken by Tofte's lawyer, DCI Helms stated that "according to my present recollection," the July 24 raid in which the documents in question were taken by CIA security was not reported to him until the following day. In the suit that Tofte filed against DCI Helms, two CIA agents, and the wife of one of them, he claimed that someone also had stolen a personal letter from DCI Helms to him from a private scrapbook at his home and that it also had been taken to headquarters. The Agency initially denied any such letter existed, then later offered Tofte a certified copy of it if he would drop his suit. But in a statement filed in district court in late February 1967, DCI Helms admitted that he had copies of *two* letters he had written Tofte, dated August 23 and September 27, 1955—ironically, one of the two letters in question reportedly encouraged Tofte to remain in the Agency as a career official "in consideration of his outstanding qualifications." In his statement, DCI Helms added that he had never seen the documents taken from Tofte's house in July 1966. Also filed in the court that same day were statements from the Slocums and a deposition claiming that a CIA security officer was "distracting" Tofte's 86-year-old mother-in-law while the Slocums were visiting.[24]

Tofte made no secret of the fact that he firmly believed that the raid on his home and the subsequent disappearance of Marlys's jewelry was a clumsily conducted cover operation to distract attention from retrieving the "offending"

Agency papers. Nor was he the only one who thought so—in mid-November 1966, a German journalist wrote an article for the *Handelsblatt*, a German-language business newspaper, talking at length about the Tofte case. Noting the tarnished reputation of CIA, the article claimed that the Agency was now also in the jewel theft business, "Namely as a 'cover' for a burglary which was concerned with secret papers. This is complicated by the circumstance that the papers stolen by the CIA belonged to it, and by the fact that one of its own officials made the accusation." The journalist also discussed Tofte's background and accomplishments, describing him as:

> An adventurous Dane, who fled before Hitler's march [into Denmark], worked his way into the intelligence service via Singapore, showed great courage in supplying Tito with ammunition and equipment, and after the war carried on honorable business transactions in paper clips and Loose Leaf office records in small US cities such as Mason City, Iowa. Friends that he made there were more than a little surprised when they read in the newspapers who he actually was—the disclosure of his identity as well as of his cover story is only one of the proofs that his accusation, that the CIA is awkwardly clumsy, may not be so completely unjustified. Because in order to defend itself against this accusation, the CIA named two more of its agents and thus compromised them.[25]

Ironically, the Moscow newspaper *Izvestiya* also commented on the case, noting that CIA "has become involved in a regular scandal" and "has been exposed in rather ignoble activities which come under the category of pure crime." Citing reports from Copenhagen, the article charged the Agency with stealing a secret document and simultaneously stealing valuables from the home. The writer described the document as "something like a diary in which Tofte, who is already an ex-agent, described his adventures much too frankly. Judging by everything, Tofte's notes promised a considerable unmasking of the activities of the U.S. intelligence service. Swedish papers hint that, embittered by the actions of his former agent-friends, Tofte will begin to unburden himself and that this will be no small thing."[26] While the Russian media didn't get all the details exactly right, they correctly characterized the case as the scandal it had become.

The whole Tofte imbroglio also prompted CIA to launch another investigation—namely, into prosecuting individuals such as Tofte who chose to openly reveal government secrets to the press. On October 7, 1966, famous—or infamous, depending on one's perspective—Counterintelligence Chief James J. Angleton confidentially advised an FBI liaison agent that CIA officials were actively meeting to explore any and all legal measures to effect this end. He noted that the Agency had its hands tied when attempting to stop former employees from freely discussing Agency business and operations. Angleton added that at the time suggestions had been made to hiring a first-rate lawyer to conduct the "necessary legal research on this thorny problem." The hope was that this research might result in a proposal for new legislation, at which point the Agency would confer with the White House and then attempt to pass legislation in Congress to that effect. Angleton admitted that the chances for such an outcome were slim, but the "CIA feels that a strong effort should be made and at least 'build a plateau' from which they can endeavor to improve on in future sessions of Congress." As a part of this legal research, CIA was seriously considering promoting an interpretation whereby government information would be accepted as government property.[27]

Much like a hand grenade, the Tofte case scattered shrapnel in multiple directions, with impacts on the Agency, its personnel, and its morale and reputation. One example of the collateral damage was Tracy Barnes, chief of the Domestic Operations Division, who, when faced with all the negative publicity that arose, retired soon after Tofte lost his lawsuit and his job.[28] Also, in July 1967, Charles Speake sued the Toftes, reporter Clark Mollenhoff, two newspapers, and DC television station WTTG for libel, asking for $750,000 in damages. In the suit, filed in DC District Court in June 1971, Speake claimed that his reputation and his future with the Agency had been damaged by the previous year's claim that he had participated in the theft of Marlys's missing jewelry. With regard to Mollenhoff, the court concluded:

> Plaintiff [Speake] cannot prove that Mollenhoff knew that the story he was reporting and its implications were false nor can he prove a reckless disregard of whether it was false or not. The record indicates that Mollenhoff received his information from what a reasonable man would consider a reliable source, a CIA agent, Hans Tofte; and this information was corroborated as much as was possible at that time by a press release from the CIA and a check with the Metropolitan Police…The record is clear there was no knowledge on any one's part at that time that the story was false and it is likewise clear that Mollenhoff was not reckless.

Metromedia, Inc., the owner of WTTG Television, did not fare as well—the court noted that their interview of Tofte, broadcasted in four separate segments between October 4 and October 7, 1966, was aired well over a month after the incident, by which time Metromedia knew that Speake had been cleared by a lie detector test, but did not broadcast that fact until its last program.[29]

As biographer Kruger put it, "The affair was a pestilence for the CIA, because in his unbridled anger, Tofte had not only revealed some of the intelligence service's front companies, but also the identity of some of his fellow agents, which was unheard of at this time." Another observer noted that Tofte was "one of the first prominent CIA agents to expose some of the shadowy actions of the intelligence service, and no one else had directly challenged the intelligence service in the same way." Some more laudatory of Tofte made comments like, "James Bond's merits are nothing compared to Tofte's." And what did his recent ex-wife have to say about the case when all was said and done? Marlys simply commented, "He is a true hero who had rendered great services to the country."[30]

After arguably taking more time and attention than was warranted, the "scandal" ended with a settlement in 1967, in which Tofte was guaranteed his pension retroactively. Although the specific rationale for this decision is not immediately apparent, biographer Kruger surmises that it is reasonable to assume that the Agency threatened some sort of reprisal against Tofte's friends who remained in CIA employ. While some regarded him as a hero, a good CIA employee with his head and his heart in the right place, "the majority of the political establishment in Washington and many CIA people saw him as a traitor."[31]

CHAPTER 9

Life After Langley

Once the considerable dust settled in the Tofte affair, DCI Helms used the unwelcome distraction as an excuse to further consolidate his power which, among other things, amounted to ridding himself of Tofte's friend Tracey Barnes. To rub salt in the wound, DCI Helms directed Lyman Fitzgerald, a friend of Barnes and another who did not, in DCI Helms's opinion, show him the proper obeisance, to fire Barnes; Fitzgerald described this as "the most difficult task of his career." Not long thereafter, Fitzgerald died of cardiac arrest while playing tennis on a hot day in July 1967.

There were those who blamed Tofte for their fates—when a writer approached Marlys on this issue, looking for a comment, she refused to speak to him, prompting him to snap, "Hans took them down!" Such a drastic judgment did not help Tofte's depressed mental state, having to get along without both CIA and Marlys—he felt that he was nothing; most of his friends had left him, and he was seldom invited out. Marlys was very worried about him, "not only because of his state of mind, but also because she feared something might happen to him." One day, Marlys met Hans, who introduced her to a man whom he had met only shortly before, but who was a Norwegian military veteran. A few days later, she sought this man out and hired him as a permanent bodyguard for Hans when he went out in the evenings, an arrangement he never knew about.

One positive was that Tofte had always kept a diary—he wrote "well and vividly," according to one account—and now, in his solitary and unexpected retirement, his thoughts turned to writing his autobiography, which he figured would be at least 800 pages in length. This was the reason for Tofte's visits to the National Archives, where he researched World War II records and worked closely with an archivist there. But his good intentions were derailed by an old habit—the "whiskey bottle got in the way time and time again." Instead of pursuing his autobiography, Tofte spent his days talking to journalists and writers, bragging too much about his accomplishments. Marlys, meanwhile, had married Brig. Gen. Chatel in 1967, though the couple were destined to spend only four years together before Brig. Gen. Chatel died of a heart attack in 1971. Even though Marlys was now alone too, she saw Hans only on a friendly basis and had no intention of ever living with him again.[1]

What followed was a substantial exodus, by one means or another, of those whom Tofte had known or worked with in the Agency, a reminder that few things in life make us feel more alone than when we outlive all our friends. His good friend Tracy Barnes suffered cerebral hemorrhages in 1969 and 1970 and died in 1972. And although there is no information to suggest that the two were close, when Bay of Pigs affair planner, long-time covert ops officer, and future Watergate burglar E. Howard Hunt retired from CIA in April 1970, the specter of the Tofte affair arose once again—authorities checked thoroughly to ensure that he was not taking any classified documents with him and he had to sign off that he did not have any others hidden elsewhere. As Richard Nixon's chief of staff, H. R. Haldeman, put it, "We want to avoid another Tofte affair."[2]

Although the widespread publicity of Tofte's firing had transfixed many, at least briefly, his illustrious past remained somewhat hidden. It was not until 1972, for example, that a local author writing of Iowa's past glories penned this entry in his book: "Hans V. Tofte, A(n) International Spy. Former Mason City businessman was disclosed to have been a longtime professional spy with the CIA…He is Hans V. Tofte, who once operated Klipto Loose Leaf Co."[3]

Seven years after Tofte was fired, his case bobbed to the surface again, in somewhat unexpected fashion. In early May 1973, a CIA employee—name and office ID redacted—sent a one-page memo to the executive secretary of the CIA Management Committee but which wound up on the desk of then-DCI William E. Colby. The subject of the memo was what the author considered "potentially embarrassing agency activities," which soon became part of the infamous "Family Jewels" file that laid out a number of gaffes committed by the Agency in the recent past, which suggested to several knowledgeable observers that CIA needed to be kept on a shorter leash. Among the cited "activities," the first was the Tofte case. As the memo's author noted, "The Tofte affair was exposed in public, of course, but the report itself is closely held within the Agency. This office was designated as the custodian of the report, and we have the only surviving copy."[4]

The shocking allegations laid at the feet of CIA, as well as the NSA, FBI, and the IRS, in the mid-1970s attracted the attention of one entity that could implement directive action—the US Congress. In 1975, the nation was transfixed by the Church Committee (formally the United States Senate Select

Committee to Study Governmental Operations with Respect to Intelligence Activities) hearings in the Senate and the parallel Pike Committee hearings in the House of Representatives, both of which highlighted indications of an intelligence apparatus in need of oversight. For the Agency, the upshot of the Church Committee hearings was a report which mandated severe personnel cuts in the Covert Operations Division and imposed a number of restrictions; Tofte was pained to see many of his old colleagues fired as a result. Not even DCI Helms could escape the winnowing fork—he was called home from his ambassadorship in Iran and when it emerged in the hearings that he had withheld information from Congress, the Department of Justice sued him and forced him to resign in 1976.

The cuts continued into the directorship of Stansfield Turner, prompting Tofte to declare in 1978:

> The two events have made my blood boil and made me decide that now I want my old accounts with the CIA settled. I have already sent some harsh letters to Helms and Turner and am currently resuming my contacts with the media so that the matters can be properly covered. My attack on Helms will be framed like this: Now that you've been convicted of being a liar, go all out and publicly admit that you fired me on a whim—and at the same time tell me what you've done about those jewelry [*sic*] that you let your people steal from my wife!" But the anticipated media gunfight never occurred, either because Hans was distracted or, more likely, because the public had moved on by then.[5]

Yet that same year, when CIA was under increasing scrutiny and attack, Tofte—despite his highly publicized dismissal from the Agency—felt compelled to write a letter to *The New York Times*, in which he simply said, "Without the CIA's covert action, America would not be where it is today. The American public owes it a debt of gratitude."[6] By the mid-1970s, Finn had resumed contact with his father, and Hans came to Denmark more often to visit his son, daughter-in-law Helle, and his grandson. A few years later, he also made the acquaintance of a woman who would be his companion in his later years. Hans seemed attracted to women of notoriety and accomplishment, and Caroline Brown was no exception. She was the sixth great-granddaughter of Abijah Gilbert, an early settler of the historic village of Gilbertsville in upstate New York, for whom the village is named. A hamlet of some 400 people, Gilbertsville is the only community in the state wholly listed as a National Register Historic Site.

Caroline's father was Admiral Alfred W. Johnson, who was a veteran of both world wars and had once been the Chief of Naval Intelligence (CNI). He and Caroline's mother, Hannah Harris Johnson, lived in Washington, DC, and Gilbertsville, and thanks to her father's career, she had seen as much of, or perhaps more, of the world than Hans. She graduated from Wellesley

College in 1926, and two years later married Foreign Service Officer James Elwyn Brown, who also had Gilbertsville ties. She and James would be among the last diplomats ousted from Cuba during Fidel Castro's revolution. During World War II, while Hans was aiding the Yugoslav partisans, Caroline was practicing cryptanalysis with the Office of Naval Intelligence (ONI). In 1962, the pair retired to Gilbertsville, where James died the following year, leaving her a widow when she and Hans met. Given their commonalities—including the fact that both were members of the exclusive Sulgrave Club in Washington, DC—Caroline and Hans hit it off, so much so that Caroline invited Hans to come live with her at "Stony Ledge," the home in Gilbertsville that had been in her family for more than a century. The house was large, beautiful, and elegantly furnished, with a park-like garden. But even in such an idyllic setting, with a woman whose company he clearly enjoyed, Hans was still unable to exorcise his demons, and turned to alcohol again to soothe the pain.[7]

"Stony Ledge," the Gilbertsville, New York, home Caroline Brown shared with Tofte in his later years. (Author's collection)

Brigadier General William Donovan, USA, director, OSS. (CIA)

There were, however, occasional moments of pleasant remembrance and celebration. One such occurred on Tuesday evening, September 25, 1979, when the Veterans of the Office of Strategic Services (OSS) convened their annual dinner, held that year in the International Ballroom West at the Washington Hilton hotel in the nation's capital. At each such annual event, the group awarded the William J. Donovan Award to "an individual who has rendered distinguished service in the interests of the United States and the cause of freedom." More specifically, the award was to be made to an individual "who, in his activities, exemplifies the spirit, the tradition and the distinguishing features which characterized General Donovan's career," generally summed-up in the phrase "citizen—soldier—diplomat."

That year, the recipient of the Donovan Award was His Excellency Jacques Chaban-Delmas, who had served as prime minister of France from 1969–72 under Georges Pompidou; of greater relevance and interest to the OSS veterans was that he had been a brigadier general in the French Resistance during World War II—the youngest French general since the late 18th century—and had fought alongside De Gaulle. Tofte was among other luminaries in the intelligence community who served in the somewhat menial role of members of the National Dinner Committee for the event, one among 126 colleagues, who included such CIA figures as James Angleton, William J. Casey, Paul and Julia Child, William Colby, Lyman Kirkpatrick, Jr., Lawrence Houston, DCI Helms, Major General John K. Singlaub, and Tofte's second in Yugoslavia, 1st Lt. Thompson.[8]

In the early 1980s, Hans developed heart problems and in 1985 flew to Denmark to have a pacemaker implanted. Finn picked him up afterwards, but was running late, and found Hans in a lively conversation with a pretty, younger woman holding flowers, who told Finn, "Your father is really incredibly charming!" Tofte had actually bought the flowers for Helle, but typically used them in his "charm offensive" instead—as Kruger put it, "There was still life in the 74-year-old womanizer." Nor was this an isolated incident—while Hans

OSS Memorial, south wall, CIA old headquarters building (OHB). (CIA)

was recovering at Skodsborg Sanatorium following the operation, he met a woman named Elly who fell for him, and with whom he had a good time. In between charming Elly, Hans also found the time to give a series of lectures at the Freedom Museum in Copenhagen. Elly wanted him to stay in Denmark, with her, but he instead returned to Gilbertsville and Caroline. The idea of writing his autobiography resurfaced, and Hans actually contacted a writer in Gilbertsville to get the process rolling; however, by this time, Hans was suffering from poor health, was walking poorly, and aging rapidly.[9]

In spring 1987, Hans wrote to Marlys, as he frequently did, and said he wanted to return to Washington, DC, to be near her, if she would help him find a place to live. Marlys was vacationing on Nantucket Island when Hans called her in August to say he was coming. She returned home to help him—but he never came. He had fallen peacefully asleep at Stony Ledge on the night of August 24, 1987, and died of heart failure in his sleep at age 76, after living a life filled with more excitement than most. He left his son, Finn, and a grandson, Carl Christian, all of Copenhagen. Caroline and her daughter kept much of what Hans had given them; Finn got only one painting, a figurine from China, and a few personal items, but not his father's scrapbook and diaries, which seemed to have disappeared.[10]

His obituary, run in several national and international papers, varied in accuracy and assessment. The primary one, that ran in *The Washington Post*, was balanced and focused on his heroic efforts in World War II and Korea. Others were more caustic, as if their comments had been written by DCI Helms, portraying Tofte as "an inept braggart who had done irreparable damage to CIA with his openness in 1966." Yet Maj. Gen. Donovan and Lt. Cmdr. Wisner both praised him; Tofte's Iowa friend, Brig. Gen. MacNider, had heard Maj. Gen. Donovan say that Tofte had been "one of his very best men in almost all branches of intelligence work during World War II," and that the spy chief "never hid the fact that he considered Tofte one of his best and most-effective agents." And the man who carried Maj. Gen. Donovan's spirit into CIA, Lt. Cmdr. Wisner, appreciated Tofte's "dynamic style and efficiency"—after all, "Why would the CIA continue to put him on big, demanding assignments if he had been incapable?"[11]

***

It is not clear if Tofte knew prior to his passing that he would be, if not immortalized in print, then at least a familiar name to millions of readers throughout the world, thanks to a renowned author. Readers of the late Tom

Clancy's 1984 smash hit, *The Hunt for Red October*, meet the illustrious Dane on page 78, or on "The Sixth Day, Wednesday, 8 December" in Clancy's timeline. Hero Dr. Jack Ryan, the Irish former US Marine and now rising young analyst/operational intelligence officer, is in a meeting in the office of the DCI, former Texas judge Arthur Moore. Also in attendance are Ryan's boss, Vice Admiral James Greer, the deputy director of intelligence (DDI), and Deputy Director of Operations (DDO) Robert Ritter. As Clancy explains Tofte's significance within the novel:

> Judge Moore pulled a cigar from his jacket pocket and lit it, looking past the flame into Ryan's eyes. The judge, everyone said, had been a hell of a field officer in his day. He'd worked with Hans Tofte during the Korean War and had been instrumental in bringing off one of the CIA's legendary missions, the disappearance of a Norwegian ship that had been carrying a cargo of medical personnel and supplies for the Chinese. The loss had delayed a Chinese offensive for several months, savings thousands of American and allied lives. But it had been a bloody operation. All of the Chinese personnel and all of the Norwegian crewmen had vanished. It was a bargain in the simple mathematics of war, but the morality of the mission was another matter. For this reason, or perhaps another, Moore had soon thereafter left government service to become a trial lawyer in his native Texas. His career had been spectacularly successful, and he'd advanced from wealthy courtroom lawyer to distinguished appellate judge. He had been recalled to the CIA three years earlier because of his unique combination of absolute personal integrity and experience in black operations. Judge Moore hid a Harvard law degree and a highly ordered mind behind the façade of a West Texas cowboy, something he had never been but simulated with ease.[12]

While Clancy did not get all of the details of TP-STOLE exactly right, his inclusion of Tofte in his initial—and some would argue best—novel is noteworthy, and it would seem likely that the mythical judge and the actual intelligence officer would have been fast friends.

***

In terms of a legacy, Tofte left probably more skeptics and cynics than friends and defenders. An example of the former is Danish associate professor Kresten Soe Christensen, who reviewed the only extant biography of Tofte—Henrik Kruger's *Den danske krigshelt, der kom til tops i CIA* [*The Danish war hero who rose to the top of the CIA*], published in Denmark in 2005, only in Danish. Christensen was not only critical of Tofte—"His way of life was extravagant and assertive, and the methods ruthless and dirty"—but also of Kruger who, according to the review, based his book on "old interviews, Tofte's lectures, conversations with loved ones, and documents and sources. The consolidation," wrote Christensen, "does not seem to me entirely convincing in terms of truth value"; a wry commentary. He added that "the text is not always convincingly substantiated despite the many notes," which he suggests might be explained by the fact that the book is "more a journalistic than investigative historical work," not surprising given Kruger's other published works, which cover a variety of pop culture topics. Also telling is Christensen's final comment in the review—"Tofte's martial gaze towards the reader on the cover sets the tone of content." Finally, even Christensen failed to comment on the title, which demonstrates the author's ignorance of CIA—while Tofte was, for a time, indeed a CIA senior executive, that hardly translated, then or now, to being at the "top of the CIA."[13]

CHAPTER 10

Looking Through a Glass, Darkly…

In the panoply of 20th-century intelligence officers, how do we characterize Hans Tofte? Does his classified documents imbroglio offset his other career achievements, or would his other flaws have unhinged his career anyway, suggesting that an ignominious end was inevitable?

From the get-go, most of those who had the opportunity to work with Tofte assessed that he had a strong sense of adventure, as evidenced from his seafaring past and continuing interest in the maritime life, strongly suggesting that life as an intelligence officer and operative was, for him, a surprising career choice for a man who had always been a mama's boy. Not surprisingly, Tofte was one among many fans of 007 within CIA—others included Tracy Barnes, Desmond Fitzgerald, DCI Dulles, and DCI Helms. Those of us who fondly remember our James Bond attaché case (and wish we still had it!) can relate, and for Tofte his life closely imitated that of his inspiration—he was a self-defense expert, a military veteran, an intelligence officer, an inveterate womanizer, a man who enjoyed and expected the finer things in life and who was seldom concerned with the cost of such, a stalwart friend to many, a man with the unique ability to please and bedevil his superiors, sometimes simultaneously. One of Tofte's acquaintances surmised that he and Barnes were the most like Bond—Barnes had been stationed in England, and he openly aped the mannerisms of MI6, and Tofte was continental by nature and heavily influenced by his time in London during the war.[1]

Tofte's relationship with women in general was…complicated, a trait he inherited from his father and practiced throughout his life. If a woman were attractive, accomplished, or especially both, Tofte was potentially interested and likely to follow up on that interest. But his "love 'em and leave 'em" philosophy, paired with his unwillingness to have any woman impede his career, meant that the women in his life often paid a high price for the "privilege" of living with him. By her own admission, Marlys was not the jealous sort—otherwise, she likely would have left him years before she actually did. Not one prone to bitterness, she once commented about Hans that "he is a true hero who has rendered great services to the country"[2] and in a 2004 interview, she mused, "Hans was a true hero, and World War II was his time. He should have stopped when it was over. He should never have allowed himself to be lured by CIA. It was the mistake of his life."[3]

As Kruger noted, "His assertiveness, charisma, and flamboyant style earned him both friends and enemies. He was a James Bond type in an intelligence community largely ruled by cold minds and dry bureaucrats, and therefore he had many friends and admirers among the like-minded active agents. But he was at the same time envied and feared by ambitious rivals in the service, and for some of his superiors he was an annoying stone in the shoe."[4] Yet, the same question remained: "Why would the CIA continue to put him on big, demanding assignments if he had been incapable?"[5]

He clearly had a particular talent for paramilitary and intelligence operations, regardless of whatever else could be said about him. Goulden notes that Tofte had a reputation among his peers as "one of the more remarkable operatives of the twentieth century," although another author's reference to Tofte in 1953 as the "head of all American covert operations at the time" is more fanciful than factual.[6] Decorated OSS veteran and future Special Forces Maj. Gen. Singlaub described Tofte as "a really brilliant, suave, and sociable guy with an extensive Asian background."[7]

Certainly, one of Tofte's greatest strengths was that he made friends easily and, at least in some cases, retained those friendships throughout his life. For example, he, Tracy Barnes, and Desmond Fitzgerald were all birds of a feather, all born in 1911, all top athletes as young men, all "made of a very special substance." Much unlike Tofte, Barnes and Fitzgerald had grown up in wealthy homes, both had studied law, and both had practiced law for a few years after the war. So, Tofte fell "a little outside" these parameters—he was not an American and did not have the same academic credentials. But, as Kruger wrote, "still they were brothers in spirit. They were warriors and loved the fight, they were adventurers and competitive people, they were strong, beautiful and wooed like the three musketeers and they were almost immortal. They believed."[8] Little wonder that they would be among his closest friends in life.

When faced with an assault upon his actions and his character—as far as he was concerned—Tofte, not surprisingly, came out swinging. In the words of an experienced reporter, in the wake of the classified documents scandal, "Tofte did what he said was 'the one thing no one had expected.' He went public. He became the spy who came out from the fold to 'fight this stupid, silent, vague, invisible government...' The papers, the jewels, Tofte's challenge of 'the entire outfit to a public showdown'—it all added up to a commando performance, to a guerrilla lunge at the CIA fortress at Langley, VA. Audacious? Unorthodox? Perhaps. But Hans Tofte had always been both."[9] He was "not a man who did things the quiet way. He wasn't afraid to fight back the supremacy, and therefore he was transformed from hero to pariah in the intelligence service."[10] In Kruger's assessment, "Hans would [not] be controlled. His almost extreme willfulness and dislike of authority was both his weakness and his strength."[11]

These negative characteristics came to the fore most prominently during the "apartment to let" fiasco—the fact that Tofte charged that the raid was a conspiracy, plain and simple, rather than a botched administrative procedure, seems overblown, almost to the point of paranoia. His ultimate decision to go public over the incident speaks of desperation and it seems incredibly naïve, especially for a career insider, to believe that when thus challenged, the Agency would not have gone on the offensive.

The messiness and ugliness of the case compromised national security and was a serious blow to the Agency's developing image, especially embarrassing for an entity that was increasingly purporting itself to be the cornerstone of the US intelligence community. It seems clear that the charges of the missing jewelry were likely false, and definitely pathetic, a move borne of desperation and deflection, just as the Agency, FBI, and the Metropolitan Police all charged. Although there were certainly other examples of such behavior in Tofte's life, it was his actions during this career-ending incident that demonstrated his penchant for discarding established policies and procedures in favor of direct action—it was almost as if any action, regardless of the consequences, was better than inaction.

His colleagues at the Agency often referred to him as "the Dynamic Dane," due to his self-will, charisma, and flamboyant style, a man who for 15 years had been considered CIA's leading expert in paramilitary operations. But the last four years of his career had been a "downer," with his being reduced to serving as an instructor for new operatives, foreign police, and anti-communist security forces. As biographer Henrik Kruger assessed, "It made him bitter."[12]

For such a talented individual, the end in terms of a fulfilling life and career came with astonishing suddenness. As one observer has noted:

> For all his distinguished service and incredible wartime feats, things eventually soured for Tofte in civilian life. Like many warriors, he discovered that the skills needed to survive in a wartime environment bear little resemblance to those needed in a peacetime bureaucracy... So ended one of the most distinguished and colorful Cold War intelligence careers. It was a

> great pity that a man who had rendered such long service had been brought down by such an apparently middling transgression, but such are the ways of large organizations. Here we see a theme played out countless times in history: a man of action, perhaps resented by his peers and having worn out his organizational welcome, finding himself given a final push out the door. Men of ability invariably arouse envy among those who prefer to lurk in obscurity behind the comfortable partitions of stifling bureaucracies. So it has always been.[13]

It would be tempting to conclude that Tofte was able to dodge the poor decisions and failures that had beset others, and thereby avoid the mental distress that plagued his colleagues Lt. Cmdr. Wisner and Tracy Barnes; however, if Kruger is to be believed, "Hans Tofte had also had his mental breakdown, but had never expressed moral objections. Perhaps he had them deep down after all, but refused to acknowledge them outwardly."[14] Or perhaps, as a man who always preferred results over protocol, the end justified the means, negating the need for regret.

Epilogue

James J. Angleton—OSS X-2 (Counterespionage) Branch during World War II, spent time in Italy before, during, and after the war; original member of CIA in 1947; Agency liaison with Mossad and Shin Bet, 1951; worked closely with Kim Philby, later uncovered as member of "Cambridge Five" spy ring; 1953, DCI Allen Dulles designates him as head of Counterintelligence Staff, tendency to see spies everywhere borders on paranoia; retired under pressure, 1974; awarded CIA's Distinguished Intelligence Medal, 1975; died of cancer, 1987.

Melvin O. "Benny" Benson—Joined Army 1942, commissioned Jan. 1943, qualified as paratrooper, joined OSS Nov. 1943; engages in espionage, sabotage in Egypt, Yugoslavia, Italy; discharged as captain, 1946; recruited and managed assets in Asia as part of SSU follow-on to OSS; transferred to CIG, then CIA; 1953, ops officer in Europe; 1955, sabotage instructor in US for Agency's Operations Directorate, testing/reporting on new demolition, incendiary devices; trainer of Cuban exiles for Bay of Pigs operation, constructing an explosive charge when materials catch fire, moves them away from other volatile items, badly burned, dies May 1961 from burns; posthumously awarded Intelligence Star by Agency.

Moe Berg—Professional baseball player (15 seasons in Major Leagues); "brainiest guy in baseball," Princeton and Columbia Law School grad., spoke several languages, read 10 newspapers daily; served in OSS during World War II, gathered info on resistance groups in Yugoslavia, interviewed number of German physicists about Reich's nuclear weapons program; 1952, Agency pays him $10,000 for information on Soviet atomic bomb program, but gets nothing in return; died 1972, aged 70, after fall at home.

Richard M. Bissell, Jr.—CIA officer put in charge of U-2 surveillance aircraft program, 1954; integral to development of A-12 follow-on; replaced

Lt. Cmdr. Wisner as deputy director for plans (DDP), 1959; organizer of anti-Castro strategy in Cuba, Bay of Pigs assault, which ultimately fails; left CIA 1962, became head of Institute for Defense Analyses, Pentagon think tank involved in weapons development; later worked for United Technologies and as consultant to Ford Foundation; 1994, died at home in Connecticut at age 84, autobiography *Reflections of a Cold Warrior: From Yalta to the Bay of Pigs* published 1996.

Martin Bormann—During World War II, head of Nazi Party Chancellery, private secretary to Hitler; fled Berlin May 2, 1945, to escape capture by Soviets; likely committed suicide in Berlin, body buried May 8; convicted and sentenced to death *in absentia* as war criminal by International Military Tribunal, Nuremberg, 1945–46; rumors of survival, supposed sightings worldwide, but body identified as his in 1973, confirmed by 1998 DNA tests; remains cremated, scattered over Baltic Sea, 1999.

Josip Broz (Tito)—Leader of Yugoslav partisans (1941–45), with Allied support post 1943; post war, serves as Yugoslav Prime Minister 1944–63, president 1953–80, president for life after 1974, Marshal of Yugoslavia in Yugoslav People's Army; open split with Stalin 1948, policies become increasingly Marxist; cult of personality surrounds him, dies 1980, age 87.

William J. Casey—Head of Secret Intelligence (SI) Branch of OSS during war; post war, business ventures, tax law lecturer, undersecretary of state for economic affairs; returns to private law practice post 1976; campaign manager for Ronald Reagan's presidential run in 1980; serves as DCI, 1981–87; suspected involvement in Iran–Contra controversy, dies of brain tumor, 1987, aged 74.

Claire Lee Chennault—American military aviator, commander of 1st American Volunteer Group (AVG, "Flying Tigers") in China, 1941, incorporated into US Army Air Forces 1942; bitter dispute with China-Burma-India (CBI) ground forces theater commander Gen. Stillwell; post war, created Civil Air Transport (CAT, later CIA asset Air America); diagnosed with lung cancer, 1957, dies July 1958 aged 64, honorary promotion to lieutenant general; inducted into National Aviation Hall of Fame, 1972.

Ray Cline—CIA official, chief Agency analyst during Cuban Missile Crisis; Harvard B.A., M.A., then volunteers for World War II service; first serves as US Navy cryptanalyst, then with OSS, chief of Current Intelligence, 1944–46;

assigned to Operations Division, General Staff, War Department, to write division history, 1946; joined CIA as analyst in 1949, same year he completed his Ph.D. at Harvard; responsible for intelligence on Korea, but failed to foresee North Korean invasion of the South, 1950; 1951–53, attaché, US Embassy, London; 1953–57, CIA desk officer charged with monitoring USSR, PRC, correctly predicted Sino-Soviet split; 1958, station chief in Taiwan; 1962, to Langley as head of Directorate of Intelligence, informs JFK that Soviets have shipped nuclear warheads to Cuba; 1966, disillusioned with LBJ, leaves CIA, becomes advisor to US ambassador in Bonn; 1969, returns to US, President Nixon appoints him as director of the Bureau of Intelligence and Research, State Dept., oversees US intelligence preparation in advance of Yom Kippur War, 1973; same year, left government to become executive director of Center for Strategic and International Studies, Georgetown; died of Alzheimer's at home, 1996, aged 77.

William J. Donovan—Known as "Wild Bill," soldier, lawyer, intelligence officer, diplomat; leader of OSS during World War II, regarded as founder of CIA; believed to be only person awarded Medal of Honor, Distinguished Service Cross, Distinguished Service Medal, and National Security Medal; recruited as prosecutor to assist William Jackson in postwar Nuremberg war crimes trials, but eventually has falling out with him; argues for postwar US domestic intelligence agency but influence declines in wake of FDR's death; 1947, founds OSS Society, which sponsors William J. Donovan Award; Feb. 1947, President Truman asks Congress to approve plans for a Central Intelligence Agency along lines Maj. Gen. Donovan proposed; wanted to lead CIA, but job given to others; 1953, accepted post as ambassador to Thailand but resigns following year; hospitalized with dementia, 1957, dies from disease, 1959, aged 76; member of Military Intelligence Hall of Fame, statue in lobby at CIA headquarters, Langley.

Allen Dulles—Lawyer recruited into OSS by Maj. Gen. Donovan, moves to Bern, Switzerland, 1941, remains based there for rest of war; maintains close contact with anti-Nazi Germans, Austrian resistance movement, involved in Operation *Sunrise*, the partial surrender of Nazi forces in northern Italy; he and brother John Foster serve as advisers to 1948 Thomas E. Dewey presidential campaign; chosen as deputy director of plans by new DCI Smith, then becomes DDCI; becomes DCI, 1952, first civilian DCI, longest-serving to date; involved in regime change in Iran, Guatemala, Cuba, though failure of Bay of Pigs and other campaigns prompts President Kennedy to compel his resignation; member of the Warren Commission, investigating JFK assassination; published *The Craft of Intelligence*, 1963; died of influenza, complicated by pneumonia, 1969, aged 75.

William Ewart Fairbairn—British soldier and police officer, developed hand-to-hand fighting techniques for Shanghai police pre-World War II; early in war, recruited by Britain's Special Operations Executive (SOE) as Army lieutenant, trained British, American, Canadian, and Dutch commandos, as well as US Army Rangers, OSS personnel; co-developer of Fairbairn-Sykes fighting knife; eventually promoted to lieutenant colonel; continued training of police officers, in Cyprus and Singapore, post war; died 1960, aged 75.

Dr. Sidney Gottlieb—American chemist and intelligence officer who began working for CIA, 1951, hired by then-DDP Dulles on recommendation of founder of Fort Detrick, MD, biological warfare program; charged with revitalizing Project BLUEBIRD, use of drugs initially on prisoners, to aid in interrogation; later renamed Project ARTICHOKE; as DCI, Dulles approves more ambitious and sweeping "brain washing" program, MK-ULTRA; researched LSD as chemical agent, took some himself, gave some to Army bacteriologist Frank Olson, resulting in the latter's suicide; as part of CIA plan, developed several means of assassinating Cuban dictator Fidel Castro, also targets politician Patrice Lumumba, in Congo; retired from CIA, 1973, believed his work ineffective; received Distinguished Intelligence Medal, 1973; died 1999, aged 80, at his home in Washington, VA, had heart problems, though wife would not disclose cause of death.

Albert R. Haney—US Army officer who spent most of his career as CIA analyst; military career started 1941, Army CI officer in Panama; CIA station chief in Seoul during Korean War, 1952; military attaché in Ecuador, Peru, Chile; deputy chief, Composite Plans Group, US Army European Command; retired 1972, received Distinguished Intelligence Medal; died 1998, aged 83, following heart attack, buried with full military honors, Arlington National Cemetery.

Richard Helms—Career intelligence officer, recruited to OSS from Navy during World War II; postwar Germany, working for Allen Dulles, Lt. Cmdr. Wisner in OSS follow-on Strategic Services Unit (SSU), then Office of Special Operations (OSO), incorporated into CIA, 1947; Helms serves as Lt. Cmdr. Wisner's deputy in Directorate of Plans; as DCI, Dulles chooses Bissell as new deputy director of plans (DDP), vice Helms, once Lt. Cmdr. Wisner resigns; Helms becomes DDP once John McCone becomes DCI; Helms involved in attempts to assassinate Castro, responds to charges against CIA made by Warren Commission; DCI, 1966–73, faces challenges of Vietnam War, war in Laos, Israeli Six-Day War; favored in LBJ administration, but influence lost to Kissinger once President Nixon elected, forced to resign post Nixon victory; becomes US ambassador to Iran, but resigns 1977; awarded National Security Medal by President Reagan, 1983; died of multiple myeloma, 2002, aged 89, interred in Arlington National Cemetery.

Henrik Kauffmann—Danish career diplomat, served in Italy, China, Norway early in his career; 1941, signed treaty with United States, latter pledged to defend Greenland from German aggression; for his actions, dubbed "King of Greenland," charged with treason, stripped of rank, but ignores both actions; once Denmark liberated in May 1945, sentence revoked by Danish Parliament, agreement legal basis for US Thule Air Base in Greenland; 1963, aged 75, suffering from prostate cancer, wife commits "mercy killing," then commits suicide.

Joseph Caldwell (J. C.) King—Military officer, intelligence officer, graduated from US Military Academy, West Point, 1923, but resigned commission following year; enrolled in diplomatic course in Paris, went to work for father's mining company in Mexico; vice president at father's chemical business, then vice president at Johnson & Johnson for Brazil, Argentina; joined Nelson Rockefeller's Office of Coordinator of Inter-American Affairs; stationed in Argentina 1941–45, fed disinformation to Japanese agents there, awarded Legion of Merit; promoted to colonel, US Army Reserve; CIA Western Hemisphere Division chief in 1950s, 1960s; retired from CIA, 1967, came back as consultant, CEO of Amazon Natural Drug Company, known CIA front; developed Parkinson's disease, died 1977, aged 76, he and his third wife buried in cemetery at West Point.

Lyman Kirkpatrick—US intelligence officer, academic, author; worked in Coordinator of Information (COI, later OSS) Office, 1942, served as London-based liaison to Allied intelligence agencies; 1943, as lieutenant, served as intelligence briefing officer for General Omar Bradley, remains in post throughout war; joins CIA, 1947, on upwardly mobile track until contracts polio while on Agency business trip to Asia, 1952; paralyzed from waist down, wheelchair-bound rest of his life; selected by DCI Dulles as

CIA inspector general, post he holds until 1961; chairman of group studying US foreign intelligence efforts, results in creation of Defense Intelligence Agency, 1961; following year, DCI McCone names him executive director of CIA; 1965, leaves CIA to become professor of political science at Brown University; wrote several books, retired from Brown, 1982; moved to Middleburg, VA, 1983; died at home, 1995.

Vincent R. Kramer—Rutgers graduate and football star, recruited by several NFL teams, but attends OCS instead, commissioned as USMC lieutenant; wounded at Guadalcanal, 1942; spent rest of war training guerrillas for Chiang Kai-Shek; post war, volunteered for CIA assignment in Taiwan; paramilitary operations chief during Korean War, developed escape-and-evasion plan for downed airmen; he and small CIA team trained North Korean guerrillas at Atsugi Air Base, Japan; July, 1951, led 100 of his guerrillas in intelligence-gathering and sabotage mission, awarded Navy Cross; guerrilla warfare advisor to French Foreign Legion in Indochina, 1952; CIA officer in Berlin prior to returning to Vietnam, served as advisor to General William Westmoreland; retired as colonel, to New Jersey, director of Rutgers Alumni Association until 1987; died 2001, aged 83, buried in Arlington National Cemetery.

Turner H. McBaine—San Francisco corporate lawyer for nearly three decades; graduated Phi Beta Kappa from University of California, Berkeley, Rhodes Scholar at Oxford; commander of Naval ROTC unit at UC Berkeley; US Navy, 1941–45, recruited into OSS, first as assistant to William Donovan, then in Mideast Theater, rises to lieutenant commander, awarded Legion of Merit, Order of the British Empire; attorney at Pillsbury, Madison & Sutro, San Francisco, 1947–77; trustee for World Affairs Council of Northern California, 1948–54; trustee founder of The Asia Foundation, non-profit international development organization; general counsel for Standard Oil of California (which later became Chevron), 1970–76; retired 1977, died 1992, aged 81.

Dragoljub "Draza" Mihailovic—Yugoslav Serb general in World War II, leader of the royalist and nationalist guerrilla element, the Chetniks; early in World War II, fought with Tito and supporters against Germans, but by 1941, strategy, ideology, general mistrust drove them apart; Allies opt to support Tito vice Mihailovic; captured March 1946, tried and convicted of high treason and war crimes, executed by firing squad, July 1946; verdict overturned on appeal by Serbian Supreme Court, 2015.

Dr. Robert Oppenheimer—American theoretical physicist, director of Manhattan Project's Los Alamos Lab during World War II, considered "father of the atomic bomb"; 1947, became director of Institute of Advanced Study, Princeton, New Jersey, and chair of General Advisory Committee of new US Atomic Energy Commission; advocate of international control of atomic weapons; opposed to development of hydrogen bomb, stances increasingly alienate him from US government and military communities; past connections with US Communist Party prompt revocation of his security clearance following 1954 investigation, brings end to his career as a nuclear physicist; legacy eventually restored, presented with Enrico Fermi Award, 1963; died of throat cancer, 1967, aged 62; 2022, federal government vacated 1954 revocation of his security clearance.

Howard J. Osborn—CIA director of security; high school classmate of Watergate burglar E. Howard Hunt in New York; attended University of Michigan, graduated from Virginia Tech; commissioned as Army lieutenant, 1941, served five years, discharged as major, 1946; CIA employee 1947–74, director of security 1964–74; went on sick leave and retired, forced to resign because he kept documents from FBI and Watergate Congressional Committee; died 1984, aged 66, lung cancer, interred in Arlington National Cemetery.

Matthew Ridgway—Served as assistant commander and commander 82nd Airborne Division during World War II; becomes Eighth Army commander, 1950, promoted to full general following 1950 relief of Gen. MacArthur as supreme commander Allied powers (SCAP); supreme commander in Europe, 1952–53; Army chief of staff, 1953–55; credited with restoring morale, going on offensive in Korean War; urged President Eisenhower to refrain from military involvement to save French in Indochina, thereby delaying US involvement in Vietnam by a decade; retired 1955, becomes author, public speaker, board member at Mellon Institute, Gulf Oil; awarded Presidential Medal of Freedom, 1986; died 1993, aged 98.

William Stephenson—Canadian soldier, fighter pilot, businessman, spymaster; senior representative of British Security Coordination (BSC) for Western Allies during World War II; wartime code name may have been "Intrepid," per author Ian Fleming, model for James Bond; conduit for wartime intelligence between FDR, Churchill; arrived in US, June 1940, BSC office in New York operates as admin center for MI6, SOE; suggests to FDR that Maj. Gen. Donovan be put in charge of all US intelligence services; set up Camp X, aka Secret Training School No. 103, Whitby, Ontario, to train British, Canadian, US covert operations personnel; knighted by King George VI, 1945; awarded Medal of Merit by President Truman, 1946, highest US civilian award at time; died 1989, aged 92, at his home in Bermuda.

Joseph "Vinegar Joe" Stillwell—US Military Academy graduate, class of 1904; US Army general, served in China-Burma-India Theater during World War II; appointed chief of staff of Chinese Nationalist Army by Chiang Kai-Shek; friction with Chiang and with Gen. Chennault over air war in China results in Gen. Stillwell being ousted; promoted to full general, 1944, but recalled by FDR, US aid to Nationalist China soon ends; died 1946, aged 63, still on active duty, after surgery for stomach cancer; cremated, ashes scattered over the Pacific.

Whitey Willauer—Lawyer who, along with Gen. Chennault, founded Civil Air Transport, 1946; CAT sold to CIA, 1950, Willauer resigned, 1954; US ambassador to Honduras, 1954–58, charged with assisting anti-Arbenz forces in Guatemala during 1954 coup; US Ambassador to Costa Rica, 1958–61; retired 1961, died 1962, aged 55.

Charles Willoughby—German-born US Army recruit and officer who served as Gen. MacArthur's chief intelligence officer (G-2) throughout World War II and in Korean War, until Gen. MacArthur relieved by President Truman; Willoughby retires after 40 years in Army, becomes champion of far-right political causes, supporter of Sen. Joseph McCarthy; stalwart defender of Gen. MacArthur personally and keeper of the "MacArthur myth"; called for an American "Foreign Legion," inveterate critic of NATO; died 1972, aged 80, buried Arlington National Cemetery.

Endnotes

Introduction

1 Henrik Kruger, *Hans V. Tofte—The Danish War Hero Who Rose to the Top of the CIA*, Google eBook translation (Copenhagen: Henrik Kruger and Lindhart and Ringhof Forlag, 2005), 5.

Chapter 1: A Danish Boy

1 "COL Hans V. Tofte," Find a Grave, https://www.findagrave.com/memorial/239043478/hans-v-tofte; "Hans Vilhelm Tofte," FamilySearch, https://ancestors.familysearch.org/en/L83M-VP4/hans-vilhelm-tofte-1911-1987.

2 Kruger, *Hans V. Tofte*, 8–9.

3 Ibid., 9–10; Joseph C. Goulden, *Korea, The Untold Story of the War* (New York: Times Books, 1982), 464; "Alien's Personal History and Statement," September 17, 1942, Entry #A1 224: Personnel Files of the Office of Strategic Services, 1942–62, Container 780, RG 226, Records of the Office of Strategic Services, Archives II, College Park, MD.

4 Kruger, *Hans V. Tofte*, 10–11; Resume, Hans V. Tofte, October 1977, Archive 15B-20393_1_1, Frihedmuseet (Museum of Danish Resistance), Copenhagen, Denmark, https://en.natmus.dk/museums-and-palaces/the-museum-of-danish-resistance, hereinafter FHM.

5 Goulden, *Korea*, 464; Kruger, *Hans V. Tofte*, 11–12; Annie Jacobsen, *Surprise, Kill, Vanish: The Secret History of Paramilitary Armies, Operators, and Assassins* (New York: Back Bay Books, 2019), 40; Richard Pearson, "Hans V. Tofte," obituary, *The Washington Post*, August 30, 1987; Clark Mollenhoff, "Hans Tofte—Superspy Caught in the Middle of a CIA Furor," *Minneapolis Tribune*, August 7, 1966; The East Asiatic Company dated to 1897 and was founded by Danish sea captain, H. N. Andersen, who, by that date, had already been involved in the teak trade with Thailand for 13 years. In the coming decades, the company flourished, becoming the leading enterprise listed on the Copenhagen Stock Exchange. As of the late 1920s, just prior to Tofte's being hired, the EAC had over 20,000 employees working on six continents to develop world trade. See https://eacfoundation.dk/en/the-each-history-eng/.

6 Kruger, *Hans V. Tofte*, 11–12.

7 Ibid., 13.

Chapter 2: The "Dynamic Dane" in World War II

1 The Second Schleswig War—among other names—lasted from February–August 1864, and was fought over the oft-disputed area known as Schleswig-Holstein. Denmark was compelled to cede most of the territory to Prussia and Austria.

2 Gavin Musynske, "Danish Citizens Resist the Nazis, 1940–1945," Global Nonviolent Action Database Case Study, Swarthmore College, 2009, https://nvdatabase.swarthmore.edu/content/danish-citizens-resist-nazis-1940-1945.
3 Kruger, *Hans V. Tofte*, 15; Folder, "TOFTE, Hans V., Capt. (Army)," Container 780, RG 226, National Archives II, 1.
4 Resume, Hans V. Tofte, compiled at The Army and Navy Club, October 1977, Archive 15B-20393_1_1, FHM; Kruger, *Hans V. Tofte*, 16.
5 Kruger, *Hans V. Tofte*, 13, 18; Gerald Schwab, *OSS Agents in Hitler's Heartland: Destination Innsbruck* (Austria: Greenwood Publishing Group, 1996), 33; Archive 15B-15516_1, FHM; Hun Ping, "The Espionage Training School in Our Backyard," *The Hunter: Location Scouting in Singapore's Filmic History* (blog), https://sgfilmhunter.wordpress.com/tag/101-special-training-school.
6 Archive 15B-15516_1, FHM.
7 Diary, Erik Nyholm, December 8, 1941, Archive 15B-15516_1, FHM.
8 The negative legacy of British colonialism meant that British military in uniform were unwelcome in the Far East at the time, especially in China.
9 Diary, Erik Nyholm, December 12, 1941, and January 5, 1942, Archive 15B-15516_1, FHM; Hun Ping, "The Espionage Training School in Our Backyard"; "Alien's Personal History and Statement," September 17, 1942, RG 226, National Archives II.
10 "Alien's Personal History and Statement," September 17, 1942, RG 226, National Archives II.
11 Kruger, *Hans V. Tofte*, 17; Archive 15B-15516_1, FHM; Maochun Yu, "'In God We Trusted, in China We Busted': The China Commando Group of the Special Operations Executive (SOE)", Abstract, *Intelligence and National Security*, Volume 16, Issue 4, 2001, 37–60.
12 "Explosive Devices," The LRDG, Long Range Desert Group, https://lrdg.hegewisch.net/bombs.html; Kruger, *Hans V. Tofte*, 19; Archive 15B-15516_1, FHM.
13 Kruger, *Hans V. Tofte*, 23–24.
14 Ibid., 24–25.
15 Kruger, *Hans V. Tofte*, 28–29; "The Position of the 'China Commando Group' Per Febr. 20th, 1942," Archive 15B-15516_1, FHM.
16 Eric Nyholm to Sir John Keswick, March 19, 1942, Archive 15B-15516_1, FHM.
17 Sir John Keswick to Eric Nyholm, April 15, 1942, Archive 15B-15516_1, FHM.
18 Review of *The Rice Paddy Navy: U.S. Sailors Undercover in China*, by Linda Kush, *World War II History*, August 2013, 66; Kruger, *Hans V. Tofte*, 30–31; Folder, "TOFTE, Hans V., Capt. (Army)," Container 780, National Archives II, 1; Yu, "'In God We Trusted, in China We Busted'."
19 Francis Russell, The Secret War (Alexandria, VA: Time-Life Books, 1981), 101–2; Special Operations Brochure, Folder 3, Box 135, RG 226, National Archives II.
20 Ibid.
21 William J. Casey, "The Clandestine War in Europe (1942–1945)" (remarks on receipt of the William J. Donovan Award at Dinner of Veterans of O.S.S., December 5, 1974), CIA archives, 5.
22 "Office of Strategic Services," US National Park Service, https://www.nps.gov/articles/office-of-strategic-services.htm; Russell, *The Secret War*, 100–1.
23 Special Operations Brochure, Folder 3, Box 135, RG 226, National Archives II; Russell, *The Secret War*, 100.
24 "Operational Groups," The OSS Primer, https://www.soc.mil/OSS/operational-groups.html. The current embodiment of the Operational Groups is found in the Operational Detachments Alpha (ODA) of Special Forces.

25 Goulden, *Korea*, 465; Duncan Bare and Siegfried Beer, University of Graz, "Building a Presence Along the Danube: A Fresh Look at OSS and SSU Austria in 1945 and 1946," *Journal of Austrian-American History*, Vol. 5, 2021, 130 n.; "The Intrepid Life of Sir William Stephenson," Stories, February 5, 2015, https://www.cia.gov/stories/story/the-intrepid-life-of-sir-william-stephenson; "Hans V. Tofte," AncientFaces, https://www.ancientfaces.com/person/hans-v-tofte-birth-1911-death-1987/16211364; Archive 15B-15516_1, FHM; John Ranelagh, *The Agency: The Rise and Decline of the CIA* (New York: Simon and Schuster, 1986), 217; Russell, *The Secret War*, 100; Authorization for Withholding of Pay, Entry #A1 224: Personnel Files of the Office of Strategic Services, 1942–62, Container 780, RG 226, Records of the Office of Strategic Services, National Archives II, College Park, MD.; Alien's Personal History and Statement, September 17, 1942, Entry #A1 224: Personnel Files of the Office of Strategic Services, 1942–62, Container 780, RG 226, Records of the Office of Strategic Services, National Archives II, College Park, MD; N. F. Allman to Major Bruce, Memorandum, December 23, 1942, Subj: Hans Vilhelm Tofte, Box 33, COI/OSS Central Files, RG 226, National Archives II; Hans V. Tofte to Mr. Howland, February 1, 1943, Box 33, COI/OSS Central Files, RG 226, National Archives II; Kenneth Baker to Major Otto C. Doering, Memorandum, February 18, 1943, Subj: Interpretation of General Order No. 12 (For the Attention of the Executive Committee), Box 33, COI/OSS Central Files, RG 226, National Archives II.

26 Kruger, *Hans V. Tofte*, 32–34; Review of *Sisterhood of Spies: The Women of OSS*, by Elizabeth P. McIntosh, *The New York Times* book review, May 31, 1998, https://archive.nytimes.com/www.nytimes.com/books.

27 Jacobsen, *Surprise, Kill, Vanish*, 40; Daniel Emilio Rojas, "Trans-Pacific Connections, World Hegemony and Asymmetric Warfare in 1950," *Le Recueil Ouvert—Projet Épopée, L'Ouvrir Litt & Arts*, 2019, 16; "Office of Strategic Services," National Park Service. Bill Casey began his intelligence career in the OSS as the chief of espionage operations in the European Theater and coordinated the deployment of 100 Allied paratrooper teams into occupied Germany in 1945. President Ronald Reagan selected Casey to be DCI in 1981. See the CIA museum site at https://www.cia.gov/legacy/museum/artifact/bust-of-william-j-casey for further information. Born in 1902, Aaron Bank joined the Army shortly after the Pearl Harbor attack, at the age of 39, his past as a lifeguard belying concerns about his age and physical prowess. He recruited partisans to fight the Nazis during World War II, led an abortive effort to assassinate Adolf Hitler had the latter attempted to flee Berlin, and mistakenly supported Vietnamese guerrilla Ho Chi Minh in the early postwar period. The irregular warfare force he called for become a reality in 1952, with the creation of the US Army Special Forces, aka the Green Berets. Banks retired as a colonel in 1958 and moved to California where, dismayed by the poor security at nuclear power plants, he worked with the *Bulletin of Atomic Scientists* to improve conditions. He died in 2004, at the age of 101. See Nicholas Slayton, "Meet the legendary 'father of Special Forces' who helped establish the Green Berets," *Task & Purpose*, June 19, 2022, https://taskandpurpose.com/news/meet-the-legendary-father-of-the-green-berets.

28 Archive 15B-20393_1_3, FHM.

29 Kruger, *Hans V. Tofte*, 37.

30 Ibid., 33, 37; "Niels Bohr," Wikipedia: The Free Encyclopedia, https://en.wikipedia.org/wiki/Niels_Bohr.

31 Folder, "TOFTE, Hans V., Capt. (Army)," Container 780, National Archives II, 1; Cabot Coville, Department of State, Washington, DC, to Officer Procurement Division, War Department, Washington, DC, February 22, 1943, Archive 15B-20393_1_3, FHM; Colonel William Mayer to Officer Procurement Division, War Department, Washington,

DC, February 20, 1943, Subject: Letter of recommendation for Mr. Hans V. Tofte, Archive 15B-20393_1_3, FHM.

32 Colonel J. M. McHugh, USMC, American Embassy, Chungking, Recommendation, February 22, 1943, Archive 15B-15516_1, FHM; "James M. McHugh papers, 1930–1965," Division of Rare and Manuscript Collection, Cornell University Library, https://rmc.library.cornell.edu/EAD/htmldocs/RMM02770.html.

33 Lt. Col. Baker to Commander of Troops, Headquarters and Headquarters Detachment, Memorandum, May 11, 1943, Box 33, COI/OSS Central Files, RG 226, National Archives II; Major Lovell to General Donovan, May 18, 1943, Memorandum, Subj: Area F Training, Box 33, COI/OSS Central Files, RG 226, National Archives II; Recruitment officer Michael Iverson to Hans Tofte, Esq., March 12, 1943, acknowledging Tofte's efforts in the Far East, Archive 15B-12197, FHM.

34 "Honorable Discharge, Hans V. Tofte, 32801604, Sergeant, Headquarters & Headquarters Detachment, Office of Strategic Services, Washington, D.C., 14 June 1943," Archive 15B-20393_1_3, FHM, and "Temporary Appointment, Sgt. Hans Vilhelm Tofte, AUS (Temp. Appointed Capt. AUS), 14 June 1943," Archive 15B-20393_1_3, FHM.

35 Folder, "TOFTE, Hans V., Capt. (Army)," Container 780, National Archives II, 1; Major Philip G. Lovell to Colonel Ellery C. Huntington, Jr., Memorandum, Subj: Operational Groups – Training, June 21, 1943, Box 33, COI/OSS Central Files, RG 226, National Archives II; Memo from Major Lovell to Col. Huntington, Memorandum, Subj: Commander Woolley's Report on Hans Tofte, June 16, 1943, Box 33, COI/OSS Central Files, RG 226, National Archives II; Lt. Col. Kenneth H. Baker to Colonel E. C. Huntington, Jr., Memorandum, Subj: Training Branch Personnel in OG Training, June 24, 1943, Box 33, COI/OSS Central Files, RG 226, National Archives II, paragraph 2.

36 Schwab, *OSS Agents in Hitler's Heartland*, 33; "W. E. Fairbairn and the Birth of Modern Gunfighting (Part 2)," *Firearms News*, October 27, 2021, https://www.firearmsnews.com/editorial/fairbairn-birth-of-modern-gunfighting/453403; Kruger, *Hans V. Tofte*, 29, 33–35, 38–39; 99th Infantry Battalion Educational Foundation, https://www.99battalion.org; "Camp Hale," Wikipedia: The Free Encyclopedia, https://en.wikipedia.org/wiki/Camp_Hale; "99th Infantry Battalion (United States)," Wikipedia: The Free Encyclopedia, https://en.wikipedia.org/wiki/99th_Infantry_Battalion_(United_States); Folder, "TOFTE, HANS VILHELM, 0525313," RG 226, Entry #A1 224: Personnel Files of the Office of Strategic Services, 1942–62, Container #780, National Archives II, College Park, MD.

Camp Hale, Colorado, opened on August 15, 1942 as an Army training facility and by 1943 there were 10,000 soldiers in residence. The facility also served as a POW camp for 400 hardcore members of Field Marshal Erwin Rommel's *Afrika Korps*. Between 1958–63, the CIA trained Tibetans at the camp, which was dismantled in 1965 and the land donated to the US Forest Service. In 1962, Pete Siebert, who had trained at the camp and had bought property nearby, founded the Vail Ski Resort. As a small, elite unit, the 99th drew much attention—it was inspected by President Roosevelt and, had a battle for Norway occurred later in the war, was intended to serve as a security force for the royal family and the government. After the war, King Haakon VII made the unit his honorary guard force. The battalion remained in the Oslo area until October 1945, when it returned to the United States. To date, it is the only US Army unit with a pure Norwegian history. NORSOG members were originally intended for action in Norway, but by 1944 were being used instead behind enemy lines in France; by early 1945, the unit was engaged in railway sabotage in Norway, where it remained until liberation. For more information, see Bruce H. Heimark, *The OSS Norwegian Special Operations Group in World War II*.

Chapter 3: Yugoslavia and Operation *Audrey*

1 Folder, "TOFTE, HANS VILHELM, 0525313," RG 226, Entry #A1 224: Personnel Files of the Office of Strategic Services, 1942–62, Container #780, National Archives II, College Park, MD; "OSE on Tito's Lines," *Failed OSS / OSE Ops in WWII* (blog), https://failedossops.blogspot.com/202/02/yugoslavia-oss-soe-1944.html; Kruger, 39.

2 "OSE on Tito's Lines," *Failed OSS / OSE Ops in WWII* (blog); Kruger, 40.

3 Ibid.

4 "OSE on Tito's Lines," *Failed OSS / OSE Ops in WWII* (blog).

5 Kruger, *Hans V. Tofte*, 41–42.

6 Ibid., 43; Kirk Ford, Jr., *OSS and the Yugoslav Resistance, 1943–1945* (College Station: Texas A&M University Press, 1992), 24; Goulden, *Korea*, 465.

7 Ibid.; Walter R. Roberts, *Tito, Mihailovic, and the Allies, 1941–1945* (Durham, NC: Duke University Press, 1994), 148; Joseph J. Jakub III, *Spies and Saboteurs: Anglo-American Collaboration and Rivalry in Human Intelligence Collection and Special Operations, 1940–1945* (New York: Springer, 1999), 133–34; R. Harris Smith, *OSS: The Secret History of America's First Central Intelligence Agency* (Berkeley: University of California Press, 1972), 145.

8 Ford, Jr., *OSS and the Yugoslav Resistance*, 26; F. N. Arnoldy, "Activities, Yugoslav Section, S.I. in Bari, Italy—From October 30, 1943 to July 12, 1944," Folder 4, Box 50, RG 226, National Archives II, 3; Kruger, *Hans V. Tofte*, 45–46; Military Record and Report of Separation, March 30, 1946, Archive 15B-20393_1_3, FHM.

9 Jakub, *Spies and Saboteurs*, 133–34; F. N. Arnoldy, "Activities, Yugoslav Section, S.I. in Bari, Italy—From October 30, 1943 to July 12, 1944," Folder 4, Box 50, RG 226, National Archives II, 9; Folder, "TOFTE, Hans V., Capt. (Army)," Container 780, RG 226, National Archives II, 2; Smith, *OSS*, 145–46; Kruger, *Hans V. Tofte*, 44, 47; "Partisan Supply Operation, September 1943–January 1944, Office of Strategic Services," Combined Arms Research Library, US Army Command and General Staff College, Ft. Leavenworth, KS; Ford, Jr.; *OSS and the Yugoslav Resistance*, 26; Hans V. Tofte to Dep. Dir., SSO, "Report of Shipping Operations from Italy to Yugoslavia, 15 Oct–31 Dec 1943," April 1, 1944, Box 33, COI/OSS Central Files, RG 226, National Archives II, 12.

10 Goulden, *Korea*, 465; Folder, "TOFTE, Hans V., Capt. (Army)," Container 780, RG 226, National Archives II, 2–3; Kruger, *Hans V. Tofte*, 49–50; Hans V. Tofte to Dep. Dir., SSO, "Report of Shipping Operations from Italy to Yugoslavia, 15 Oct–31 Dec 1943," Box 33, COI/OSS Central Files, National Archives II, 2.

11 Brig. Gen. F. H. R. McLean, Commanding Officer, Allied Military Mission to Partisan Forces, "The Partisan Movement in Yugoslavia," November 12, 1943, Folder 3, Box 43, RG 226, National Archives II, 1–2, 4.

12 Kruger, *Hans V. Tofte*, 50–51.

13 Folder, "TOFTE, Hans V., Capt. (Army)," Container 780, RG 226, National Archives II, 3.

14 Lt. Cmdr. Morgan Giles, Royal Navy, to Capt. Hans Tofte, USA, Message, December 2, 1943, Container 780, RG 226, National Archives II.

15 "World War II: German Raid on Bari," Historynet, www.historynet.com/world-war-ii-german-raid-on-bari; Lt. Cmdr. Morgan Giles, Royal Navy, to Capt. Hans Tofte, USA, Message, December 2, 1943, 3–4.

16 Special Forces Roll of Honour, www.specialforcesroh.com; Ford, Jr., *OSS and the Yugoslav Resistance*, 26, 28; *Aero Digest*, Vol. 52, 150; OSS Personnel Files, Entry 224, RG 226, Records of the OSS, National Archives II; Kruger, *Hans V. Tofte*, 48.

17 Narrative of Lt. John Hamilton, USMCR, November 2, 1944, Box 108, RG 226, National Archives II, 3–4; Kruger, *Hans V. Tofte*, 48.
18 Kruger, *Hans V. Tofte*, 49; "Liaison with Tito and Operations in Yugoslavia, Capt. M.O. Benson, OSS-SO," Folder 4, Box 50, RG 226, National Archives II, 38.
19 Narrative of Lt. John Hamilton, 4; Kruger, *Hans V. Tofte*, 52.
20 Kruger, *Hans V. Tofte*, 53.
21 Ibid., 55.
22 Tim Wilding, review of *Prinz Eugen: The Story of the 7.SS-Freiwilligen-Gebirgs-Division 1942–1945*, by Bohumir Kudlicka and Radoslaw Szewczyk, IPMS/USA Reviews, https://reviews.ipmsusa.org/review/Prinz-Eugen-The-Story-of-the-7-SS-Freiwilligen-Gebirgs-Division-1942-1945/; Kruger, *Hans V. Tofte*, 56–57.
23 Kruger, *Hans V. Tofte*, 59.
24 Narrative of Lt. John Hamilton, 5; Kruger, *Hans V. Tofte*, 58.
25 Hans V. Tofte to Dep. Dir, SSO, "Report of Shipping Operations from Italy to Yugoslavia, 15 Oct–31 Dec 1943," Box 33, COI/OSS Central Files, RG 226, National Archives II, 3–4, 22.
26 "Occupation and Resistance on Hvar During WWII: The Jelsa Raid," Total Croatia News, accessed December 8, 2023, https://total-croatia-news.com/destinations/destinations-hvar/blog-hvar/hvar-news/occupation-and-resistance-on-hvar-during-wwii-the-jelsa-raid; Kruger, *Hans V. Tofte*, 58, 60.
27 Hans V. Tofte to Director of Strategic Services, Report, Subj: OSS Shipping Operations from 9 October 1943 to 1 Jan 1944, January 2, 1944, Box 135, Folder 2, OSS, SO Shipping Operation Italy to YO, 1943, Hans V. Tofte, Captain, AUS, RG 226, National Archives II.
28 Narrative of Lt. John Hamilton, USMCR, November 2, 1944, Box 108, RG 226, National Archives II, 6; Kruger, *Hans V. Tofte*, 60.
29 Ford, Jr., *OSS and the Yugoslav Resistance*, 28; Jakub, *Spies and Saboteurs*, 135; Captain M. O. Benson, A.C., to Deputy Director, SSO, Report, Subj: Work and Experiences with Tito and Yugoslav Partisans, 22 Jun 1944, CIA archives; Kruger, *Hans V. Tofte*, 52; Hans V. Tofte to Dep. Dir, SSO, "Report of Shipping Operations from Italy to Yugoslavia, 15 Oct–31 Dec 1943," Box 33, COI/OSS Central Files, RG 226, National Archives II, 19.
30 Folder, "TOFTE, Hans V., Capt. (Army)," Container 780, RG 226, National Archives II, 4.
31 Archive 15B-20393_1_1, FHM.
32 Archive 15-B, 20393_1_3, FHM.
33 First Lieutenant Thompson to Lt. S. G. Percy Wood, Chief Ops Officer, Cairo, February 15, 1944, Folder 2, OSS, SO Shipping Operations Italy to YO, 1943, Hans V. Tofte, Captain, AUS, Box 135, RG 226, National Archives II.
34 Major John E. Burke, The Essex Regiment, to Hans V. Tofte, November 5, 1943, Folder 2, OSS, SO Shipping Operations Italy to YO, 1943, Hans V. Tofte, Captain, AUS, Box 135, RG 226, National Archives II. The Essex Regiment is a storied line infantry unit in the British Army, operating from 1881 to 1958.
35 Lt. Cmdr. Morgan Giles, Royal Navy, to Hans V. Tofte, January 28, 1944, Folder 2, OSS, SO Shipping Operations Italy to YO, 1943, Hans V. Tofte, Captain, AUS, Box 135, RG 226, National Archives II.
36 OSS Personnel File, Hans V. Tofte, SN 525313, Box 780, RG 226, National Archives II; Special Forces Roll of Honour, https://www.specialforcesroh.com.
37 Roberts, *Tito, Mihailovic, and the Allies*, 151; Kruger, *Hans V. Tofte*, 56.
38 Ford, Jr., *OSS and the Yugoslav Resistance*, 28.

39 J. M. Scribner to Col. G. Edward Buxton, Memorandum, Subj: Attached Letter dated 15 March from J. E. Toulmin, March 25, 1944, Box 33, A1 Entry 92A NN3-226-94-001, COI/OSS Central Files, RG 226, National Archives II.

40 F. Catherine Rigsbee to Mrs. Begg, SI-Portugal, Field Report, September 26, 1945, CIA archives (https://www.cia.gov/readingroom/docs/DOC_0005341597.pdf), 1; Kruger, *Hans V. Tofte*, 61–62; F. N. Arnoldy, "Activities, Yugoslav Section, S.I. in Bari, Italy—From October 30, 1943 to July 12, 1944," Folder 4, Box 50, RG 226, National Archives II, 35.

41 "Operation Rosselsprung," Military Wiki, https://military-history.fandom.com/wiki/Operation_Rosselsprung_(1944).

Chapter 4: Man of Action: Austria, Scandinavia, Mason City

1 Clark Mollenhoff, "Hans Tofte—Superspy Caught in the Middle of a CIA Furor," *Minneapolis Tribune*, August 7, 1966; Application for Marriage License, Duval County, Florida, April 4, 1944, "Florida Marriages, 1830–1993"; Hans V. Tofte to Mr. Van Buren, Security Officer, Note concerning Certificate of Naturalization No. 6031975, July 24, 1943, Box 33, COI/OSS Central Files, RG 226, National Archives II; Kruger, *Hans V. Tofte*, 39, 63, 65.

2 Kruger, *Hans V. Tofte*, 65–66, 68.

3 Whitney Shephardson, Chief, SI, to Major Carl O. Hoffmann, Chief, SO, Memorandum, Subj: Captain Hans Tofte, May 16, 1944, Folder 486, Box 33, RG 226, National Archives II, n.p.; Kruger, *Hans V. Tofte*, 68–69.

4 Kruger, *Hans V. Tofte*, 69; WN# 24629, Entry 214, Box 5, RG 226, National Archives.

5 Kruger, *Hans V. Tofte*, 70–71.

6 Personnel file, Hans V. Tofte, Container 780, RG 226, National Archives II.

7 Kruger, *Hans V. Tofte*, 71–72; John Mancini, "Hitler's Nightmare: Meet America's Spies in Nazi Germany," *The National Interest*, April 25, 2020 (https://nationalinterest.org/blog/buzz/hitlers-nightmare-meet-americas-spies-nazi-germany-148301); James R. Forgan, Colonel, GSC, Commanding, Report, Entry #A1 224: Personnel Files of the Office of Strategic Services, 1942–62, Container 780, National Archives II.

8 Hans V. Tofte, Chief, Scandinavian Section, SI to Lt. Col. C. C. Bowman, Executive Officer, SI, Subj: Launching of V-1 Against New York, November 10, 1944, Container 303, UD 190, Field Station Files, RG 226, National Archives II; Todd H. Rider, *Forgotten Creators—How the German-Speaking Scientists and Engineers Invented the Modern World, and What We Can Learn From Them*, December 31, 2021 (https://riderinstitute.org/revolutionary-innovation/), 4122.

9 Hans V. Tofte to Lt. Col. C. C. Bowman, November 10, 1944; Rider, *Forgotten Creators*, 4123.

10 Ibid.

11 Major Winkelhorn to Major Tofte, Memorandum, Subj: Information *re* German Intentions of Launching V-1's Against New York, December 20, 1944, Folder "V-1 Against New York," Container 303, UD 190, Field Station Files, RG 226, National Archives II.

12 Rider, *Forgotten Creators*, 4124.

13 Ibid.

14 Ibid.

15 Casey, "The Clandestine War in Europe," 7.

16 Kruger, *Hans V. Tofte*, 72–73.

17 Ibid., 74.

18 James R. Forgan, Report, Container 780, National Archives II; Kruger, *Hans V. Tofte*, 74–75.
19 Kruger, *Hans V. Tofte*, 76–77; Excerpt from John Whiteclay Chambers II, *OSS Training in the National Parks and Service Abroad in World War II*, www.nps.gov/articles/a-wartime-organization-for-unconventional-warfare.htm.
20 Kruger, *Hans V. Tofte*, 77; Lorraine Boissoneault, "The Nazi Werewolves Who Terrorized Allied Soldiers at the End of World War II, *Smithsonian Magazine*, October 30, 2018, www.smithsonianmag.com/history/nazi-werewolves-who-terrorized-allied-soldiers-end-wwii-180970522/.
21 Kruger, *Hans V. Tofte*, 79, 81.
22 Major Louis Huot, *Guns for Tito*, Folder 3, Box 50, National Archives II, College Park, MD.
23 James R. Forgan, Report, Container 780, National Archives II; Kruger, *Hans V. Tofte*, 83–84.
24 Kruger, *Hans V. Tofte*, 87; Whitney H. Shepardson, Chief, SI, to Personnel Branch, Memorandum, Subj: Extension of Services for Major Hans V. Tofte, November 23, 1945, ASN O-525313, Folder 486, Box 33, RG 226, National Archives II.
25 Kruger, *Hans V. Tofte*, 82–84.
26 Major Hans Tofte to Lt. Col. R. W. Estey, OSS Property Board, Memorandum, Subj: Accountability of Pocket and Wrist Watches, October 25, 1945, Folder 486, Box 33, RG 226, National Archives II.
27 Whitney Shephardson, SSU, General letter, November 29, 1945, Archive 15B-20393_1_3, FHM.
28 Bare and Beer, "Building a Presence Along the Danube," 130, 147.
29 Jacobsen, *Surprise, Kill, Vanish*, 40.
30 Ibid., 155.
31 OSS Form 802D, January 29, 1946, in Personnel file, Hans V. Tofte, RG 226, Entry #A1 224: Personnel Files of the Office of Strategic Services, 1942–62, Container #780, National Archives II, College Park, MD; Emergency Addressee and Personal Property Card, in folder "TOFTE, HANS VILHELM, 0525313," RG 226, Entry #A1 224: Personnel Files of the Office of Strategic Services, 1942–62, Container #780, National Archives II, College Park, MD; Army of the United States Certificate of Service, Major Hans V. Tofte, Archive 15B-20393_1_3, FHM; Military Record and Report of Separation, Certificate of Service, Maj. Hans V. Tofte, March 30, 1946, Archive 15B-20393_1_3, FHM.
32 Major Carleton Coon, OSS Interoffice Memorandum, Subj: Commendation of Capt. Hans V. Tofte, Chief, S.O. Shipping Operations Italy–Yugoslavia 1943–44, July 6, 1944, Container 780, RG 226, National Archives II.
33 Citation for Bronze Star Medal, Archive 15B-20393_1_3; "Citation relative to LEGION OF MERIT, United States Army presented to Major Hans Tofte by Major General Wm. J. Donovan in New York, March 30, 1946," Archive 15B-20393_1_1, FHM; Strategic Services Unit Memorandum, Subject: Award of the Legion of Merit and the Bronze Star Medal to Major Hans V. Tofte, AUS, O-525313," Archive 15B-20394_1_1, FHM.
34 Chambers, *OSS Training in the National Parks and Service Abroad in World War II*; Kruger, *Hans V. Tofte*, 92–93.
35 Kruger, *Hans V. Tofte*, 88–89; John Ranelagh, *The Agency*, 218.
36 Ibid., 88–89, 92–93.
37 Jacobsen, *Surprise, Kill, Vanish*, 40; Goulden, *Korea*, 465; *Aero Digest*, Vol. 52, 150; Resume, Hans V. Tofte, compiled at The Army and Navy Club, October 1977, Archive 15B-20393_1_1, FHM; Kruger, *Hans V. Tofte*, 90–91; Biographic sketch, "Hanford MacNider (1889–1968)," Office of the Historian, United States Department of State, https://history.state.gov/departmenthistory/people/macnider-hanford; Biographic sketch, "General Hanford 'Jack' MacNIDER,"

IAGenWeb, https://iagenweb.org/boards/cerrogordo/biographies/index.cgi?read=333853; "Marlys Josephine Leister Chatel," Find a Grave, www.findagrave.com. Although records are sketchy, the marriage between Hans and Marlys ended sometime shortly before 1967, the year she married retired French army Brigadier General Jean C. Chatel, her fourth marriage. Marlys died in 2007, aged 101, and her obituary ran in the *The Washington Post* on August 21, 2007.

Chapter 5: The Korean War

1 Goulden, *Korea*, 466; Clark Mollenhoff, "Hans Tofte—Superspy Caught in the Middle of a CIA Furor," *Minneapolis Tribune*, August 7, 1966; Kruger, *Hans V. Tofte*, 94. The Sulgrave Club, which is still in operation, describes itself as "a gracious club experience in a lovely, historical Beaux Arts mansion" at 1801 Massachusetts Avenue, NW. It opened in 1902, is one of only two remaining mansions on Dupont Circle, and is listed on the National Register of Historic Places.

2 Ibid.; Col. Michael E. Haas (USAF, Ret.), "The Clandestine Services in Korea," *Intelligencer: Journal of U.S. Intelligence Studies*, winter/spring 2005, 98; DA Form 1058, Application for Short Tour of Active Duty Training, Lt. Col. Hans Vilhelm Tofte, May 1, 1950, Archive 15B-20393_1_1, FHM.

3 Michael Warner, ed., *CIA Cold War Records: The CIA Under Harry Truman* (Washington, DC: History Staff, Center for the Study of Intelligence, Central Intelligence Agency, 1994), 173–75.

4 Ibid., 214–16; Haas, "The Clandestine Services in Korea," 97; Frank G. Wisner to Director of Central Intelligence, Memorandum, "Interpretation of NSC 10/2 and Related Matters," October 12, 1950, in Warner, ed., *The CIA Under Harry Truman*, 347.

5 Frank G. Wisner, to Director of Central Intelligence, Memorandum, OPC Projects, October 29, 1948, 241–42, CIA archives.

6 Major Steve Fondacaro, "A Strategic Analysis of US Special Operations During the Korean Conflict, 1950–1953," M.A. thesis, US Army Command and General Staff College, Ft. Leavenworth, KS, 1988, 49.

7 Goulden, *Korea*, 467; Kruger, *Hans V. Tofte*, 95–96.

8 Mollenhoff, "Hans Tofte," *Minneapolis Tribune*, August 7, 1966. Lieutenant General Hanford MacNider was a Mason City native, the national commander of the American Legion in 1921–22, the assistant secretary of war in 1925–28, a man who fought in both world wars, served as a US diplomat, and was one of only four men ever elevated to the rank of lieutenant general following his retirement. Considered one of Iowa's greatest war heroes, he was one of only a very few who was awarded three Distinguished Service Crosses.

9 Kruger, *Hans V. Tofte*, 95; Charles H. Briscoe, "CIA Paramilitary Operations, Korea, 1950–1951," US Army Special Operations Command History Office, https://mail.arsof-history.org/articles/pdf/v9n1_cia_paramilitary.pdf, 70–71; Goulden, *Korea*, 467.

10 Stephen Endicott and Edward Hagerman, *The United States and Biological Warfare: Secrets from the Early Cold War and Korea* (Bloomington, IN: Indiana University Press, 1998), 134; Goulden, *Korea*, 468.

11 Goulden, *Korea*, 468; "Hans Tofte," WikiSpooks, https://wikispooks.com/w/index.php?title=Hans_Tofte&oldid=245935, 1; Endicott and Hagerman, *The United States and Biological Warfare*, 96. Colwell Beers served in CIA from the late 1940s until he retired in 1964 as assistant deputy director of supply after engaging in covert operations in Korea and Southeast

Asia. In retirement, he operated several small businesses in the greater Washington, DC, area, including bakeries, auto repair shops, gift shops, and a restaurant. He died on April 25, 1988, at the age of 79. See his obituary, "Colwell Edward Beers," *The Washington Post,* April 27, 1988.

12 Goulden, *Korea*, 468.

13 Ibid., 469; Kruger, *Hans V. Tofte*, 98; Commendation for Meritorious Civilian Service, Mr. Hans V. Tofte, Archive 15B-20393_1_3, FHM; Gen. Walter Bedell Smith to Gen. Matthew Ridgway, March 31, 1951, Archive 15B-20394_1_1, FHM.

14 Kruger, *Hans V. Tofte*, 97–98; Briscoe, "JACK Operations and Activities, Korea, 1950–1953," *Veritas*, Vol. 9, No. 1, 2013.

15 Kruger, *Hans V. Tofte*, 107.

16 Kruger, *Hans V. Tofte*, 99, 103; Dr. Richard P. Hallion, "US Navy Special Operations in the Korean War," Naval History and Heritage Command, https://www.history.navy.mil/research/library/online-reading-room/title-list-alphabetically/u/usnavy-special-operations-korean-war/; Goulden, *Korea*, 469–71; Tim Weiner, *Legacy of Ashes: The History of the CIA* (New York: Doubleday, 2007), eBook; Endicott and Hagerman, *The United States and Biological Warfare,* 134. Weiner's *Legacy of Ashes* is a generally unreliable and inaccurate account of the history of the CIA—as former CIA History Staff member Dr. Nick Dujmovic noted in a thorough book review, "His bias overcomes his scholarship. One cannot learn the true story of CIA from *Legacy of Ashes*." However, his book is one of only a few sources which includes these details of the guerrilla forces and so is included here, with a strong caveat to readers. Weiner noted the claims of a much more reliable witness to CIA history, John Ranelagh, but says that the latter's claims of Tofte's having successfully placed agents throughout Korea, China, and Manchuria are "false," just as Agency operational histories demonstrate, and that Tofte was "a fabricator."

17 Kruger, *Hans V. Tofte*, 100. There was a lot of underestimating the North Korean and Chinese threats going around—for a more sweeping example of how this myopia was practiced by MacArthur's G-2, see this author's *Loyalty First: The Life and Times of Charles A. Willoughby, MacArthur's Chief Intelligence Officer* (Philadelphia and Oxford: Casemate Books, 2023).

18 Goulden, *Korea*, 470; Kruger, *Hans V. Tofte*, 102.

19 Nicholson Baker, *Baseless: My Search for Secrets in the Ruins of the Freedom of Information Act* (New York: Penguin Books, 2021, 183–84.

20 Goulden, *Korea*, 471. Kruger, *Hans V. Tofte*, 105–6.

21 Fondacaro, "A Strategic Analysis," 51, 53, 88, 90; Goulden, *Korea*, 468–69; G. J. A. O'Toole, *The Encyclopedia of American Intelligence and Espionage: From the Revolutionary War to the Present* (New York: Facts on File, 1988), 267; G. J. A. O'Toole, *Honorable Treachery: A History of U.S. Intelligence, Espionage, and Covert Action from the American Revolution to the CIA* (New York: Atlantic Monthly Press, 1991), 450; Evan Thomas, *The Very Best Men: Four Who Dared: The Early Years of the CIA* (New York: Simon and Schuster, 1995), 53.

22 Thomas, *The Very Best Men*, 53.

23 Kruger, *Hans V. Tofte*, 104–5.

24 Kruger, *Hans V. Tofte*, 105.

25 Gordon Thomas, *Secrets and Lies: A History of CIA Mind Control and Germ Warfare* (Old Saybrook, CT: Octavo Editions, 2007), 47. By 1951, Gottlieb had created a CIA enclave within Fort Detrick, Maryland, the Army's secret base to develop biological weapons. In response to 1942 reports that the Japanese were using such weapons in China, the Army hired University of Wisconsin biochemist Ira Baldwin to run the program and find it a home, which he did

at a mostly abandoned National Guard base below Catoctin Mountain in Maryland, then known as Detrick Field. In March 1943, the Army renamed the facility Camp Detrick and designated it as the headquarters of the Army Biological Warfare Laboratories. In the spring of 1949, the Army created a small, secretive team of chemists at Camp Detrick, called the Special Operations Division, with the mission of finding military uses for toxic bacteria. By 1956, the freezers at now Fort Detrick housed biological agents that could cause smallpox, tuberculosis, and anthrax, as well as such organic toxins as snake venom and paralytic shellfish toxins. Fort Detrick also became known as the home of CIA mind control experiments—in 1951, future CIA director Allen Dulles, stunned by apparent Soviet mind control experiments on the world stage, tasked Gottlieb with investigating mind control. This project, ultimately known as MK-ULTRA, was later abandoned after the inadvertent death of one of the scientists involved and the resulting hue and cry. For further information, see Stephen Kinzer, "The Secret History of Fort Detrick, the CIA's Base for Mind Control Experiments," *Politico*, September 15, 2019, 1–5.

26 Baker, *Baseless*, 183–84; Stephen C. Mercado, Review *of Rikugun Noborito Kenkyujo no shinjitsu* [*The Truth About the Army Noborito Research Institute*], by Ban Shigeo, in *Studies in Intelligence*, Vol. 46, No. 4, 2002. Ariga also discovered that Ban had worked on "unspecified projects" inside the United States from 1955–59 before returning to Japan to enter the private sector. He died in 1993, shortly after completing his manuscript, published in Tokyo in 2001.

27 Charles H. Briscoe, "JACK Operations and Activities, Korea, 1951–1953," https://arsof-history.org/articles/v9n1_jack_operations_page_1.html, 102, 106, 118. Major Kramer would be awarded the Navy Cross for extraordinary heroism during CIA agent recovery missions in North Korea on June 30 and July 2, 1951. See fn 5 in Briscoe, above.

28 Goulden, *Korea*, 467–68, 471; O'Toole, *The American Encyclopedia of Intelligence and Espionage*, 494–95; Curtis Peebles, *Twilight Warriors: Covert Air Operations Against the USSR* (Annapolis, MD: Naval Institute Press, 2005), 77.

29 Haas, "The Clandestine Services in Korea," 98.

30 Fondacaro, "A Strategic Analysis," 49.

31 Allan R. Millett, *The War for Korea, 1950–1951: They Came From the North* (Lawrence, KS: University Press of Kansas, 2010), 241; "Inchon 1950: Operation 'Trudy Jackson,'" Korean War Weapons & History, koreanwaronline.com/arms/Clark.htm; John Toland, *In Mortal Combat: Korea, 1950–1953* (New York: William Morrow and Company, Inc., 1991), 182. Sasebo had been an important naval base since 1889 and was the home port for the Japanese fleet that sank 34 Russian naval vessels in the 1905 battle of Tsushima Straits, the major naval engagement of the Russo-Japanese War, a defeat which shocked the world and served as a dismissed foreshadowing of Asiatic military dominance. Currently, the US Seventh Fleet and the Japan Maritime Self-Defense Force share the port, home to US Fleet Activities Sasebo, which was established in 1946, https://cnrj.cnic.navy.mil/About/History.

32 Goulden, *Korea*, 471.

33 Jacobsen, *Surprise, Kill, Vanish*, 40–41; Goulden, *Korea*, 472.

34 Kruger, *Hans V. Tofte*, 113.

35 Goulden, *Korea*, 472.

36 Ibid., 472–73; Kruger, *Hans V. Tofte*, 112.

37 Kruger, *Hans V. Tofte*, 112.

38 Haas, "The Clandestine Services in Korea," 98; Thomas, *The Very Best Men*, 53; Kruger, *Hans V. Tofte*, 114.

39 O'Toole, *Honorable Treachery*, 450; Andrew Burt, "Your Future is Very Dark," *Slate*, November 19, 2014, https://slate.com/news-and-politics/2014/11/john-downey-cia-agent-captured-by-the-China-during-the-korean-war-the-story-of-the-longest-held-american-pow.html; Robert Burns, "CIA Operative From New Britain Had Role in Failed Cold War Spy Mission in China," *Hartford [CT] Courant*, June 19, 2010, http://www.courant.com/news/connecticut/hc-new-britain-cia-ambushed-in-china-20100619%2C0%2C7029400%2Cfull.story; Kruger, *Hans V. Tofte*, 105–6.

40 Goulden, *Korea*, 473; Kruger, *Hans V. Tofte*, 108–9.

41 Baker, *Baseless*, 183–84; "Members of Unit 731," *Pacific Atrocities Education* (blog), https://www.pacificatrocities.org/blog/members-of-unit-731, April 21, 2018.

42 Briscoe, "CIA Paramilitary Operations," 71.

43 Baker, *Baseless*, 183–84, 364.

44 *Lockwood's Directory of the Paper and Allied Trades* (United States: Vance Publishing Corporation, 1963.

45 Ibid., 104; "Psychological Strategy Board," Harry S. Truman Papers, The Harry S. Truman Library and Museum, https://www.trumanlibrary.gov/library/truman-papers/harry-s-truman-papers-staff-member-and-office-files-psychologicalstrategy. The records of the PSB were in CIA possession until they were turned over to the National Archives circa 1980.

46 Baker, *Baseless*, 104.

47 Ranelagh, *The Agency*, 218.

48 Goulden, *Korea*, 463–64, 474; Fondacaro, "A Strategic Analysis," 93; John Prados, *Safe for Democracy: The Secret Wars of the CIA* (Chicago: Ivan R. Dee, 2006), 129. The "TP" prefix was the Agency's nomenclature for Korea.

49 Goulden, *Korea*, 474.

50 Ibid., 463, 474; Prados, *Safe for Democracy*, 129.

51 Ibid., 474–75; Prados, *Safe for Democracy*, 129; Catherine Churchman, "Nationalist Ambitions and Covert Activities," in Tessa Norris-Suzuki, ed., *The Korean War in Asia: A Hidden History* (Lanham, MD: Rowan and Littlefield, 2018), 82.

52 Fondacaro, "A Strategic Analysis," 93.

53 James Barron, "Hans Tofte, World War II Spy Later Dismissed by the C.I.A.," *The New York Times*, August 28, 1987, https://www.nytimes.com/1987/08/28/obituaries/hans-tofte-world-war-ii-spy-later-dismissed-by-the-cia.html.

54 Goulden, *Korea*, 475.

55 Alec Smith, "Air America: The History of the CIA's Covert Airline," Grey Dynamics, September 30, 2022, https://greydynamics.com/air-america-the-history-of-cias-covert-airline. In 1959, Civil Air Transport became the more familiar Air America, to avoid undue scrutiny from Japanese tax investigators looking into the company's origins and its financial backers, and soon adopted the slogan "Anything, Anywhere, Any Time, Professionally." Since its ties to the CIA were still a closely guarded secret, Air America had to appear to be a legitimate US airline, with qualified pilots, bona fide passengers and/or cargo, and aircraft—as the 1950s ended, Air America had a small inventory of about a dozen fixed- and rotary-wing aircraft. Air America would continue until the mid-1970s before closing down in the *denouement* of the Vietnam War—perhaps appropriately, the helicopter that evacuated civilians from the US Embassy in Saigon when it fell in 1975 was an Air America asset. Air America continued to operate until 1978, when the Agency shed the air transport and logistics enterprise—its pilots became deniable assets, and the aircraft were sold, destroyed, or repatriated. The sale of Air

America resulted in a $30 million "profit" for the US Treasury—as CIA General Counsel Larry Houston noted, "That was one of our more successful business ventures." Smith, Chapter 2.5 and Ranelagh, *The Agency*, 217n.

56 Smith, Chapters 2.1; 2.2; 2.3; Ranelagh, *The Agency*, 217n.

57 Kruger, *Hans V. Tofte*, 119.

58 Barron, "Hans Tofte," 475; Kruger, *Hans V. Tofte*, 118–19.

59 Kruger, *Hans V. Tofte*, 115–17, 119.

60 CIA Deputy Director to Major General Charles A. Willoughby, Acting Chief of Staff, G-2, Headquarters, Far East Command, April 14, 1951, CIA archives.

61 Hans V. Tofte to Lieutenant General Walter Bedell Smith, April 25, 1951, CIA archives.

62 Kruger, *Hans V. Tofte*, 120–21.

63 Jacobsen, *Surprise, Kill, Vanish*, 49–52.

64 Ibid., 42–43.

65 Ibid., 52.

66 Jeremy Kuzmarov, "Police Training, 'Nation Building,' and Political Repression in Postcolonial South Korea," *The Asia-Pacific Journal*, Vol. 10, Issue 27, No. 3, Article ID 3785, July 1, 2012, 5, 10.

67 Jacobsen, *Surprise, Kill, Vanish*, 52.

68 Richard Harwood, "O What a Tangled Web the CIA Wove," *The Washington Post*, February 26, 1967, and "CIA Reported Ending Aid to Some Groups," *The Washington Post*, February 22, 1967; Kruger, *Hans V. Tofte*, 121–22.

69 Jacobsen, *Surprise, Kill, Vanish*, 53.

70 Ibid., 54; Samuel F. Wells, Jr., "Korean War: Myths and Misconceptions," *Wilson Quarterly*, summer 2020, 4–6.

Chapter 6: The "Dynamic Dane" and Regime Change

1 Gregory F. Treverton, "Covert Action and Open Society," *Foreign Affairs*, summer 1987, 47.

2 Ibid., 48.

3 Nick Cullather, *The CIA's Classified Account of its Operation in Guatemala, 1952–1954* (Stanford, CA: Stanford University Press, 2006), 39.

4 "Tommy Corcoran," Spartacus Educational, https://spartacus-educational.com/JFKcorcoran.htm, accessed March 8, 2024.

5 Christopher Andrew, *For the President's Eyes Only: Secret Intelligence and the American Presidency from Washington to Bush* (New York: Harper-Collins Publishers, Inc., 1995), 206; Kruger, *Hans V. Tofte*, 122–23, 125–27; "Tommy Corcoran."

6 Kruger, *Hans V. Tofte*, 123–24; "Tommy Corcoran."

7 Kruger, *Hans V. Tofte*, 124.

8 Ibid., 125; Report, Washington, October 8, 1952, as recorded in *Foreign Relations of the United States, 1952–1954, Guatemala* (Washington, DC: Office of the Historian, Department of State), 29; Jacobsen, *Surprise, Kill, Vanish*, 52; "Operation PBFORTUNE," Military Wiki, https://military-history.fandom.com/wiki/Operation-PBFortune; "Operation PB Fortune," Wikipedia: The Free Encyclopedia, https://en.wikipedia.org/wiki/Operation_PBFortune, accessed October 9, 2023; Memorandum for the Record, Washington, September 4, 1952, SUBJ: Impressions of PBFORTUNE, *Foreign Relations of the United States, 1952–1954, Guatemala* (Washington: US Government Printing Office, 2003), 96–97.

9 Andrew, *For the President's Eyes Only*, 206; Evan Thomas, "You Can Own the World, Part I," *The Washington Post*, October 22, 1995.

10 Cullather, *Operation PBSUCCESS: The United States and Guatemala, 1952–1954* (Washington, DC: History Staff, Center for the Study of Intelligence, Central Intelligence Agency, 1994), 25–26; Kruger, *Hans V. Tofte*, 127.

11 Memorandum, "PBFORTUNE, Essential Elements," September 1, 1953, https://www.cia.gov/readingroom/docs/DOC_0000924025.pdf; Andrew, *For the President's Eyes Only*, 206.

12 Hans V. Tofte, Memorandum for the Record, Washington, September 3, 1953, as recorded in *Foreign Relations of the United States, 1952–1954*, (Washington, DC: Office of the Historian, Department of State), 96; Cullather, *The CIA's Classified Account of its Operation in Guatemala*, 39 and *Operation PBSUCCESS*, 107.

13 Kruger, *Hans V. Tofte*, 127–28.

14 Cullather, *The CIA's Classified Account of its Operation in Guatemala*, 41; Andrew, *For the President's Eyes Only*, 206.

15 Prados, *Safe for Democracy*, 109–10; Thomas, "You Can Own the World, Part I"; Cullather, *Operation PBSUCCESS*, 28–29; J. C. King, chief, Western Hemisphere Division, Memorandum of Conversation, September 15, 1953, Subj: PBSUCCESS, in *Foreign Relations of the United States, 1952–1954, Guatemala* (Washington, DC: US Government Printing Office, 2003), 109.

16 Memorandum for the Record, Washington, DC, September 18, 1953, Subj: PBSUCCESS, in *Foreign Relations of the United States, 1952–1954, Guatemala* (Washington, DC: US Government Printing Office, 2003), 112–13.

17 Hans V. Tofte, Chief, PP/OPS, Memorandum for the Record, Washington, November 1153, Subj: PBSUCCESS, in *Foreign Relations of the United States, 1952–1954, Guatemala* (Washington, DC: US Government Printing Office, 2003), 135.

18 Andrew, *For the President's Eyes Only*, 206.

19 Alfonso Chardy, "Florida Opa-locka Field Was Once Site of Secret CIA Base," *Miami Herald*, April 22, 2013.

20 Kruger, *Hans V. Tofte*, 128–29.

21 Thomas, "You Can Own the World."

22 Kruger, *Hans V. Tofte*, 130.

23 Ibid., 131.

24 Ibid., 132–34.

25 Ibid., 135–37.

26 Jerome C. Dunbar to chief of station, Guatemala, LINCOLN, Subj: KUGOWN/WASHTUB, Publicity in Guatemalan Press, May 19, 1954, CIA Historical Review Program, Released in Full 2003, CIA archives; Kruger, *Hans V. Tofte*, 137; "Abbreviations and Cryptonyms," Office of the Historian, Department of State, Foreign Relations of the United States, 1952–54, Guatemala, https://history.state.gov/historicaldocuments/frus1952-54Guat/terms.

27 Kruger, *Hans V. Tofte*, 138–39.

28 Ibid., 139–40; "The CIA and Guatemala," Digital History, http://www.digitalhistory.uh.edu/disp_textbook.cfm?smtID=3&psid=1119, 56, derived from Cullather, *The CIA's Classified Account of its Operation in Guatemala.*

29 Kruger, *Hans V. Tofte*, 141–42; The Assistant Secretary of State for Inter-American Affairs (Holland) to the Secretary of State, Memorandum, May 18, 1954, in *Foreign Relations of the United States, 1952–1954, The American Republics,* Volume IV, 1112; "M.S. Alfhem," Wikipedia: The Free Encyclopedia, (https://en.wikipedia.org/wiki/MS_Alfhem).

30 Kruger, *Hans V. Tofte*, 142–43; "Liberation Air Force," Guatemala Air Force Unit History, https://www.aeroflight.co.uk/waf/americas/guatemala/Guatemala-af-home.com.

31 Kruger, *Hans V. Tofte*, 129; "William 'Rip' Robertson," Wikipedia: The Free Encyclopedia, https://en. Wikipedia.org/wiki/William_"Rip"_Robertson. Robertson's career at the CIA ended after he sunk a British cargo ship misidentified as a Soviet freighter shipping arms to Cuba. He stayed in Nicaragua, bought a parcel of land, and became a coffee farmer—good cover for training Brigade 2506 guerrillas for the Bay of Pigs operation. He was later in Laos, but had to be evacuated due to the malaria which ultimately killed him in 1970, at the age of 50. Originally buried in Culpepper National Cemetery, his body was moved to Arlington National Cemetery in 1977.

32 Prados, *Safe for Democracy*, 112.

33 Andrew, *For the President's Eyes Only*, 206, 208, 210–11; Treverton, "Covert Action and Open Society,"48–49; Kruger, *Hans V. Tofte*, 144–45, 149.

34 Kruger, *Hans V. Tofte*, 146, 148.

35 Treverton, "Covert Action and Open Society," 49; Ranelagh, *The Agency*, 219; Kruger, *Hans V. Tofte*, 146–47.

36 Kruger, *Hans V. Tofte*, 162–63; Charles H. Briscoe, "Plan Lazo: Evaluation and Execution," *Veritas*, Vol. 2, No. 4, 2006, https:arsof-history.org/articles/v2n4_plan_lazo_page_1.html; Dennis M. Rempe, *The Past as Prologue? A History of U.S. Counterinsurgency Policy in Colombia, 1958–1966* (Carlisle, PA: Strategic Studies Institute, Army War College, 2020), 4–6.

37 Rempe, *The Past as Prologue*, 4; Charles H. Briscoe, "Plan Lazo: Evaluation and Execution"; Rojas, "Trans-Pacific Connections," 16; Major Manuel F. Ramirez, "The Colombian Awakening: President Alvaro Uribe's Integrated Action Approach to Counterinsurgency," Air University thesis, Maxwell AFB, Alabama, June 2010, 32.

38 Rempe, *The Past as Prologue*, 4–6; Rojas, "Trans-Pacific Connections," 15; Briscoe, "Plan Lazo."

39 Kruger, *Hans V. Tofte*, 163–65.

40 Ibid., 165–66; Rempe, *The Past as Prologue*, 5; Kruger, *Hans V. Tofte*, 166. The Escuela de Lanceros had its pilot course in 1956 and shares common origins, traditions, goals, culture, and training with the US Army's Rangers. This close US–Colombian partnership dates to the Korean War, when Colombia was the only South American nation who supported the United Nations mission on the Korean Peninsula, deploying nearly 20 percent of its army's manpower to the fight. During the war, the Colombian Army unit suffered 163 KIA, 448 wounded, 60 missing, and 30 captured. Shortly after the Korean War, the then-president of Colombia asked the US Army Mission in Colombia to help design a type of Ranger school to build leaders who could help end "La Violencia" and provide peace and stability to the populace. For further information, see Capt. Nicholas Naquin, "Learning the *Lancero* Way: U.S. Helped Develop Elite Colombian Training," Association of the United States Army, https://www.ausa.org/articles/learning-lancero-way-us-helped-develop-elite-colombian-training.

41 Rojas, "Trans-Pacific Connections," 18; "Hans Tofte," Wiki Spooks, https://wikispooks.com/w/index.php?title=Hans_Tofte&oldid=245935.

42 Briscoe, "Plan Lazo: Evaluation and Execution."

43 Kruger, *Hans V. Tofte*, 166–67.

44 Director, FBI to Special Agent-in-Charge (SAC), Washington Field Office (WFO), Memorandum, Subj: Hans Vilhelm Tofte, Espionage, December 31, 1964; Director, FBI to SAC, WFO, Memorandum, Subj: Hans Vilhelm Tofte, Espionage, December 30, 1964; Director, FBI to SAC, WFO, Memorandum, Subj: Hans Vilhelm Tofte, Espionage, January 6, 1965, with Enclosure; John Edgar Hoover, Director [FBI] to Director, Central Intelligence

Agency, Memorandum, Attention: Chief, Personnel Security Division, Subj: Hans Vilhelm Tofte, Espionage, January 13, 1965. All references from https://documents2.theblackvault.com/documents/fbifiles/cia/hanstofte-fbi1.pdf. The Black Vault site was created and is operated by John Greenewald, Jr., and describes itself as the largest Freedom of Information Act (FOIA) clearinghouse in the world.

Chapter 7: Mason City Interlude

1 *Hearings Before the United States Senate Committee on Interstate and Foreign Commerce*, 83rd Congress, Second Session (Washington, DC: US Government Printing Office), 332; Jessie Merrill Dwelle and Ruth H. Wagner, *Iowa Beautiful Land: A History of Iowa* (Mason City, IA; Klipto Loose Leaf Co., 1954), 6.
2 *School and Community*, Vols. 41–42, Missouri State Teachers Association, 1954, 6; *The Texas Outlook*, Vol. 39, 1955, Texas State Teachers Association, 31.
3 Kruger, *Hans V. Tofte*, 149.
4 Clark Mollenhoff, "Hans Tofte—Superspy Caught in the Middle of a CIA Furor," *Minneapolis Tribune*, August 7, 1966; Julian Morrison, "The Strange Saga of a CIA Sleuth," *The Washington Daily News*, August 5, 1966; Kruger, *Hans V. Tofte*, 150–51; director, FBI to SAC, WFO, Memorandum, Subj: Hans Vilhelm Tofte, Subj: Espionage, December 30, 1964, https://documents2.theblackvault.com/documents/fbifiles/cia/hanstofte-fbi1.pdf.
5 Kruger, *Hans V. Tofte*, 152.
6 Ibid., 152–54.
7 Ibid., 154; Senior Airman Ryan Whitney, "'Air Commando One' to be Honored for Work, Impact on AFSOC Community," Air Force Special Operations Command, https://www.afsoc.af.mil/News/Article-Display/Article/162900/air-commando-one-to-be-honored-for-work-impact-on-afsoc-community/, June 23, 2010; Jane Steele, "Adolf Galland: The Luftwaffe Air Ace Who Survived Being Shot Down Four Times," War History Online, https://www.warhistoryonline.com/world-war-ii/adolf-galland.html, October 31, 2023.
8 Kruger, *Hans V. Tofte*, 157–58. Tofte's information about Bormann was correct, if incomplete. A *New York Times* article of November 28, 1972, reported that Bormann had bought his freedom and his passage to Argentina with the assistance of Juan and Eva Peron, and the promise of a substantial share of $500 million in Nazi loot. Bormann had entered Argentina on May 17, 1948, using a passport issued by the Vatican Office of Stateless Persons, traveling under the name Eliezer Goldstein.
9 Kruger, *Hans V. Tofte*, 159–60. Shepherd and Enoch Pratt Hospital, in the northern Baltimore suburb of Towson, Maryland, is a psychiatric hospital that opened in 1853 and is one of the oldest such medical facilities in the nation. Ranked in the top 10 psychiatric hospitals in the United States by *US News & World Report*, it still provides what is now referred to as electroconvulsive therapy (ECT) to patients suffering from severe depression, psychoses, and other mental illnesses.
10 Thomas, *The Very Best Men*, 187; Kruger, *Hans V. Tofte*, 161.
11 Kruger, *Hans V. Tofte*, 162.
12 Ibid., 171.
13 Thomas, *The Very Best Men*, 313; Kruger, *Hans V. Tofte*, 172.
14 Kruger, *Hans V. Tofte*, 174–75.
15 Ibid., 176.

16 Ibid., 182; Marcos Napolitano, "The Brazilian Military Regime, 1964–1985," Oxford Research Encyclopedia, https://doi.org/10.1093/acrefore/9780199366439.013.413; Matias Spektor, "The United States and the 1964 Brazilian Military Coup," Oxford Research Encyclopedia, https://doi.org/10.1093/acrefore/9780199366439.013.551.

17 Spektor, "The United States and the 1964 Brazilian Military Coup"; Napolitano, "The Brazilian Military Regime, 1964–1985"; CIA Intelligence Information Cable, Subj: "Plans of Revolutionary Plotters in Minais Gerais," March 30, 1964; Kruger, *Hans V. Tofte*, 185; "Operation Brother Sam" and "1964 Brazilian Coup D'Etat," Wikipedia: The Free Encyclopedia, https://en.wikipedia.org/wiki/Operation_Brother_Sam and https://en.wikipedia.org/wiki/1964_Brazilian_coup_d%27%C3%A9tat.

18 Kruger, *Hans V. Tofte*, 189; FBI response to FOIA Request No. 1485587-000, Subj: TOFTE, HANS V., January 22, 2021, in https://documents2.theblackvault.com/documents/fbifiles/cia/hanstofte-fbi1.pdf.

19 Kruger, *Hans V. Tofte*, 190–91.

20 Ibid., 193.

Chapter 8: Apartment to Let

1 Kruger, *Hans V. Tofte*, 193–94; Chatel Real Estate, https://www.chatelrealestate.com. In 1966, the GS-16 pay range was from $20,075 per year (Step 1) to $25,435 per year (Step 9). The original 1949 General Schedule that set the pay of Federal employees spanned GS-1 to GS-18; until 1978, the top three grades, GS-16–18, were considered "super grades." See www.govinfo.gov, Public Law 89-504, July 18, 1966, for details. Millicent and Jean Chatel founded the company in 1950, with offices in Georgetown and Dupont Circle. The firm's website describes it as "family owned and operated for three generations" and counts among its distinguished clientele General Ulysses S. Grant and inventor Thomas A. Edison. The same firm is still extant in the Washington, DC/Northern Virginia area.

2 Richard Pearson, "Hans V. Tofte," Obituary, *The Washington Post*, August 30, 1987; James Barron, "Hans Tofte, World War II Spy Later Dismissed by the C.I.A.," *The New York Times*, August 28, 1987, https://www.nytimes.com/1987/08/28/obituaries/hans-tofte-world-war-ii-spy-later-dismissed-by-the-cia.html; Clark Mollenhoff, "Hans Tofte—Superspy Caught in the Middle of a CIA Furor," *Minneapolis Tribune*, August 7, 1966; "Judge Orders Tofte to Name Questioners," *The New York Times*, December 30, 1966; "CIA Suspends Duties of Tofte During Probe," *The Washington Star*, August 4, 1966; Morton Mintz, "CIA Aide Reports Gems Missing Following Visits by Colleagues," *The Washington Post and Times-Herald*, August 3, 1966, and "Tofte Case Blew Covers High and Low," *The Washington Post*, September 14, 1966; Julian Morrison, "The Strange Saga of a CIA Sleuth," *The Washington Daily News*, August 5, 1966; "Exposed Classified Documents Under CIA Investigation," Corpus Christi *Times*, August 3, 1966; FBI report, "Hans Vilhelm Tofte, Employee, Central Intelligence Agency," August 3, 1966, and W. C. Sullivan to [redacted], Memorandum, Subj: REPORTED JEWEL THEFT BY CENTRAL INTELLIGENCE AGENCY (CIA) EMPLOYEE, HANS V. TOFTE, VALUED AT $20,000 TO $30,000, INTERSTATE TRANSPORTATION OF STOLEN PROPERTY, both from https://documents2.theblackvault.com/documents/fbifiles/cia/hanstofte-fbi1.pdf; Kruger, *Hans V. Tofte*, 195–96.

3 Hans V. Tofte, interview by Bill Diehl, "Bizarre Chain of Events," *The World Tonight*, WTOP Radio, Washington, DC, August 3, 1966, 6:00 p.m.

4 "Hypnotic Propensity for Publicity," *Huntley-Brinkley Report*, WRC-TV, Washington, DC, August 4, 1966, 6:30 p.m.

5 [Redacted] to W.C. Sullivan, Memorandum, Subj: HANS VILHELM TOFTE, ESPIONAGE, INTERSTATE TRANSPORATION OF STOLEN PROPERTY, August 4, 1966, https://documents2/theblackvault.com/documents/fbifiles/cia/hanstofte-fbi1.pdf.

6 Mollenhoff, "Hans Tofte," *Minneapolis Tribune*, August 7, 1966; "Judge Orders Tofte to Name Questioners," *The New York Times*, December 30, 1966; Clark Mollenhoff, "Tofte Threatens to Expose CIA Blunders," *The Des Moines Register*, August 12, 1966; "CIA Suspends Duties of Tofte During Probe," *The Washington Star*, August 4, 1966; Mintz, "Tofte Case Blew Covers High and Low," *The Washington Post*, September 15, 1966.

7 Kruger, *Hans V. Tofte*, 197–99.

8 Julian Morrison, "Tofte: CIA Favors Plotters," *The Washington Daily News*, August 12, 1966, CIA archives; Clark Mollenhoff, "Tofte Threatens to Expose CIA Blunders," *The Des Moines Register*, August 12, 1966, CIA archives; Mintz, "Tofte Case Blew Covers," *The Washington Post*, August 12, 1966, https://archive.org/download/nsia-CIAGeneral/CIA%20General%20115_text.pdf., accessed May 15, 2024.

9 Clark Mollenhoff, "Tofte Threatens to Expose CIA Blunders," *The Des Moines Register*, August 12, 1966; "Tofte: CIA Favors Plotters," *The Washington Daily News*, August 12, 1966; Clark Mollenhoff, "Tofte Refuses to Go to CIA for Inquiry," *Minneapolis Tribune*, September 15, 1966; Mintz, "Tofte Case Blew Covers High and Low," *The Washington Post*, September 15, 1966. Mollenhoff had earned a reputation as "one of Washington's most feared as well as respected investigative reporters," who at one time or another had aroused the anger of presidents Eisenhower, Kennedy, and Johnson, as well as leading members of Congress, the Cabinet, and civil society. Despite a law degree from Drake University, his writing always needed help, and he had a disconcerting habit of not attributing statements—but others had assisted, and Mollenhoff won 30 awards over the years, including a Pulitzer Prize for National Reporting in 1958 for a story on fraud and racketeering within the International Brotherhood of Teamsters.

10 Mintz, "CIA Aide Reports Gems Missing," *The Washington Post and Times-Herald*, August 3, 1966, and "Tofte Case Blew Covers High and Low," *The Washington Post*, September 15, 1966; "CIA Expert Says Gems Were Taken," *The New York Times*, August 3, 1966; Clark Mollenhoff, "Jewel Theft Creates Problem for Helms," *Minneapolis Tribune*, August 2, 1966; "Exposed Classified Documents Under CIA Investigation," Corpus Christi *Times*, August 3, 1966; [Redacted] to W. C. Sullivan, Memorandum, REPORTED JEWEL THEFT BY CENTRAL INTELLIGENCE AGENCY (CIA) EMPLOYEE, HANS V. TOFTE, VALUED AT $20,000 TO $30,000, August 3, 1966, https://documents2/theblackvault.com/documents/fbifiles/cia/hanstofte-fbi1.pdf. With inflation, that $20,000 worth of jewelry would now be worth more than $185,000. Interestingly, media reporting indicated that Marlys owned nearly $100,000 worth of jewelry at the time, but there was only $25,000 worth of insurance coverage because, as Tofte remarked, "that is about all she wears or has out at any one time."

11 SAC, WFO to Director, FBI, Memorandum, Subj: HANS VILHELM TOFTE, aka Hans V. Tofte, Employee, Central Intelligence Agency (CIA), MISCELLANEOUS – INFORMATION CONCERNING, August 3, 1966; FBI report, "Mrs. Hans Vilhelm Tofte, Employee, Central Intelligence Agency," August 3, 1966, both from https://documents2/theblackvault.com/documents/fbifiles/cia/hanstofte-fbi1.pdf.

12 [Redacted] to W. C. Sullivan, Memorandum, REPORTED JEWEL THEFT BY CENTRAL INTELLIGENCE AGENCY (CIA) EMPLOYEE, HANS V. TOFTE, VALUED AT $20,000

TO $30,000, August 3, 1966, https://documents2/theblackvault.com/documents/fbifiles/cia/hanstofte-fbi1.pdf. Osborn worked for the CIA for 27 years, 1947–74, and served as the director of security from 1964–74. He was ultimately forced to resign because he withheld documents

13 Baker, *Baseless*, 185.

14 "Investigation of Top Official," *Newsday*, August 3, 1966, 1:00 p.m., WTOP-TV, Washington, DC.

15 Director, FBI to SAC, WFO, Memorandum, Subj: Hans Vilhelm Tofte, Interstate Transportation of Stolen Property, August 4, 1966, https://documents2/theblackvault.com/documents/fbifiles/cia/hanstofte-fbi1.pdf.

16 W. C. Sullivan to [Redacted], Memorandum, Subj: Hans Vilhelm Tofte, Interstate Transportation of Stolen Property, August 10, 1966, https://documents2.theblackvault.com/documents/fbifiles/cia/hanstofte-fbi1.pdf; Kruger, *Hans V. Tofte*, 199.

17 Clark Mollenhoff, "Tofte Refuses to Go to CIA for Inquiry," *Minneapolis Tribune*, September 15, 1966; *The Philadelphia Inquirer*, August 5, 1966; "Administration Endorses CIA's Secret Funds," St. Petersburg, Fla. *Times*, February 24, 1967.

18 Baker, *Baseless*, 185; Mintz, "Tofte Case Blew Covers High and Low," *The Washington Post*, September 15, 1966.

19 Director, FBI to SAC, WFO, Memorandum, Subj: HANS VILHELM TOFTE, ESPIONAGE, INTERSTATE TRANSPORTATION OF STOLEN PROPERTY, September 14, 1966, and [Redacted] to W. C. Sullivan, Memorandum, same subject and date, both from https://documents2.theblackvault.com/documents/fbifiles/cia/hanstofte-fbi1.pdf; Mintz, "Tofte Case Blew Covers High and Low," *The Washington Post*, September 15, 1966; "CIA Serves Dismissal Notice on Veteran Agent Hans Tofte," *Daily Illini,* 16 September 1966, 12.

20 "Camera Team is Detained by CIA," October 3, 1966, CIA archives, NFI.

21 Clark Mollenhoff, "Hans Tofte," *Minneapolis Tribune*, August 7, 1966.

22 "Not in on Tofte Raid, CIA Chief Helms Says," *The Washington Daily News*, February 25, 1967; "Ex-Agent Tofte's Lawyer Says CIA Offered Deal," *The Washington Star*, November 24, 1966; "Ousted Tofte Sues CIA Director," *The Washington Post*, October 26, 1966; "Sarah," *Washington Weekly*, October 21, 1980.

23 Stephen S. Rosenfeld, "Suspended CIA Operative Insists That IF He is Judged It Be in Open," *The Washington Post and Times-Herald*, August 13, 1966.

24 Ibid.; "Judge Orders Tofte to Name Questioners," *The New York Times*, December 30, 1966; "Tofte Sues CIA," *Berlingske Tidende*, October 27, 1966. *Berlingske Tidende* is the former name of the Danish national daily newspaper, published since 1749.

25 Heinz Paechter, "CIA Agents Among Themselves," *Handelsblatt*, November 15, 1966, 32.

26 G. Deynishenko, "CIA Agent Expected to 'Unburden' Self," *Izvestiya*, August 7, 1966.

27 [Redacted] to W. C. Sullivan, Memorandum, Subj: CENTRAL INTELLIGENCE AGENCY (CIA), October 10, 1966, https://documents2.theblackvault.com/documents/fbifiles/cia/hanstofte-fbi1.pdf.

28 Prados, *Safe for Democracy*, 295.

29 "CIA Man Sues Tofte, Others," *The Washington Daily News*, July 28, 1967; *Speake v. Tofte*, United States District Court, District of Columbia, June 1, 1971, https://casetext.com/case/speake-v-tofte.

30 Kruger, *Hans V. Tofte*, 202–3.

31 Ibid., 204.

Chapter 9: Life After Langley

1 Kruger, *Hans V. Tofte*, 206–7.
2 Ibid., 207.
3 George Mills, *Rogues and Heroes From Iowa's Amazing Past*, (Ames, IA: Iowa State University Press, 1972), 45.
4 Scott C. Monje, *The Central Intelligence Agency: A Documentary History* (Greenwood Publishing Group, 2008), 49. The author mistakenly claims that the classified documents were found in the basement apartment and also asserts that Tofte was not authorized to have classified documents at home, period, a claim subject to some question, especially during that era.
5 "Church Committee," Wikipedia: The Free Encyclopedia; Kruger, *Hans V. Tofte*, 210.
6 Baker, *Baseless*, 185.
7 Kruger, *Hans V. Tofte*, 211; "Gilbertsville Village," Living Places, https://www.livingplaces.com/NY/Otsego_County/Gilbertsville_Village.html; "Caroline Brown," obituary, https://www.legacy.com/us/obituaries/legacy remembers/caroline-brown-obituary?id=29608460. After a life almost as exciting as Hans's, Caroline passed away in 2006, at the age of 102. Not surprisingly, there is no mention of Hans in her obituary.
8 Invitation, Veterans of the OSS dinner, 1979, CIA archives.
9 Kruger, *Hans V. Tofte*, 211–12.
10 Richard Pearson, "Hans V. Tofte," Obituary, *The Washington Post*, August 30, 1987; James Barron, "Hans Tofte, World War II Spy Later Dismissed by the C.I.A.," *The New York Times*, August 28, 1987, https://www.nytimes.com/1987/08/28/obituaries/hans-tofte-world-war-ii-spy-later-dismissed-by-the-cia.html; "Hans V. Tofte," Find A Grave, https://www.findagrave.com/memorial/239043478/hans-v-tofte; Kruger, *Hans V. Tofte*, 213.
11 Kruger, *Hans V. Tofte*, 95.
12 Tom Clancy, *The Hunt for Red October* (Annapolis, MD: Naval Institute Press, 1984), 78.
13 Book review comments by Kresten Soe Christensen on Henrik Kruger's *Den danske krigshelt, der kom til tops i CIA* [*The Danish war hero, who rose to the top of the CIA*], https://ereolen.dk/content/lydboerger, n.p.

Chapter 10: Looking Through a Glass, Darkly…

1 Kruger, *Hans V. Tofte*, 179.
2 Ibid., 203.
3 Goulden interview with Marlys Tofte, November 15–16, 2004, n.p.; Kruger, *Hans V. Tofte*, 215.
4 Ibid., 7.
5 Ibid., 95.
6 Goulden, *Korea*, 464; Richard Falk, "Iran and American Geopolitics in the Gulf," *Race and Class*, 21 (1), 41.
7 Briscoe, "CIA Paramilitary Operations, Korea, 1950–1951," 72.
8 Kruger, *Hans V. Tofte*, 177–78.
9 Morton Mintz, "Tofte Case Blew Covers High and Low," *The Washington Post*, September 15, 1966.
10 Kruger, *Hans V. Tofte*, 7.
11 Ibid., 14.

12 Ibid., 7.

13 Quintus Curtius, "The Covert Operations of Hans Tofte During the Korean War," December 22, 2014, blogsite https://theredarchive.com/blog/Return-of-Kings/the-covert-operations-of-Hans-Tofte-during-the-Korean-War.

14 Kruger, *Hans V. Tofte*, 215.

Bibliography

Primary Sources

Record Group 226, Records of the Office of Strategic Services, National Archives II, College Park, Maryland.

Secondary Works

Andrew, Christopher. *For the President's Eyes Only: Secret Intelligence and the American Presidency from Washington to Bush*. New York: Harper-Collins Publishers, Inc., 1995.

Baker, Nicholson. *Baseless: My Search for Secrets in the Ruins of the Freedom of Information Act*. New York: Penguin Press, 2020.

Churchman, Catherine. "Nationalist Ambitions and Covert Activities," in *The Korean War in Asia: A Hidden History*, edited by Tessa Monis-Suzuki. Lanham, MD: Rowan and Littlefield, 2018.

Clancy, Tom. *The Hunt for Red October*. Annapolis, MD: US Naval Institute Press, 1984.

Colledge, J. J. *Ships of the Royal Navy: The Complete Record of All Fighting Ships of the Royal Navy*. London: Chatham Publishing, 1969.

Critchlow, Donald T. and Emilie Raymond, eds. *Hollywood and Politics: A Sourcebook*. New York: Routledge, 2009.

Cullather, Nick. *The CIA's Classified Account of its Operations in Guatemala, 1952–1954*. Stanford, CA: Stanford University Press, 2006.

———. *Operation PBSUCCESS: The United States and Guatemala, 1952–1954*. Washington, DC: History Staff, Center for the Study of Intelligence, Central Intelligence Agency, 1994.

Dwelle, Jessie Merrill. *Iowa Beautiful Land: A History of Iowa*. Mason City, IA: Klipto Loose Leaf Co., 1958.

Endicott, Stephen and Edward Hagerman. *The United States and Biological Warfare: Secrets from the Early Cold War and Korea*. Bloomington, IN: Indiana University Press, 1998.

Ford, Kirk. *OSS and the Yugoslav Resistance, 1943–1945*. College Station, TX: Texas A & M University Press, 1992.

Goulden, Joseph C. Korea. *The Untold Story of the War*. New York: Times Books, 1982.

Haas, Michael. *In the Devil's Shadow: UN Special Operations During the Korean War*. Annapolis, MD: Naval Institute Press, 2000.

Jacobsen, Annie. *Surprise, Kill, Vanish: The Secret History of CIA Paramilitary Armies, Operators, and Assassins*. New York: Back Bay Books, 2019.

Jakub, Joseph J. III. *Spies and Saboteurs: Anglo-American Collaboration and Rivalry in Human Intelligence Collection and Special Operations, 1940–1945*. New York: Springer, 1999.

Kruger, Henrik. *Den danske krigshelt, der kom til tops I CIA* (*The Danish War Hero Who Rose to the Top of the CIA*). Translation of Google eBook. Copenhagen: Henrik Kruger and Lindhart and Ringhof Forlag, 2005.

Leary, William. *Perilous Missions: Civil Air Transport and CIA Covert Operations in Asia*. Tuscaloosa, AL: University of Alabama Press, 1984.

Lockwood's Directory of the Paper and Allied Trades. United States: Vance Publishing Corporation, 1963.

Millett, Allan R. *The War for Korea, 1950–1951: They Came From the North*. Lawrence, KS: University Press of Kansas, 2010.

Mills, George. *Rogues and Heroes From Iowa's Amazing Past*. Ames, IA: Iowa State University Press, 1972.

Monje, Scott C. *The Central Intelligence Agency: A Documentary History*. Westport, CT: Greenwood Publishing Group, 2008.

O'Toole, G. J. A. *The American Encyclopedia of Intelligence and Espionage: From the Revolutionary War to the Present*. New York: Facts on File, 1988.

———. *Honorable Treachery: A History of U.S. Intelligence, Espionage, and Covert Action from the American Revolution to the CIA*. New York: Atlantic Monthly Press, 1991.

Peebles, Curtis. *Twilight Warriors: Covert Air Operations Against the USSR*. Annapolis, MD: Naval Institute Press, 2005.

Prados, John. *Safe for Democracy: The Secret Wars of the CIA*. Chicago: Ivan R. Dee, 2006.

Ranelagh, John. *The Agency: The Rise and Decline of the CIA*. New York: Simon and Schuster, 1986.

Rempe, Dennis M. *The Past as Prologue? A History of U.S. Counterinsurgency Policy in Colombia, 1958–1966*. Carlisle, PA: Army War College Strategic Studies Institute, 2002.

Roberts, Walter R. *Tito, Mihailovic, and the Allies, 1941–1945*. Durham, NC: Duke University Press, 1994.

Russell, Francis. *The Secret War*. Alexandria, VA: Time-Life Books, 1981. NARA Still Pictures Branch reference volume, National Archives II, College Park, MD.

Russo, Gus. *Live By the Sword: The Secret War Against Castro and the Death of JFK*. Baltimore, MD: Bancroft Press, 1998.

Schwab, Gerald. *OSS Agents in Hitler's Heartland: Destination Innsbruck*. Austria: Greenwood Publishing Group, 1996.

Singlaub, John K. *Hazardous Duty: An American Soldier in the Twentieth Century*. New York: Touchstone, 1992.

Smith, R. Harris. *OSS: The Secret History of America's First Central Intelligence Agency*. Berkeley, CA: University of California Press, 1972.

Thomas, Evan. *The Very Best Men: Four Who Dared: The Early Years of the CIA*. New York: Simon and Schuster, 1995.

Thomas, Gordon. *Secrets and Lies: A History of CIA Mind Control and Germ Warfare*. Old Saybrook, CT: Octavo Editions, 2007.

Toland, John. *In Mortal Combat: Korea, 1950–1953*. New York: William Morrow and Company, Inc., 1991.

Warner, Michael, ed. *The CIA Under Harry Truman*. Washington, DC: History Staff, Center for the Study of Intelligence, Central Intelligence Agency, 1994.

Weiner, Tim. *Legacy of Ashes: The History of the CIA*. New York: Doubleday, 2007.

Theses and Dissertations

Fondacaro, Steve, Major, US Army. "A Strategic Analysis of U.S. Special Operations During the Korean Conflict, 1950–1953," M.A. thesis, US Army Command and General Staff College, Ft. Leavenworth, KS, 1988.

Archival Sources

Article, CIA Clandestine Service Domestic Operations Division survey notes, 1966, CIA archives.

Beer, Siegfried. "Target Central Europe: American Intelligence Efforts Regarding Nazi and Early Postwar Austria," Working Paper, August 1997.

"CIA Involvement of Danish Company Reported in Tofte Case," CIA-RDP75-00001R000400390023-7, approved for release, December 2, 2012, CIA archives.

"The Clandestine War in Europe (1942–1945)," Remarks of William J. Casey on Receipt of the William J. Donovan Award at Dinner of Veterans of O.S.S., December 5, 1974, CIA archives.

Danish Press Attaché Announcement CIA-OK (diagonal through the first "O"), August 6, 1966, CIA archives.

Foreign Relations of the United States, 1952–1954, Guatemala. Washington, DC: US Government Printing Office, 2003.

Hearings Before the United States Senate Committee on Interstate and Foreign Commerce, 83d Congress, Second Session, April–July 1954. Washington, DC: United States Government Printing Office.

"Investigation of Top Official," *Newsday* Public Affairs Staff article, WTOP-TV, Washington, DC, August 3, 1966, CIA archives.

Invitation to O.S.S. 1979 Dinner, September 1979, CIA archives.

Letter from Allen W. Dulles to Major General Charles A. Willoughby, April 14, 1951, CIA archives.

Letter from Hans V. Tofte to Lieutenant General Walter Bedell Smith, April 25, 1951, CIA archives.

"Partisan Supply Operation, September 1943–January 1944," Office of Strategic Services, Combined Arms Research Library, US Army Command and General Staff College, Ft. Leavenworth, Kansas.

Peters, Gerhard and John T. Woolley, Harry S. Truman, Directive Establishing the Psychological Strategy Board, June 20, 1951, The American Presidency Project, https://www.presidency.ucsb.edu/node/230148, accessed June 17, 2024.

"Plans of Revolutionary Plotters in Minas Gerais," CIA Intelligence Information Cable IN 50 182, 30 March 1964, George Washington University.

"Psychological Strategy Board," Harry S. Truman Papers Staff Member and Office Files, https://www.trumanlibrary.gov/library/truman-papers/harry-s-truman-papers-staff-member-and-office-files-psychological-strategy, accessed June 11, 2024.

"Report to Deputy Director, SSO from Capt. M. O. Benson, A.C., 22 Jun 1944," Subj: Work and Experiences with Tito and Yugoslav partisans, CIA archives.

Select archival records of the *Frihedsmuseet* (Museum of Danish Resistance), Copenhagen, Denmark.

Rider, Todd H., *Forgotten Creators—How German-Speaking Scientists and Engineers Invented the Modern World, and What We Can Learn From Them,* December 31, 2021.

Veterans of the OSS 1979 Dinner invitation, CIA archives.

Wisner, Frank G., "Memorandum for the Director of Central Intelligence," OPC Projects, October 29, 1948, CIA archives.

Newspapers/Media

Aero Digest, Vol. 52. Ann Arbor, MI: Aeronautical Digest Publishing Corporation, 1946.

Barron, James. "Hans Tofte, World War II Spy Later Dismissed by the CIA," obituary, *The New York Times*, August 28, 1987.

"Bizarre Chain of Events," Public Affairs Staff, *The World Tonight*, WTOP Radio, Washington, DC, August 3, 1966.

Burns, Robert. "CIA Operative From New Britain Had Role in Failed Cold War Spy Mission in China," *Hartford [CT] Courant*, June 19, 2010.

"Camera Team is Detained by CIA," October 3, 1966, NFI.

Chardy, Alfonso. "Florida Opa-locka Field Was Once Site of Secret CIA Base," *Miami Herald*, April 22, 2013.

"C.I.A. Expert Says Gems Were Taken," *The New York Times*, August 3, 1966.

"CIA Man Sues Tofte, Others," *The Washington Daily News*, July 28, 1967.

"CIA Serves Dismissal Notice on Veteran Agent Hans Tofte," September 16, 1966.

"CIA Suspends Duties of Tofte During Probe," *The Washington Star*, August 4, 1966.

"C. Tracy Barnes Dies at 60; Former Aide With CIA, Yale," *The Washington Post*, February 20, 1972.

"Colwell Edward Beers," obituary, *The Washington Post*, April 27, 1988.

"Col. Hans V. Tofte," obituary, *Orlando Sentinel*, August 30, 1987.

"C. Tracy Barnes Dies at 60; Former Aide with CIA, Yale," *The Washington Post*, February 20, 1972.

Elizabeth P. McIntosh, *Sisterhood of Spies: The Women of OSS*, *The New York Times* book review, https://archive.nytimes.com/www.nytimes.com/books, accessed July 9, 2024.

"The East Asiatic Company Foundation," https://eacfoundation.dk/en/the-each-history-eng/, accessed February 20, 2024.

"Ex-Agent Tofte's Lawyer Says CIA Offered Deal," *The Washington Star*, November 24, 1966.

"Exposed Classified Documents Under CIA Investigation," Corpus Christi *Times*, August 3, 1966.

Harwood, Richard. "O What a Tangled Web the CIA Wove," *The Washington Post*, February 26, 1967.

"Hypnotic Propensity for Publicity," *Huntley-Brinkley Report*, August 4, 1966, 6:30 p.m., WRC-TV, Washington, DC.

"Inchon 1950: Operation 'Trudy Jackson,'" koreanwaronline.com/arms/Clark.htm.

"The Intrepid Life of Sir William Stephenson," February 5, 2015, https://www.cia.gov/stories/story/the-intrepid-life-of-sir-william-stephenson, accessed February 23, 2024.

"Judge Orders Tofte to Name Questioners," *The New York Times*, December 30, 1966.

Mancini, John. "Hitler's Nightmare: Meet America's Spies in Nazi Germany," *The National Interest*, https://nationalinterest.org/blog/buzz/hitlers-nightmare-meet-americas-spies-nazi-germany-148301, accessed April 19, 2024.

Mintz, Morton. "CIA Aide Reports Gems Missing Following Visits by Colleagues," *The Washington Post and Times-Herald*, August 3, 1966.

Mollenhoff, Clark. "Hans Tofte—Superspy Caught in the Middle of a CIA Furor," *Minneapolis Tribune*, August 13, 1966.

———. "Jewel Theft Creates Problems for Helms," *Minneapolis Tribune*, August 2, 1966.

———. "Tofte Refuses to go to CIA for Inquiry," *Minneapolis Tribune*, September 15, 1966.

———. "Tofte Threatens to Expose CIA Blunders," *The Des Moines Register*, August 12, 1966.

Morrison, Julian. "The Strange Saga of a CIA Sleuth," *The Washington Daily News*, August 5, 1966.

———. "Tofte: CIA Favors Plotters," *The Washington Daily News*, August 12, 1966.

Musynske, Gavin, "Danish Citizens Resist the Nazis, 1940–1945," Global Non-Violent Action Database Case Study, Swarthmore College (2009), https://nvdatabase.swarthmore.edu/content/danish-citizens-resist-Nazis-1940-1945, accessed April 24, 2024.

Naquin, Capt. Nicholas, "Learning the Lancero Way: U.S. Helped Develop Elite Colombian Training," March 2, 2020, https://www.ausa.org/articles/learning-lancero-way-us-helped-develop-elite-colombian-training, accessed January 26, 2024.

"Not in on Tofte Raid, CIA Chief Helms Says," *The Washington Daily News*, February 25 1967.

"Ousted Tofte Sues CIA Director," *The Washington Post and Times-Herald*, October 26, 1966.

Pearson, Richard. "Hans V. Tofte, 76, Dies," *The Washington Post*, August 30, 1987.

The Philadelphia Inquirer, August 5, 1966.

Review of Linda Kush, *The Rice Paddy Navy: U.S. Sailors Undercover in China*, in *World War II History*, August 2013, 66.

Rosenfeld. Stephen S., "Suspended CIA Operative Insists That If He is Judged It Be in Open," *The Washington Post and Times-Herald*, August 13, 1966.
"Sarah," *Washington Weekly*, October 21, 1980.
Smith, Alec. "Air America: The History of the CIA's Covert Airline," September 30, 2022, https://greydynamics.com/air-america-the-history-of-cias-covert-airline/, accessed January 11, 2024.
Steele, Jane. "Adolf Galland: The Luftwaffe Air Ace Who Survived Being Shot Down Four Times," War History Online, October 31, 2023.
"The CIA Had the OK (diagonal slash) Listed as a Communist Blind," *Berlingske Tidende*, August 5, 1966.
Thomas, Evan. "You Can Own the World, Part I," *The Washington Post*, October 22, 1995.
"Tofte Sues CIA," *Berlingske Tidende* (Danish national daily newspaper), October 27, 1966.
Whitney, Ryan, Senior Airman, "'Air Commando One' to be Honored for Work, Impact on AFSOC Community," Air Force Special Operations Command, June 23, 2010.

Periodical Sources

Bare, Duncan and Siegfried Beer, University of Graz. "Building a Presence Along the Danube: A Fresh Look at OSS and SSU Austria in 1945 and 1946." *Journal of Austrian-American History*, Vol. 5, (2021): 122–56.
Boissoneault, Lorraine. "The Nazi Werewolves Who Terrorized Allied Soldiers at the End of World War II." *Smithsonian Magazine*, October 30, 2018, https://www.smithsonianmag.com/history/nazi-werewolves-who-terrorized-allied-soldiers-end-wwii-180970522/, accessed March 18, 2024.
Briscoe, Charles H. "CIA Paramilitary Operations, Korea, 1950–1951." *Veritas*, Vol. 9, No. 1 (2013): 69–83, https://mail.arsof-history.org/articles/pdf/v9n1_cia_paramilitary.pdf, accessed April 3, 2024.
———. "JACK Operations and Activities, Korea, 1951–1953." *Veritas*, Vol. 9, No. 1 (2013): https://arsof-history.org/articles/v9n1_jack_operations_page_1.html, accessed April 3, 2024.
———. "Plan Lazo: Evaluation and Execution." *Veritas*, Vol. 2, No. 4 (2006): https://arsof-history.org/articles/v2n4_plan_lazo_page_1.html, accessed April 3, 2024.
Chambers, John Whiteclay II. "OSS Training in the National Parks and Service Abroad in World War II." Excerpt. www.nps.gov/articles/a-wartime-organization-for-unconventional-warfare.htm, accessed December 4, 2023.
Curtius, Quintus. "The Covert Operations of Hans Tofte During the Korean War." *Return of Kings*, 22 December 2014, www.TheRedArchive.com, accessed July 16, 2024.
Falk, Richard. "Iran and American Geopolitics in the Gulf." *Race and Class*, 21 (1): 41–55, https://doi.org/10.1177/030639687902100105, accessed November 14, 2023.
Haas, Col. Michael E. "The Clandestine Services in Korea." *Intelligencer: Journal of U.S. Intelligence Studies* (Winter/Spring 2005): 97–103.
Kinzer, Stephen. "The Secret History of Fort Detrick, the CIA's Base for Mind Control Experiments," *Politico*, September 15, 2019, 1–5.
Kiper, Richard L. "Unconventional Warfare in Korea: Forgotten Aspect of the Forgotten War." *Special Warfare* (August 2003): 26–37.
Kuzmarov, Jeremy. "Police Training, 'Nation Building,' and Political Repression in Postcolonial South Korea." *The Asia-Pacific Journal*, Vol. 10, Issue 27, No. 3, Article ID 3785 (July 1, 2012): 1–26.
Mercado, Stephen C. "Intelligence in Recent Public Literature," review of *Rikugun Noborito Kenkyujo no shinjitsu* [*The Truth About the Army Noborito Research Institute*] by Ban Shigeo, *Studies in Intelligence*, Vol. 46, No. 4 (2002).

"The Mollenhoff Cocktail." *Time* magazine, August 12, 1966.

Rojas, Daniel Emilio. "Trans-Pacific Connections, World Hegemony and Asymmetric Warfare in 1950." *Le Recueil Ouvert—Projet Epopee, L'Ouvroir Litt & Arts* [*The Open Compendium/Epic Project, Research in the Arts and Practices of Text, Image, Screen and Stage*], University of Grenoble Alpes (2019): 1–25.

School and Community, Vols. 41–42. Missouri State Teacher's Association, 1954.

Slayton, Nicholas. "Meet the legendary 'father of Special Forces' who helped establish the Green Berets." *Task and Purpose*, June 19, 2022, https://taskandpurpose.com/news/meet-the-legendary-father-of-the-green-berets, accessed October 26, 2023.

Spektor, Matias. "The United States and the 1964 Brazilian Military Coup." *Oxford Research Encyclopedia of Latin American History*, April 26, 2018, https://doi.org/10.1093/acrefore/9780199366439.013.551, accessed January 18, 2024.

"The Texas Outlook," Texas State Teacher's Association, Vol. 39, 1955.

Treverton, Gregory F. "Covert Action and Open Society." *Foreign Affairs*, summer 1987, 46–65.

Wells, Samuel F., Jr., et al. "Korean War: Myths and Misconceptions," *Wilson Quarterly*, summer 2020, 1–6.

Yu, Maochun. "'In God We Trusted, in China We Busted': The China Command Group of the Special Operations Executive (SOE)." Abstract. *Intelligence and National Security*, Volume 16, Issue 4 (2001).

Websites

http://www.courant.com/news/connecticut/hc-new-britain-cia-ambushed-in-china-20100619%2C0%2C7029400%2Cfull.story, accessed February 2, 2024.

https://ancestors.familysearch.org/en/L83M-VP4/hans-vilhelm-tofte-1911-1987, accessed September 20, 2023.

https://boggaragen.dk/produkt/henrik-kruger-hans-v-tofte-den-danske-krigshelt-der-kom-til-tops-i-cia/, accessed February 7, 2024.

https://casetext.com/case/speake-v-tofte, accessed January 22, 2024.

https://cnrj.cnic.navy.mil/About/History, accessed November 14, 2023.

https://covertactionnmagazine.com/2021/11/28/theres-something-rotten-in-denmark-frank-olson-and-the-macabre-fate-of-a-CIA-whistleblower-in-the-early-cold-war/, accessed December 14, 2023.

https://documents2.theblackvault.com/documents/fbifiles/cia/hanstofte-fbi1.pdf, accessed September 5, 2023.

https://doi.org/10.1093/acrefore/9780199366439.013.413, accessed December 8, 2023.

https://doi.org/10.1093/acrefore/9780199366439.013.551, accessed December 8, 2023.

https://en.wikipedia.org/wiki/99th_Infantry_Battalion_(United_States), accessed March 9, 2024.

https://en.wikipedia.org/wiki/Operation_PBFortune, accessed January 15, 2024.

https://ereolen.dk/content/lydboerger, accessed February 16, 2024.

https://failedossops.blogspot.com/2020/02/yugoslavia-oss-s0e-1944.html, accessed October 19, 2023.

https://history.state.gov/departmenthistory/people/macnider-hanford, accessed January 17, 2024.

https://iagenweb.org/boards/cerrogordo/biographies/index.cgi?read=333853, accessed January 24, 2024.

https://lrdg.hegewisch.net/bombs.html, accessed January 29, 2024.

https://military-history.fandom.com/wiki/Operation-PBFortune, accessed October 26, 2023.

https://reviews.ipmsusa.org/review/Prinz-Eugen-the-story-of-the-7-SS-Freiwilligen-Gebirgs-Division-1942-1945, accessed June 10, 2024.

https://riderinstitute.org/revolutionary-innovation/, accessed May 13, 2024.

https://rmc.library.cornell.edu/EAD/htmldocs/RMM02770.html, accessed February 21, 2024.

https://sgfilmhunter.wordpress.com/tag/101-special-training-school, accessed March 12, 2024.

https://slate.com/news-and-politics/2014/11/john-downey-cia-agent-captured-by-the-China-during-the-korean-war-the-story-of-the-longest-held-american-pow.html, accessed December 14, 2023.

https://theredarchive.com/blog/Return-of-Kings/the-covert-operations-of-hans-tofte-during-the-korean-war, accessed October 20, 2023.

https://spartacus-educational.com/JFKcorcoran.htm, accessed April 17, 2024.

https://total-croatia-news.com/destinations/destinations-hvar/blog-hvar/hvar-news/occupation-and-resistance-on-hvar-during-wwii-the-jelsa-raid, accessed May 9, 2024.

https://www.aeroflight.co.uk/waf/americas/guatemala/Guatemala-af-home.com, accessed May 4, 2024.

https://www.ancientfaces.com/person/hans-v-tofte-birth-1911-death-1987/16211364, accessed September 19, 2023.

https://www.chatelrealestate.com, accessed May 14, 2024.

https://www.cia.gov/legacy/museum/artifact/bust-of-william-j-casey, accessed December 20, 2024.

https://www.cia.gov/stories/story/the-intrepid-life-of-sir-william-stephenson, accessed December 20, 2024.

https://www.cia.gov/readingroom/docs, accessed November 9, 2023.

http://www.digitalhistory.uh.edu/disp_textbook.cfm?smtID=3&psid=1119, accessed May 23, 2024.

https://www.familysearch.org/en/wiki/Florida,_Marriage_Records_-_FamilySearch_Historical_Records, accessed October 18, 2023.

https://www.firearmsnews.com/editorial/fairbairn-birth-of-modern-gunfighting/453403, accessed September 28, 2023.

https://www.legacy.com/us/obituaries/legacyremembers/caroline-brown-obituary?id=29608460, accessed June 11, 2024.

https://www.livingplaces.com/NY/Otsego_County/Gilbertsville_Village.html, accessed February 21, 2024.

https://www.nytimes.com/1987/08/28/obituaries/hans-tofte-world-war-ii-spy-later-dismissed-by-the-cia.html, accessed September 21, 2023.

https://www.99battalion.org, accessed March 9, 2024.

https://www.nps.gov/articles/office-of-strategic-services.htm, accessed September 29, 2023.

https://www.soc.mil/OSS/operational-groups.html, accessed April 24, 2024.

https://www.trumanlibrary.gov/library, truman-papers/harry-s-truman-papers-staff-member-and-office-files-psyc, accessed June 11, 2024.

https://wikispooks.com/w/index.php?title=Hans_Tofte&oldid=245935, accessed October 13, 2023.

https://www.findagrave.com/memorial/239043478/hans-v-tofte, accessed November 17, 2023.

https://www.findagrave.com/memorial/29408576/marlys-josephine-chatel, accessed May 20, 2024.

https://wikispooks.com/w/index/.php?title=Hans_Tofte&oldid=245935, accessed October 17, 2023.

https://www.pacificatrocities.org/blog/members-of-unit-731, accessed November 21, 2023.

https://www.warhistoryonline.com, accessed December 19, 2023.

koreanwaronline.com/arms/Clark.htm, accessed December 5, 2023.

www.govinfo.gov, accessed March 1, 2024.
www.history.navy.mil, accessed October 11, 2023.
www.historynet.com/world-war-ii-german-raid-on-bari, accessed November 6, 2023.
www.smithsonianmag.com/history/nazi-werewolves-who-terrorized-allied-soldiers-end-wwii-180970522/, accessed April 16, 2024.
www.afsoc.af.mil, accessed January 16, 2024.
www.specialforcesroh.com, accessed November 15, 2023.

Index

Advisory Council, 75
Aderholt, Capt. Harry "Heinie" Clay (US), 134–35
Air America, 99, 172. *See also* Civil Air Transport
"Alum" team, 28–29
American Madsen Corporation, 10
American Overseas Airlines (AOA), 70
American Volunteer Group (AVG), 99, 172. *See also* "Flying Tigers"
Angleton, James Jesus, 132, 155, 156, 163, 171
Argentina, 105, 126, 133, 134–38, 175
Armas, Carlos Castillo, 109–13, 115–16, 118–19, 121–23
Armed Forces Security Agency (AFSA), 93
Atsugi Air Force Base (Japan), 78, 81, 82, 84, 86, 98, 176
Aurell, George, 77

Bank, Col. Aaron (US), 20
Bari (Italy), 30, 33–34, 36–45, 47–48, 52, 68–69
Barnes, Tracy, 96, 111, 114, 122–23, 136, 138–39, 147, 156, 160, 167–68, 170
Beers, Colwell, 78
Benson, Capt. Melvin "Benny" (US), 28, 33, 35, 39–41, 43–45, 47, 53, 55, 63–65, 171
Berg, Morris "Moe," 28, 171
Berlin (Germany), 4–6, 53, 172, 176
Bissell, Maj. Gen. Clayton, 57, 85, 114, 122, 136–39
Bissell, Richard M., Jr., 171–72, 174
Bohanan, Maj. Charles T. R. (US), 126
Bohr, Dr. Neils (DA), 21
Bormann, Martin (GE), 134, 136, 172
Brazil, 139–40, 175
Brown, Capt. Julian (USMC), 3
Brown, Caroline, 161–62
Broz, Josip, 27, 172. *See also* Tito
"Buffalo," 90–91
Burke, Maj. John E. (UK), 46
Burma Road, 7, 10–11, 35, 39, 66, 98
Buxton, Col. G. Edward (US), 48, 52

Cairo (Egypt), 9, 25, 29–30, 33, 41–44, 46–48, 52, 66
Calcina, Marlys Leister (later Tofte and Chatel), 3, 4, 6–7, 21, 25, 33, 51, 64–65, 70–72, 94–96, 102, 105, 123, 131–35, 137–38, 141–44, 147–51, 154, 156–57, 159–60, 164, 168
Camargo, President of Colombia Alberto Lleras, 125, 127
Casey, DCI William J., 16, 20, 55, 60–61, 163, 172
Castro, Fidel, 108, 124, 137, 162, 172, 174, 175
Central Intelligence Agency (CIA), 70, 73–75, 146, 173
  Covert Operations Division, 138, 161
  Directorate of Plans (DDP), 96, 110–11, 174
  Office of Policy Coordination (OPC), 70, 78, 89
  Office of Special Operations (OSO), 96, 174
  Security Division, 128, 132
Chaban-Delmas, Jacques, 163
Chatel, Jean Charles, 141
Chennault, Gen. Claire Lee, 12, 14, 99–100, 172, 178

Chetniks, 27–28, 48, 176
Chiang Kai-Shek, "Generalissimo," 7–9, 14–16, 22, 93, 98–99, 110, 176
Chigasaki (Japan), 78, 82
China Commando Group, 9, 12–13, 19, 110
Chongqing (China), 8, 10, 12, 15
Church Committee, US Congress, 161
Churchill, Prime Minister Winston (UK), 6, 17, 28, 177
Churchill, Randolph, 35
Civil Air Transport (CAT), 82–83, 172, 178. *See also* Air America
Clancy, Tom, 165
Clark, Lt. Eugene F. (USN), 82–83, 89
Cline, Ray, 142, 172–73
Colby, DCI William E., 160, 163
Colepaugh, William Curtus (German spy), 58
Colombia, 124–28, 137
Coon, Maj. Carleton (US), 32, 47, 52, 68
Corcoran, Tommy "The Cork," 108–10
Cox, Al, 98–99
Cummings, Samuel, 121, 123

Dalmatia, 28, 30, 34–35, 40, 42, 66
"Documents Research Section V," 89
Donovan, Maj. Gen. William (US), 5, 12, 14–17, 19–21, 23–25, 27–28, 30–31, 38, 48, 51–52, 60, 65, 69–70, 77, 162–64, 173, 176–77
Dulles, DCI Allen, 101, 102, 105, 109, 171, 173–74
Dulles, Secretary of State John Foster, 109, 119

East Asiatic Company (EAC), 1, 22, 132, 133
Eisenhower, Gen. Dwight D. (US), 18, 30, 57, 109, 113, 116, 120, 122–23, 177
escape-and-evasion (E&E) program, Korea, 78, 176
Executive Order 9621 (dissolution of OSS), 70

Fairbairn, Lt. Col. William Ewart (UK), 7, 19–21, 24, 66, 174
Farrish, Maj. Linn (US), 28
"Faust Plan," 55
Federal Bureau of Investigation (FBI), 20, 58, 70, 126, 128, 133, 141, 143, 146–47, 149–51, 155, 160, 169, 177
Fifteenth Air Force, 37
Fitzgerald, Desmond, 20, 73, 159, 167–68
"Flying Tigers," 100, 172. *See also* American Volunteers Group
Fuerzas Armadas Revolucionarias de Colombia (FARC), 125

Galland, Gen. Adolf (*Luftwaffe*), 135
Garcia, Anastasio Somoza, 109–10, 118–19, 121–23, 141
Gestapo (*Geheimestaatspolizei*), 5, 62
Giles, Lt. Cdr. Morgan (UK), 36, 46
Goldberg, Arthur, 55
Gottlieb, Dr. Sidney, 86, 174
Goulart, Joao ("Jango"), 139–40
Guatemala, 107–15, 118–25, 137–38, 173, 178
guerrillas, Korean War, 75–76, 79–87, 89, 92–95, 104, 112, 176
guerrillas, South America, 127
guerrillas, World War II, 8–10, 12, 14, 16, 19, 28, 30, 33, 61, 176
Guzman, Jacobo Arbenz, 108–9, 111, 113, 116–24, 178

Hamilton, Lt. John/Sterling Hayden (US), 16, 38–39, 41–43, 45, 47, 48
Haney, Col. Albert, 104, 106, 110, 114–15, 118, 174
Helms, Maj. Richard (US), 53, 67, 101, 106, 131–32, 136, 139, 142, 145, 149, 151–52, 154, 159, 161, 163–64, 167, 174–75
Hunt, E. Howard, 115, 160, 177
Hunter, Edward, 90–91
Huntington, Col. Ellery C., Jr. (US), 18, 24
Huntley, Chet, 146
Huot, Maj. Louis (US), 29–30, 32–33, 39, 45–48, 52, 63

Ibsen, Thor and Sonia, 3, 71
Ilic, Col. Pavle (YO), 32–33
Italy, 18, 21, 25, 27–31, 33, 37–38, 42, 45, 68–69, 73, 171, 173

Iversen, Capt. Michael W. (DA), 23–24

Jajce (YO), 33, 35, 49
Jedburgh teams, 20, 64, 104
"Joan-Eleanor" communications system, 62
Johnson, Adm. Alfred W. (US), 161
Joint Advisory Commission Korea (JACK), 78
Joint Chiefs of Staff, 16, 30, 62, 75, 89, 95, 100
Joint Technical Advisory Group (JTAG), 84

Kauffmann, Henrik, 21, 64, 175
Kennedy, President of the United States John F., 127, 137–39, 148–49, 173
Keswick, Sir John, 8–9, 11–15, 18
King, Col. Joseph Caldwell (J. C.) (US), 107, 110, 112–14, 118, 128–29, 137, 175
Kirkpatrick, CIA Inspector General Lyman, 101, 138, 142, 163, 175
Kitano, Masaji, 94
Klipto Loose Leaf Company, 72, 95–96, 131
Koch, Maj. Robert (US), 21, 33, 38–39, 41–43, 47, 52
Korea, North, 80–83, 85–86, 88–94, 98, 101, 103, 105–6, 173, 176
Korea, South, 74, 80–81, 83, 106
Kramer, Lt. Col. Vincent "Dutch" (USMC), 81, 83, 87, 176

Lashio (CH), 11
Leister, Charlott, 133, 143–44, 147
"Liberation Air Force," 123
Luftwaffe, 37, 53
Lund, Lt. Col. Ragnvald "Alfred" Roscher, 54

MacArthur, Gen. Douglas (US), 76–77, 79, 85, 88–90, 92, 95, 99–102, 125, 177–78
McBaine, Lt. Cdr. Turner (USN), 30, 39, 41, 47, 52, 176
McCarthy, Senator Joseph (D-MN), 132, 152, 178
McCone, John, DCI, 138, 149, 175, 176
McClure, Gen. Robert A. (US), 105–6
McHugh, Lt. Col. (USMC), 22
McLean, Brigadier General Fitzroy (UK), 35
MacNider, Maj. Gen. Hanford (US), 72, 76–77

Makiedo, Sergei (YO), 45
Manchuria, 3–4, 20, 22, 76–78, 80–81, 84–85, 90–91, 94, 132
Mason City, Iowa, 72–73, 76–77, 95–96, 102, 123, 131, 139, 141, 148, 155, 160
Mihailovic, Gen. Draza (YO), 27–28, 176
Miles, Capt. Milton "Mary" Miles (US), 14–15
MK-ULTRA, 91, 174
Molloy, Melitta, 143–44
Monopoli (YO), 40–41, 45
motor torpedo boat (MTB), 34, 136

National Security Council, 96, 106, 109, 111
National Security Council (NSC) 4-A, 74
National Security Council (NSC) 10/2, 74–75
New York, 6, 10, 18, 19, 21, 28, 51, 56–59, 69–70, 105, 113, 132, 161–62, 177
Noborito Research Institute, 86–87
Norwegian Special Operations Group (NORSOG), 25
Nyholm, Erik and Betty, 3, 6–15, 18–19, 110

Office of Strategic Services (OSS), 2, 16, 21, 30, 69, 162
- Area "A" (Catoctin Mountain Park), 17, 189
- Area "C" (Chopawamsic Recreation Demonstration Area), 17
- Area "F" (Congressional Country Club), 17, 20, 21
- Operational Groups (OG), 17–18, 23–24
- Secret Intelligence (SI), 16–17, 67, 172
- Special Operations (SO), 16–18, 21, 28, 30, 43, 48

Operation *Able/Force X* (CO), 127
Operation *Audrey*, 27, 30, 33–35, 40, 43–44, 48–49, 51, 53, 132, 137
Operation *Aviary*, 103, 105
Operation *Brother Sam*, 140
Operation *Lincoln*, 113–15, 118
Operation *Mockingbird*, 103
Operation *Rösselsprung*, 49
Operation *Sherwood*, 119
Operation TP-AJAX, 107, 109, 111, 114, 124
Operation TP-STOLE, 97
Operation *Tropic/Third Force*, 93

Operation *Trudy Jackson*, 89
Operation *Washtub*, 118
Osborn, CIA DOS Howard, 128–29, 150–51, 177

PAINTER agent team, 63
partisans/partizans, 27–31, 34–37, 39–46, 49, 52, 66, 69, 162, 172
Partridge, Gen. Earl (USAF), 84
PBFORTUNE, 110–12, 124
PBSUCCESS, 110–11, 113–16, 118–19, 121–22, 124
P808 explosive, 10
Peking (CH), 3, 6, 8, 94
Peking Club, 3
Powers, Francis Gary, 138
Psychological Strategy Board (PSB), 96

Rand, Iris Elizabeth, "Musse," 2, 4–5, 21
Rangers, U.S. Army, 126, 174
Rangoon (BM), 8–11, 66, 100
Ridgway, Gen. Matthew (US), 79–80, 97, 99, 101–2, 177
Rockefeller, Nelson, 125, 132, 140, 175
Roosevelt, Kermit ("Kim"), 107, 114
Royal Navy (UK), 34, 36, 39, 41–42, 46

Scribner, Joseph M. (US), 47–48, 52
Shanghai (CH), 3, 7–8, 20, 22, 94
Sicily, 27, 29–30, 34
Singapore, 7–10, 12, 23, 66, 155, 174
Sino-American Special Technical Cooperative Organization (SACO), 14
Slocum, Kenneth and Judy, 143–45, 150–51, 154
Smith, Gen. Walter Bedell ("Beetle") (US), 80, 95–96, 100–2, 104, 106, 109–10, 173
Smodlaka, Dr. Josip (YO), 45
Soderbom, KG (SW), 9–11
Sorensen, Theodore ("Ted"), 148
South Pole, 135
Speake, Charles D., 144, 154, 156
Special Mission Group (SMG), 87
Special Operations Executive (SOE) (UK), 6, 16, 174
SS *Galeb*, 36
SSU Austria, 67
State Department (US), 22, 70, 75, 101, 108, 110, 113, 120
Stephenson, Sir William (UK), 6
Stillwell, Gen. Joseph "Vinegar Joe" (US), 13–15, 73–74, 76, 172, 178
Strickland, Charles E., 148
Sulgrave Club, 73, 162
Sweet-Escott, Lt. Col. (UK), 46

Tai Li, Gen. (CH), 14–15
Thompson, Lt. Robert E. S. (US), 29–30, 34, 38, 40–46, 48, 55, 60–61, 63, 163
Tito, 27–28, 30–35, 39–42, 48–49, 63, 66, 69, 155, 172, 176. *See also* Josip Broz
Tofte, Finn, 4–5, 64, 71, 134, 136, 161, 163–64
Tofte, Hans Vilhelm
- and Operation TP-STOLE, 97–99
- classified documents raid, 144–45, 147, 149, 151–55
- filmmaking in Korea, 91–92
- head of CIA covert operations in Korea, 74
- in British Army, 7, 18, 23
- involvement in public education, 131
- in Office of Training, 139
- in US Army, 19–69
- marries Marlys Leister Calcina, 51
- personality, 23, 55, 66, 71, 83, 138, 167–68
- severs North Korean cable, 94
- with the partizans in Yugoslavia, 27–49

Tofte, Teresa, 7, 70–71, 133
Toulmin, Lt. Col. J. E. (UK), 31, 43, 48
Truman, President of the United States Harry, 70, 79, 89, 95–96, 101, 109–10, 173, 178
Turner, DCI Stansfield, 161

U-boats, 56–58, 60
United Fruit Company (GT), 107, 109, 114, 123
Ustashi, 27, 42, 49

Valeriano, Col. Napoleon (RP), 125
Vis Island (YO), 36, 42
V-1 rockets, 56

Washington Field Office (WFO), FBI, 128, 133, 146, 151
Weil, Lt. Col. Richard (US), 28, 38–39, 41, 47, 52
Werwolf movement (GE), 62–63
White, Lawrence K. ("Red"), 115
Willauer, Whiting, 100, 178
Willoughby, Maj. Gen. Charles A. (US), 76–77, 79, 85, 88–89, 91–92, 95, 101–2, 178
Wilson, Gen. Henry Maitland (UK), 30
Wingate, Col. Orde Charles (UK), 15, 66
Wisner, Lt. Cdr. Frank (US), 29, 67, 70, 73–77, 85, 90, 92, 96, 101, 103–6, 110–11, 113–15, 118–19, 123, 131, 134, 136, 141, 164, 170, 172, 174–75
Wood, Struthers & Winthrop, 105, 132

Yokosuka (JA), 78, 86–87
Yugoslavia, 18, 27–30, 34–36, 39–42, 44, 45–49, 55, 65, 68–69, 73, 80, 111, 132, 163, 171, 172

Zemurray, Sam, 107–8